COMPASSIONATE COMMUNITY WORK

COMPASSIONATE COMMUNITY WORK

AN INTRODUCTORY COURSE FOR CHRISTIANS

DAVE ANDREWS

Réseau Michée
Rede Miquéias
Red Miqueas
Micah Network

First published in Great Britain in 2006
Second edition, 2009

Piquant Editions Ltd
PO Box 83, Carlisle, CA3 9GR
Website: **www.piquanteditions.com**

British Library Cataloguing in Publication Data

Andrews, Dave
  Compassionate community work : an introductory course for
  Christians
  1.Community development - Religious aspects - Christianity
  2.Church work 3.Religion and social problems
  I.Title
  261.8'3

  ISBN-13: 9781903689363
  ISBN-10: 1903689368

Scripture quotations, unless otherwise stated, are from the Holy Bible, New
International Version, copyright © 1973, 1978, 1984 by the International Bible
Society. Used by permission of Hodder & Stoughton Publishers, a Member of
Hodder Headline Plc Group. All rights reserved. "NIV" is a registered trademark of
the International Bible Society. UK trademark number 1448790.

Cover photograph: CCC La Palmera, Trinidad Beni, Bolivia
Cover design by Projectluz
Book design by To a Tee (www.2at.com)

CONTENTS

PART I: Compassionate Community Work Principles

PART II: Compassionate Community Work Skills

DIAGRAMS

FOREWORD

In *Compassionate Community Work* Dave Andrews has provided a truly remarkable and comprehensive resource for teaching and learning about community development. This "introductory course on community work for Christians" is much more than a textbook. It is an invitation to participate in an experiential, highly practical, spiritually rich, and potentially life-changing learning process.

This exceptional resource has been written by someone who has dedicated much of his life to nurturing, in himself and others, a commitment to work with those whom society so often ignores, neglects, and sometimes even despises. Dave Andrews is also a gifted teacher, and he employs a learning methodology which maximizes the opportunity for students to fully own and internalize what they discover. I find this particularly exciting and refreshing, because this approach takes into account how much of our really important learning actually occurs. Not surprisingly, it reflects an approach to discovery and learning that also lies at the heart of successful community development.

There are many profound insights in this resource, because Dave is a particularly reflective scholar and practitioner. This also means that he draws on a very discerning selection of information and thoughts from other scholars, development workers, and recent research.

The course ensures that the essential skills, principles, practices and competencies of community development are properly covered. As a result, it fully meets the relevant criteria required by the Australian National Training Authority. This is what Dave calls the "outer dimension of the course." But what makes this course so exceptional is its "inner dimension," or what Dave refers to as the "soul" of the course. In my experience, it's rare in any sphere of endeavour to discover teachers or learning resources which truly integrate the spiritual dimension into the learning experience. More often than not, the so-called "spiritual" is merely tacked on – sidelined and undervalued, reinforcing the compartmentalization of our lives and reducing the influence of the Spirit.

In this regard, Dave's course is utterly different. Prayer, meditation, vigorous engagement with biblical material, private and communal reflection, are all central activities. Within this context, the constant questioning is sometimes provocative, but there is also a grace and gentleness in the process – a beautiful pastoral quality. And behind it all? A love and respect for the church, but also a longing to see churches, whatever shape they take, develop as rich communities where we love God, love and sustain one another, and truly love our neighbour.

In all of this, the course is incredibly user-friendly. Explanations and instructions are given with great clarity. It's all so easy to follow. Moreover, the material would be easy to adapt to different contexts. Many years of living and working in a low-income country has done much to inform and shape Dave's understanding of church and community development.

In producing this manual Dave has done us a great service.

Steve Bradbury

National Director, TEAR Australia

Chairman, Micah Network*

* For more information about the Micah Network, see p. 340

ABOUT THIS COURSE

Compassionate Community Work is an introductory course on Christ-like community work. It can be studied formally as a subject for university or seminary – or informally at home in your own church or community. The *Compassionate Community Work* course has an inner dimension and an outer dimension.

The inner dimension, or "soul," of the course is my passion for *in situ*, spiritual, experiential, personal, relational, ethical, action-reflection community development education. It seeks to provide people with the opportunity to explore a dynamic spirituality that is essential for developing a healthy faith-based community. The Trinity is the model, Christ is the example, the Gospel is the process, and the Spirit is the power for healthy faith-based community development.

In his study of *Basic Communities*, David Clark says:

> Community (is) essentially a sentiment which people have about themselves in relation to themselves: a sentiment expressed in action, but still basically a feeling. People have many feelings, but there are two essentials for the existence of community: a sense of significance and a sense of solidarity. The strength of community within any given group is determined by the degree to which its members experience both a sense of solidarity and a sense of significance within it.[1]

In his book on community, psychologist Scott Peck writes:

> If we are going to use the word [community] meaningfully we must restrict it to a group of individuals who have learned to communicate honestly with each other, whose relationships go deeper than their masks of composure, and who have developed some significant commitment to "rejoice together, mourn together," "delight in each other, make others' conditions our own."[2]

After researching five different Christian communities in depth, sociologist Luther Smith wrote:

---

[1] D. Clark, *Basic Communities* (London: SPCK, 1975), pp. 4–5.
[2] S. Peck, *The Different Drum* (London: Rider and Co., 1988), p. 59.

> The primary indicator of communal well-being is that members feel their fellowship approximates the qualities of a caring family. Hardship and failures will be the occasion for creative solutions. But loss of mutual respect and steadfast caring strikes a deathblow at the very heart of a community.[3]

It is my hope that, through this course, you will discover the significance and solidarity which are at the heart of community; that you will develop deep mutual respect for people in your community – as in a healthy extended family; and that you will learn to rejoice and mourn more fully with your neighbours.[4]

The outer dimension of the course deals with community development knowledge, skills, principles, practices and competencies, seeking to impart:

a) Underpinning knowledge, in areas such as

- The nature and the dynamics of community
- Community development principles and practices
- Community development strategies and tactics
- Methods for encouraging community participation
- Concepts of effective community leadership
- Organizational systems
- Program guidelines
- Project budgets
- Funding options.

b) Underpinning skills, such as

- Formal and informal networking
- Liaising with a range of people
- Researching community issues
- Developing community policies
- Facilitating community meetings
- Negotiating community agreements
- Preparing community budgets

---

[3] Luther E. Smith, Jr., *Intimacy and Mission* (Scottsdale, PA: Herald Press, 1994), pp. 98–100.
[4] R.W. Woodman and W.A. Pasmore, *Research in Organizational Change and Development*, I (Greenwich, CT: JAI Press, 1996), pp. 129–69.

- Promoting community activities
- Evaluating community programs
- Writing community reports.

1. OUTCOMES, OBJECTIVES AND CONTENT

When you complete *Compassionate Community Work*, you will be able to:

1. Demonstrate a developed and biblical understanding of community and community development
2. Articulate a broad understanding of general theories related to community and community development
3. Analyze with insight the issues involved in doing church-based community development
4. Identify and develop opportunities for church and community leadership
5. Appreciate Christian responses which enhance human dignity, community solidarity, and effective witness
6. Articulate and value the uniquely Christian contribution to community and community development.

The content of the course, as set out in the Table of Contents, is divided into 28 sessions. Part I (Sessions 1 through 17) helps students to explore and understand the principles of compassionate community work. Building on these principles, then, Part II (Sessions 18 through 28) sets out the practices of compassionate community work in a way that enables students to use and hone these skills in their own particular contexts.

2. LEARNING STRATEGIES AND LEARNING PARTNERS

Compassionate Community Work includes processes, exercises, a set text, study notes, additional readings, and a simple series of community tasks that you can work through, step-by-step, in the context of your own community.

The course includes a set of instructions to assist you in self-managed study. However, no course on community work could possibly be done in total isolation. So you will need to identify someone who could be your learning partner for this course. Whether this partner is a new acquaintance or an old friend, what's important is that you think you can work with, feel comfortable with, collaborate with and be accountable to this person.

This learning partner does not need to be present when you do most of the study sessions. But for some sessions it will be absolutely essential that you have one or two learning partners with you, in order to be able to explore the subject at hand with integrity (Sessions 18, 20 and 22 in particular, and you will need two people in order to complete each of the latter two sessions). The learning partners for these sessions do not necessarily have to be learning partners you have chosen for the whole course.

3.   Learning Responsibilities and Resources for Informal Study

1)   You are responsible for your own learning. To get the most out of *Compassionate Community Work,* you will need to follow the instructions in each session. This includes reading the materials, talking things over with a learning partner, answering the questions, completing the set community tasks and writing up the working notes – on a weekly basis.

2)   In order to successfully complete all of the work that the course entails, you will need to dedicate at least 2½ hours to working through the material in each session and an additional 2½ hours to the tasks associated with each session. The total number of hours required each week, then, is five.

3)   At the end of each session you are encouraged to complete set *community tasks.* These activities provide the basis for the action and reflection that are at the heart of the course.

4)   The *working notes* that you are encouraged to keep will consist of informal personal reflections on the course and your engagement with community development theory and practice in your community. These working notes function much like a journal, giving you the space and discipline to reflect on some of the thoughts, feelings and issues that the course raises for you to consider. Although they are an important element of the course, if you are doing the course informally, you are not required to share these notes with anyone else. If you are doing the course formally, you will be required to share these notes

with your examiner, but the notes will not be graded. You will be given an automatic pass if you have kept a record of your working notes, and an automatic fail if you have not.

5)   While reading widely on the topic of community development is strongly encouraged, we have tried to provide enough resources for you to read without having to access a library. Additional *articles* (Appendix A) and *stories* (Appendix B) have been provided for you on our website: www.daveandrews.com.au

4.   TRAINING RESPONSIBILITIES AND RESOURCES FOR FORMAL STUDY

This section outlines the requirements for facilitating the delivery of this course for formal study and accreditation.

1)   Your responsibilities are to help students: clarify their understanding of biblical material related to community and community development; consider general theories related to community and community development in the context of today's world; analyze the issues involved in doing church-based community development; appreciate Christian responses which enhance human dignity, community solidarity and effective witness. You will address the following:

•   The principles of compassionate community development
•   The practices of compassionate community development
•   The church as a subject for community development
•   The church as an agent of community development
•   Opportunities for church community leadership
•   Support for leadership structures and processes in the church community
•   Support for leadership training and learning in the church community
•   Appropriate participation in community activities
•   Appropriate participation by groups and individuals in community activities

2)   You need to encourage students to study *Compassionate Community Work*, to follow the instructions in each session (including reading the materials, talking things over with a learning partner,

answering the questions, and writing up the working notes) on a weekly basis where possible.

3)   If students are studying the course for accreditation you will also need to encourage them to:

- Participate in a *residential intensive* (if required)
- Complete the weekly *community tasks*
- Work on weekly *working notes*
- Complete the *essays* and *reports*.

Students should be encouraged to dedicate at least 2½ hours for working through the material in each session, 2½ hours for the tasks associated with each session, 3 hours a week for additional reading, and 2 hours for writing. This means that students should aim to dedicate at least ten hours per week to this course.

4)   The best way of encouraging students is to meet with them at least once every week (as a group) for a couple of hours. If that is not possible, you may want to consider staying in touch with them by phone or email – and organize a *residential intensive* once or twice during the course.

A *residential intensive* is a two or three day face-to-face facilitated learning experience.

What a residential intensive *is*	What a residential intensive is *not*
One important aspect of the student's learning experience.	The main learning event for this course.
An opportunity for the student to withdraw briefly from their context to reflect on and discuss the themes and emphases of this course, after which they will return to their *in situ* engagement.	The place to receive the content of the course.
A gathering of fellow travellers who have unique and valuable perspectives and contributions to make to each other's learning.	A place for students to be lectured to by an "expert."
A facilitated, interactive process.	A passive, receptive process.
A "whole- person" engagement with God, each other and the themes of this course.	An academic exercise only.[5]

[5] Garry Hills, *Residential Facilitators Handbook* (Brisbane: ACOM, 2004).

5)   The *community tasks* that need to be completed are explained at the end of each session. These activities provide the basis for the action and reflection that are at the heart of the course. The *reports* that students are expected to write are based on the *working notes* they keep on these community tasks.

6)   The *working notes* that the students need to keep updated are informal (but legible) personal reflections students make on specific lessons they learn from this course through their engagement with community development, theory and practice in their community. The working notes are not the reports but, rather, form the basis for the student's reports. Working notes are not an objective reporting of events, per se, but more subjective, personal reflections.

Note: Working notes should *not* be graded – but they should be submitted as evidence of the student's personal learning progress.

7)   Two formal *reports* are to be submitted – one for each half of the course. These should be framed around:

- The weekly tasks attempted
- Strategies tried
- Successes
- Failures
- Lessons learned along the way.

The reports should demonstrate the student's theoretical and practical understanding of community work within the framework of the student's own spirituality. Reports should be based on the weekly working notes they have kept on their community tasks. Honesty, authenticity and creativity in these presentations should be rewarded. But students should be reminded that while these reports may be personal and practical, reports are assessable pieces of work. References and research need to be adequately cited, and a bibliography appended.

Reports by degree students should be 2,000 words and by diploma students should be 1,500 words.

8)   Two *essays* are to be written – one for each half of the course – demonstrating an in-depth understanding of one aspect of compassionate community work. Students may either suggest a topic for approval to the facilitator, or choose *one* of the following suggested topics:

- The principles of compassionate community development
- The practices of compassionate community development
- The church as a subject for community development
- The church as an agent of community development
- Gender equity in community development
- Indigenous people in community development
- Migrants and refugees in community development
- Disadvantaged people in community development.

Essays by degree students should be 3,000 words and by diploma students should be 2,500 words.

9)   Facilitators need to understand that not all students have access to good libraries. While library research is strongly encouraged where possible, we have tried to provide the resources needed for students to be able to complete essay writing without accessing a library. Additional stories and articles have been provided for students on our website: www.daveandrews.com.au

5.   CHECKLIST

In addition to *Compassionate Community Work*, you will need the following additional materials to complete the course. The articles, stories and assignments and assessment guidelines are all available on www.daveandrews.com.au

- D. Andrews, *Not Religion but Love* (Oxford: Lion, 2001/Cleveland: Pilgrim Press, 2003/ Armidale: Tafina, 2005) is the set text for *Compassionate Community Work*. The page numbers to the 2005 Australian Tafina Press edition is separated with a "/" from the page numbers quoted for the Lion (UK)=Pilgrim Press (USA) editions.
- Articles for *Compassionate Community Work* (listed in Appendix A)
- Stories for *Compassionate Community Work* (listed in Appendix B)
- Assignments and assessment guidelines (Training Responsibilities and Training Resources for Formal Study)

Dave is also available, by arrangement, to run workshops, seminars and residential intensives. See the final page for contact information.

ACKNOWLEDGEMENTS

I would like to acknowledge my elders who have helped me develop my approach to *Compassionate Community Work* – my parents, Frank and Margaret Andrews; my parents-in-law, James and Athena Bellas; Doris Bailey; Howard and Betty Barclay; Rita Barwick; Paul and Cherry Bavinton; Rob and Lois Bellingham; Colin and Janet Blair; Chris and Marilyn Brown; Rod and Kay Bullpitt; Ernie and Elfie Campbell; Murray and Florence Carter; Charles and Hilary Elliott; Frank and Val Garlick; Alan and Naideen Halladay; Jim and Maureen Hunter; Tony Kelly; Lalchuangliana; Alan Norish; Arthur and Betty McCutchan; Floyd and Sally McClung; Margaret Parkinson; John Richards; Charles and Rita Ringma; Michael and Betty Roemmele; Sabodh Sahu; Basil and Shirley Scott; Joe and Marietta Smith; Tony and Bertha Stone; and Ray and Gwen Windsor.

I would especially like to thank Rod and Kay Bullpitt for their tireless work in helping me develop the course material on which *Compassionate Community Work* is based; Steve Bradbury for writing his wholehearted foreword; Olive, George Lovell and Stephen Covey for the use of their very helpful insights and diagrams*; Tara Smith for her toil in editing the text; Pieter and Elria Kwant for their willingness to publish the book; and TEAR Australia and the Micah Network for promoting it worldwide.

Dave Andrews

*   Olive (Organisation Development & Training <www.oliveodt.co.za>). *Project Planning for Development* (Durban, 1994), pp. 38, 41, 46, 47, 66, 75, 76. Used with permission; George Lovell. *The Church and Community Development* (Pinner: Grail Publications <www. avecresources.org>), pp. 8, 9, 12, 13, 34, 42, 44, 45, 47, 48, 50, 51, 53, 55. Used with permission; Stephen Covey, 7 *Habits of Highly Effective People* (Melbourne: The Business Library, 1989) pp. 81, 82, 83

PART I

COMPASSIONATE COMMUNITY WORK PRINCIPLES

INTRODUCTION TO COMMUNITY

1. PREPARATION

1.1. Objectives

- To establish guidelines for the course
- To introduce the course, its content and process
- To establish learning partnerships for the course
- To introduce the underpinning concept of community

1.2. Time

- 2 hours completing this session
- 3 hours in community activities (see 1.3, below)

1.3. Guidelines

Compassionate Community Work is an introductory course on Christ-like community work. The course includes processes, exercises, a set text, study notes, additional readings and a simple series of community tasks that you can work through, step-by-step, in the context of your own community. If you have not read "About this Course" at the beginning of this book, you need to read it before you proceed.

If you want to want to work through this book informally, you will need to read section 3, "Learning Responsibilities and Resources for Informal Study," but you can skip section 4, "Training Responsibilities and Resources for Formal Study."

If you want to want to work through this book formally for accreditation, you need to read both sections 3 and 4, "Learning Responsibilities and Resources for Informal Study" and "Training Responsibilities and Resources for Formal Study."

Learning partner

Jesus encouraged his disciples to operate in pairs. *"The Lord . . . sent them two by two ahead of him to every town and place where he was about to go"* (Lk. 10:1).

You will need to find a learning partner for this course. For details and guidelines see section 3, "Learning Strategies and Learning Partners" in "About this Course" above.

Community tasks

At the end of each study session you will be assigned a community task. These tasks are simple activities that will help you put what you are learning into practice. As such, they are a crucial part of the course. These tasks will form the basis of your working notes and any report(s) you may write.

Working notes

You will keep these notes in the context of learning activities. These "rough scribblings" are part of your permanent record of the underpinning knowledge and skills presented during the training sessions, and you should file them in a suitable folder as part of a portfolio of your learning. These documents don't have to be neat, but they must be readable. If you are doing the course for accreditation your working notes won't be assessed for a mark or grade, but you will be required to submit them to document your learning experience.

2.   EXPECTATION

10 minutes

◊ What are your expectations of the course? What do you hope to get out of it?

◊ How realistic are those expectations? (Check them against the course contents.)

◊ How can you make the most of the course? What do you need to put into it?

If you feel that the course will help you meet your goals, then let's get started...

3.   MEDITATION

10 minutes

◊ Read the following passages from the book of Acts, and then think for a few minutes about the picture of the early church community painted here.

The church community at Pentecost

With many other words he warned them; and he pleaded with them, "Save yourselves from this corrupt generation." Those who accepted his message were baptized, and about three thousand were added to their number that day.

They devoted themselves to the apostles' teaching and to the fellowship, to the breaking of bread and to prayer. Everyone was filled with awe, and many wonders and miraculous signs were done by the apostles. All the believers were together and had everything in common. Selling their possessions and goods, they gave to anyone as he had need. Every day they continued to meet together in the temple courts. They broke bread in their homes and ate together with glad and sincere hearts, praising God and enjoying the favour of all the people. And the Lord added to their number daily those who were being saved. (Acts 2:40–47)

All the believers were one in heart and mind. No-one claimed that any of his possessions was his own, but they shared everything they had. With great power the apostles continued to testify to the resurrection of the Lord Jesus, and much grace was upon them all. There were no needy persons among them. For from time to time those who owned lands or houses sold them, brought the money from the sales and put it at the apostles' feet, and it was distributed to anyone as he had need. (Acts 4:32–35)

◊ Close your eyes and imagine what it would have been like to be in the church community in the days just after Pentecost. *Then record your reflections in your working notes.*

1. What do you see?
2. What do you hear?
3. What would it be like to be "one in heart and mind"?
4. What would it be like to have "no needy person among us, because we gladly met all of one another's needs?"

4.   INTRODUCTION

10 minutes

Reflect on the following: Where have you lived in the past ten years? What church community have you been a part of? What is your first *positive* memory of a *healthy church community experience*?

If you are with one or more other people, talk about your answers. If you are on your own, jot down a few notes to answer the final question above.

5.   VISION EXERCISE

20 minutes

Draw a picture of your ideal church community – the kind you'd like to be a part of.

This exercise is not an art competition – and is *not* for assessment. But keep a copy of your picture in your working notes.

◊ After you have drawn your picture, consider the community you have depicted. Look at it and listen to what it says about the kind of church community of which, deep down, you'd really like to be a part.

◊ Then write down what the picture says to you about your ideal church community. *Keep a copy of what you write in your working notes.*

6.   VALUES EXERCISE

20 minutes

◊ Read the following verse and make a list of all the values that you consider to be crucial to the development of your ideal church community.

> *Whatever is true, whatever is noble [has dignity], whatever is right [or is just], whatever is pure [has integrity], whatever is lovely [or is lovable], whatever is admirable [or is kind] – if anything is excellent [has quality] or praiseworthy [has credibility] – think about such things.* (Phil. 4:8)

◊ List the four priority values that you think are most important for developing your ideal church community.

◊ Then answer the following questions and record your conclusions in your working notes.

1. What are the values you nominated as top priority?

2. Why do you consider these values to be so important?

3. What are the similarities between your own values and the values that other people have listed below?

4. What are the differences between your own values and the values that other people have listed below?

5. What values listed by other people would you like to add to your list?

6. What would you nominate as your top four values now?

7. Are they same or different? Explain the reasons for your selections.

Examples of values other people have nominated include:

- Faith
- Love
- Respect
- Support
- Honesty
- Safety
- Hope
- Acceptance
- Compassion
- Help
- Equality
- Freedom

7.   A CHARTER FOR HEALTHY COMMUNITY

20 minutes

◊ Read the following, which is my translation of Romans 12:9–21 – Paul's "charter for healthy community."

A charter for healthy community

Love needs to be sincere.
Renounce what is evil; embrace what is good.
Be devoted to one another in love.
Honour one another above yourselves.
Make sure you don't lack in enthusiasm,
but maintain your spiritual passion, serving the Lord.
Be joyful in hope, patient in affliction, faithful in prayer.
Be careful to do what is right in the eyes of everybody.
Do not be conceited but live in harmony with one another.
Do not be proud but associate with marginalized people.
Share with those who are in need. Practise hospitality.
Rejoice with those who rejoice; mourn with those who mourn.
As far as it depends on you, live at peace with everyone.
Do not take revenge.
If your enemies are hungry, feed them;
If they are thirsty, give them something to drink.
Do not repay anyone evil for evil.
Bless those who persecute you;
bless and do not curse.
Do not be overcome by evil, but overcome evil with good.
(Rom. 12:9–21)

◊ Make a list of the points that strike you as being particularly important. Then list beside each point the reason(s) why you think they are so important for the development of healthy community. *Keep this list in your working notes.*

8.   CONCLUSION

20 minutes

Plan to begin each week from now on with a review of the work from the previous week. This will include a review of your responses to the issues raised in the course notes and the follow-up readings, as well as your experiences of set community tasks.

Your working notes serve as a journal of reflections on your experiences, thoughts and feelings about your experiences, and on your growing understanding of the nature of community and community development. You should aim to write at least one hundred words each week, incorporating all aspects of your learning experiences. Keep your working notes handy at all times, as learning experiences are not always predictable or scheduled!

The follow-up reading for this session is:
- Andrews, Dave, *Building a Better World* (Sutherland: Albatross, 1996), pp. 52–68. (Reading 1)

Finding a learning partner

◊ You need to identify a learning partner, then get together with him/her and discuss the partnership.

◊ As a starting point, address the following questions with your learning partner. *Record your conclusions in your working notes.*

1. What are some characteristics of a good partnership?
2. How will you assess whether it is working well?
3. How will you agree to communicate about any problems that might arise?
4. What do you think you need most help with?
5. What do you feel you can help most with?

Community activity

It might be helpful for you to talk with leadership in your church about your doing this course, and to enlist their help in finding places to do research and tasks.

◊ Your first task is to attend a large open, public meeting of your church this week – like a Sunday service. Find an unobtrusive place to sit and just observe the people and their relationships.

1. What do you see?

2. What do you hear?

3. What conclusions can you draw about your community based on your observations?

◊ Then meet with your learning partner to discuss your observations of your community in the light of the issues raised in this session and clarified in the reading.

◊ *Record your insights in your working notes.*

COMMUNITY DEVELOPMENT

1. PREPARATION

1.1. Objectives

- To review your understanding of a healthy church community
- To introduce an understanding of community development principles and practices, including a Trinitarian approach

2. REVIEW

15 minutes

Review your work from Session 1.

Review the issues raised in the course notes in the previous session, particularly your understanding of the nature of a healthy church community.

Review the reading:

Building a Better World (Sutherland: Albatross, 1996), pp. 52–68.

Review the tasks:

1. Did you identify a learning partner? If so, good. If not, find someone to fulfil this role.

2. Did you get together with this person to discuss the learning partnership?

If so, what terms did you agree to?

3. Which meeting of your church did you attend this week? Were you able to find an unobtrusive place to sit and observe the people and their relationships?

4. What are the most important things you learned about community from your observation of this meeting?

5. How did it go getting together with your learning partner to discuss your observations of your community in the light of the issues raised in this session and clarified in the reading?

The famous German martyr-theologian, Dietrich Bonhoeffer, said: "Those who love community, destroy community. Those who love people, build community" (quoted in **Building a Better World**, p. 63).

If we try to build the perfect church community at the expense of the people in it, we will destroy the very church community we are trying to build. It is only as we lay aside our obsession with building bigger, brighter and better churches and simply love the people in them as sincerely as we can, that we will be able to build healthy church communities. What do you think about that?

◊ *Record your reflections in your working notes.*

3. COMMUNITY DEVELOPMENT PRACTICE

10 minutes

◊ Read the following statement by Tony Kelly, Senior Lecturer in community work at the University of Queensland, on community development practice:

> Community development describes a way of working with people that is based on a set of values. These values emphasize the right (and the responsibility) of people to participate in decisions that will affect their lives.
>
> Community development is concerned first and foremost with poverty and power. It is concerned with giving people – particularly the poorest – the knowledge, skills, opportunity and resources so that they can control their own lives. It emphasizes the process that enables maximum decision making for people where they are – at the grass-roots where they live.
>
> A community development worker is anyone with these values who works with people where they live. A community development worker therefore can work with the people on any task that the community sees as important. In this sense, the

choice of the task is of secondary importance, the way in which the task is approached is of primary importance.

◊ Jot down your answers to the following questions:

1. How does Tony Kelly define community development?

2. How does his definition compare or contrast with the view of Paul, as seen in Session 1?

3. What ideas about community development do they share?

4. Which of these ideas are most important for developing your community?

5. How do you think these themes may apply to the work that you want to do?

4. COMMUNITY DEVELOPMENT PRINCIPLES

10 minutes

◊ Read the following statement on community development principles adapted from a community forum of the Young Men's Christian Association (YMCA) in Fiji. As you read through this list, put a tick beside the principles that you agree with, and a cross beside the ones with which you disagree.

Community development principles

1. People are more important than things; people are more important than programs.
2. Growth comes from within people; all people have talents waiting to be developed.
3. People grow in responsibility as they are helped to accept greater responsibilities.
4. The most effective venue for training the community is in the community itself.
5. People learn most effectively when what they are learning is relevant and built on the basis of their experiences.
6. As communities are integrated, they are best served by integrated development rather than by departmentalized units working in isolation from one another.
7. The most effective helper is a person who strongly identifies with the community and who develops a relationship with that community based on trust.
8. Communities know their own problems and the solutions that will work better than others from outside the community do.

9. The energy a community will put into any activity will be in proportion to their involvement in the planning of that activity.
10. The pace of development will be determined by the community; a particular change will only become permanent if a community is ready for it.
11. People should be helped only in so far as this assistance enables them to become more self-reliant.
12. There are resources in each community that are under-utilized and waiting to be released.

◊ In your working notes, name the principles that you disagree with, and why.

◊ Name the principles you agree with, and why.

◊ Record the answers to these two further questions in your working notes:

1. Which of these principles do you practise well? (Give examples.)

2. Which of these do you need to develop more? (Give an example.)

5.   THE TRINITY AS A MODEL FOR COMMUNITY

30 minutes

5.1. An Introduction to the Trinity

> *The LORD our God, the LORD is one! (Deut. 6:4)*

However, the one true God is not a simple entity, but a Trinity of three persons living together in one community for all of eternity.

Jesus expected his disciples to baptize people into the community of the Trinity *in the name of the Father and of the Son and of the Holy Spirit* (Matt. 28:19).

5.2. Some Images of the Trinity

a) H_2O

This is an old favourite. The one substance expressed in three states: solid – like the Father; liquid – like the son; gas – like the Spirit.

b) "Big Mac"

This is a new favourite. The one object comprised of three parts: the Father – bun; the Son – meat; the Spirit – mayonnaise.

Both these images are totally impersonal, non-relational and unbiblical! So let's look at another image, "The Rublev Icon," a fifteenth-century image of the Trinity.

Figure 1. Icon of the Holy Trinity *by Andrei Rublev*

What strikes you about this particular picture of the Trinity?
Write a page of reflections on this picture in your working notes.

5.3. The Nature of the Trinity as a Community

The Trinity is a community of three Persons devoted to love and justice, living in harmony for all of eternity. In this community:

a) People are safe

Jesus called out with a loud voice, "Father, into your hands I commit my spirit." (Lk. 23:46)

b) People are accepted

And a voice from heaven said, "This is my Son, whom I love; with him I am well pleased." (Matt. 3:17)

c) Both unity and diversity are respected

God is not prejudiced, but respects people from all countries, cultures and backgrounds . . . (Acts 10:34–35 [author's version])

d) All are special – none are expendable

[God] is patient . . . not wanting anyone to perish. (2 Pet. 3:9)

e) Each one can participate in decisions

I tell you the truth, my Father will give you whatever you ask . . . Ask and you will receive. (Jn. 16:23–24)

f) There is a commitment to doing justice to disadvantaged people, both locally and globally

The Father . . . causes his sun to rise on the evil and the good, and sends rain on the righteous and the unrighteous. (Matt. 5:45)

5.4. The Trinity as a Model of Community

For Jesus . . . the Trinity is the divine model for human community. In praying for his disciples, Jesus says:

My prayer is not for them alone. I pray also for those who will believe in me through their message, that all of them may be one, Father, just as you are in me and I am in you. (Jn. 17:20–23)

So in our community we should aim that:

a) People should feel safe

Practise hospitality. . . . As far as it depends on you, live at peace with everyone. (Rom. 12:13, 18)

b) People should be accepted

Not only "love your neighbour as yourself," but also "as I have loved you, so you must love one another." (Jn. 13:34)

c) Both unity and diversity should be respected

There is no us and them, no gender, class or race divisions; for you are all united in Christ! (Gal. 3:28 [author's version])

The church is the "body" of Christ. The body is not made up of one part.

If they were all one part, where would the body be? As it is, there are many parts, but one body. (1 Cor. 12:19–20)

d) All should know they are special – none are expendable

Whatever you did [or did not do] for one of the least of these . . . you did [or did not do] for me. (Matt. 25:40, [45] [author's version])

e) Each one should be able to participate in decisions

Why don't you judge for yourselves what is right? (Lk. 12:57)

Do what is right in the eyes of everybody. (Rom. 12:17)

f) There should be a commitment to doing justice to marginalized people, both locally and globally

Give to the one who asks you. (Matt. 5:42)

Lend . . . without expecting to get anything back. (Lk. 6:35)

Sell everything you have and give to the poor. (Luke 18:22)

The righteous will shine like the sun. (Matt. 13:43)

◊ The following questions raise issues from this material for you to discuss. *Record your conclusions in your working notes.*

1. How relevant is the Trinity as a model of community?
2. What are the values that characterize the Trinity as a community?

3. How do they compare/contrast with the values you selected in the values exercise in Session 1?

4. What are the values in your church community that are most like those of the Trinity?

5. What are the values in your church community that are least like those of the Trinity?

6. How can you nurture the Trinitarian values in your church community?

7. What do you need to keep doing to help this take place?

8. What do you need to change (what do you need to stop doing or start doing) in order to help this happen?

6.   THE TRINITY AS A MODEL FOR COMMUNITY DEVELOPMENT

45 minutes

The Trinity is not just a model for community, it is also a model for community development. Jesus sent his disciples out "two by two," to look for a third person, the so-called "person of peace," with whom the disciples could form a trinity as the building block for community (Lk. 10:1, 5).

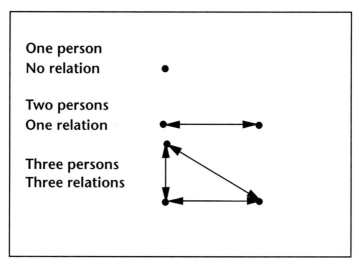

One person
No relation

Two persons
One relation

Three persons
Three relations

Figure 2. A trinity creates multiple relations

A trinity is a building block for establishing community for at least three reasons:

a) A trinity creates the "stability" and "security" necessary for community development

Two are better than one . . .

A cord of three strands is not quickly broken. (Eccl. 4:9, 12)

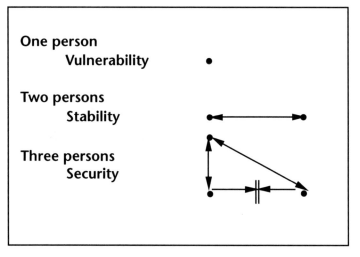

One person
     Vulnerability

Two persons
     Stability

Three persons
     Security

Figure 3. A trinity creates "stability" and "security"

b) A trinity creates the "subjectivity" and "objectivity" necessary for community development

Every matter may be established by the testimony of two or three witnesses. (Matt. 18:16)

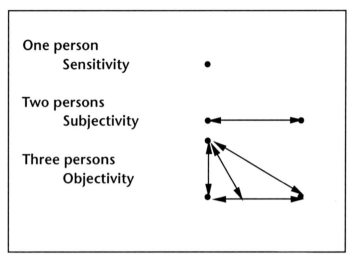

Figure 4. A trinity creates "subjectivity" and "objectivity"

c) A trinity creates the "possibility" or the "opportunity" for community development

"Where two or three come together in my name, there am I with them." (Matt. 18:20)

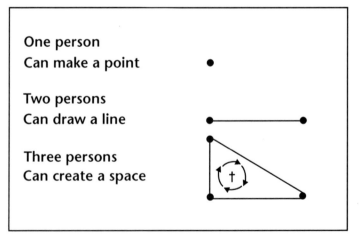

Figure 5. A trinity creates the "possibility" or "opportunity"

6.1. Trinitarian Community Development

There are many kinds of development programs. Three of the most common kinds in churches are:

- Individual/charismatic development
- Institutional development
- Community development

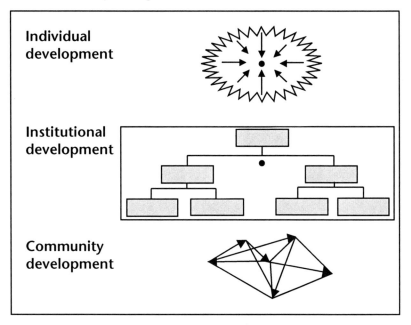

Figure 6. Three community development models

1. What are the similarities between these approaches?
2. What are the differences between these approaches?
3. Which of these approaches is a Trinitarian approach?
4. What part do you imagine the Trinitarian approach might play in the development of community?

Consider, for example, developing a visiting program.

1. What would an individual visiting program like look?
2. What would an institutional visiting program look like?
3. What would a community visiting program look like?

Note the following diagrams of visiting programs:

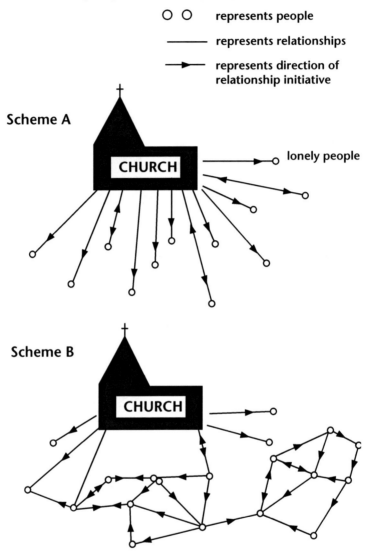

Scheme A

CHURCH

lonely people

Scheme B

CHURCH

Figure 7. Two visiting program schemes

1. Which of these schemes is a community program?
2. Which are the disadvantages in a community program?

3. What are the advantages in a community program?

Note the following diagrams of holiday camping programs:

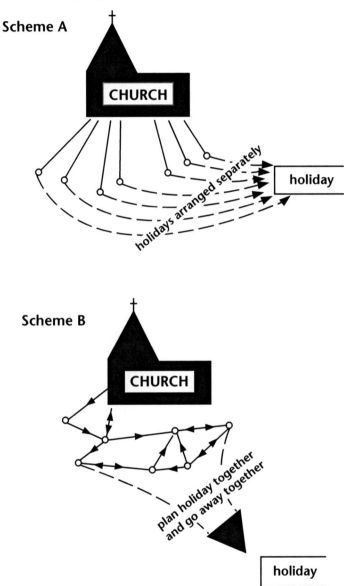

Figure 8. Two holiday camping schemes

Now, consider a program that your church runs.

1. Think of a program that your church currently runs (visiting, camping, counselling, welfare).

2. How does your church run this program (according to the individual, institutional, or community model)?

3. If it is a community program, how well do you think that it is working?

4. If it is not a community program, how do you think it would work as one?

7.   CONCLUSION

The follow-up reading for this session is:
- Dave Andrews, *Building a Better World* (Sutherland: Albatross, 1996), pp. 163–65. (Reading 2)

The set community tasks for this session are:

◊ Attend a couple of meetings in your church – a large gathering and a small group. Record your observations of the people and their relationships.

1. What do you observe that – at their best – are indicators of a healthy church community?

2. What do you observe that – at their best – are indicators of a healthy church community development?

3. What do you observe that is Trinitarian about your church community?

◊ Get together with your learning partner to discuss how you could practise principles of community development and support the development of the healthy dynamics at work in your church.

◊ *Record your actions, reflections and conclusions in your working notes.*

THE CHURCH AND COMMUNITY DEVELOPMENT

1. PREPARATION

1.1. Objectives

- To review your understanding of healthy community and healthy community development, particularly "Trinitarian community development"
- To consider dominant ideas, images and models of church and how they impact the church's potential to be an agent of community development

2. REVIEW

15 minutes

Review your work from the previous session.

Review the issues raised in Session 2 – especially your understanding of healthy community and healthy community development and, in particular, "Trinitarian community development."

Review the reading:

Building a Better World (Sutherland: Albatross, 1996), pp. 163–72.

Review the tasks:

1. How did you find observing the groups at church?

2. What was the most important thing you learned while doing the community tasks for the last session?

◊ *Record your reflections in your working notes.*

3.   CHANGING THE CHURCH

If the church is to become an effective catalyst for community development in our locality, we need to change three things: our *idea* of church, our *image* of church, and our *model* of church.

3.1. Changing our Idea of Church

30 minutes

I was taught that the key to understanding the church was the Greek word *ecclesia,* which we translate into English as "church." This is the word Jesus used when he said, in Matthew 16:18:

> *I tell you that . . . on this rock I will build my church, and the gates of hell will not overcome it.*

I was taught that the word *ecclesia* means "called out." So the church was "those called out of the society," "apart from the society," "to stand for the truth against the false values of the society," "in the hope that even the forces of hell itself would not prevail against it."

Note that this definition of the church is essentially "separate." It sees "church" as:

- Not only apart from the society,
- But also over against the society.

It is this "separate" idea of church that still affects the way many of us see the church in relationship to society – at a respectable distance from society.

So churches contribute to society through:

- Denominational agencies
- Congregational activities
- Congregants' occupations.

But churches tend to keep society at a respectable distance. Of church attendees surveyed one Sunday morning in churches all over Australia, 40% said they had contact with no more than two people in the locality for more than 15 minutes per week – and 16% said they had no contact at all. Moreover, 78% said they weren't involved in serving the locality that they were located in outside church activities.

However, when Jesus first used the word *ecclesia* it was not a religious term; it was a political term. It referred to a "community council," or people in a locality who were "called aside" for a while, to consider how to promote the welfare of their locality.

The church was never intended to be "those called out of the society." The church was called to be "in it" – but "not of it." Not "apart from the society" – but "a part of the society" that "promotes the welfare of the society." Not fighting "against flesh and blood" but against "principalities and powers" in the society that oppress people.

Note that this definition of church is essentially "connected." It sees church as:

- A *part of* the society,
- *Working for* the welfare of the society.

To connect with society we need to move from bonding to bridging.[6]

Bonding

- Bonds are strong, inward-looking connections, like those in a marriage, that are exclusive.
- Bonds produce deep, "thick trust" and are essential for people who are nurturing and supporting one another to "get by."

Churches, with their emphasis on family, do bonding pretty well.

Bridging

- Bridges are weak, outward-looking connections, like those made by the civil rights movement, that are inclusive.
- Bridges produce broad, "thin trust" and are crucial for people co-operating and campaigning with others to "get on."

Churches, with their suspicion of others who are not considered to be brothers or sisters in the family of faith, do not generally do bridging very well.

Churches need to continue to bond, but not at the expense of building bridges to people in our communities.

◊ *Consider the following questions and record your answers in your working notes.*

---

[6] Adapted from R. Putnam, *Bowling Alone* (Sydney: Simon & Schuster, 2000), pp. 361–62.

1. What is the difference between understanding the church as "apart from the society" and understanding the church as "a part of the society"?

2. What difference, if any, do you think that this understanding makes?

3. What is the difference between "bonding" and "bridging" behaviour?

4. How is your church doing with building bridges to people in your locality?

3.2. Changing our Image of Church

30 minutes

I used to see the church as "the light of the world," a "city of virtue set high on top of a hill," shining brightly for the whole world to see.

Maybe that is what Jesus had in mind when he told his disciples that they were the "light of the world." With one church scandal after another blazoned across the tabloid headlines today, however, it would be ridiculous for us to present the church as "the light of the world."

The Scriptures present another, humbler, image of the church. Consider the Parable of the yeast and the flour.

Jesus said that:

> *The kingdom of heaven is like yeast that a woman took and mixed into a large amount of flour until it worked all through the dough.* (Matt. 13:33)

Modest as it is, this is in fact a significant image that has the potential to not only reframe the role of the church, but also to restore its reputation in the community. For the purposes of our discussion, think of the "church" as the "yeast" and the "community" as the "dough."

Note that the yeast only does its work when it is mixed into the flour. It is only then that the yeast makes a difference. And what difference does it make? It causes everything into which it has been mixed to rise!

There are two time-honoured ways of mixing with people in the community that the Jews refer to in Yiddish as *schmoozing* and *maching* (pronounced "mucking").[7]

---

[7] Adapted from Putnam, *Bowling Alone*, pp. 92–94.

Schmoozing

- *Schmoozers* take an informal approach to mixing.
- *Schmoozers* like to visit family, drop in on friends, invite newcomers over for barbecues, or go for picnics with old friends.

Maching

- *Machers* tend to take a more formal approach to mixing.
- *Machers* are more likely to attend a workshop on community, start a community group, or implement a community project.

Interestingly, one will often find that people are *schmoozers* or *machers* at different stages in life. As Putnam says:

> "Schmoozing" peaks among young adults, enters a long decline as family and community obligations press in, then rises again with retirement; while "maching" is relatively modest early in life, peaks in late middle age, and declines with retirement.

The two types of involvement overlap. *Schmoozers* can be *machers* and *machers* can be *schmoozers*. Most of the time, however, we tend to be mainly one or the other.

1. Do you think you are a **schmoozer** or a **macher**?
2. Think of five individuals in your church community. Can you identify their different mixing styles?

◊ *Record your reflections in your working notes.*

To mix effectively, we do need to be both *schmoozers* and *machers*. We need to take an informal approach to mixing:

- Visiting family
- Dropping in on friends
- Inviting newcomers over for barbeques
- Going on picnics with old friends.

We also need to take a formal approach to mixing:

- Attending seminars on community
- Starting community organizations
- Implementing community projects.

We don't all have to do everything the same way. Different people will play different roles at different times. Whatever we choose to do will but begin the process of mixing that will slowly but surely ferment change in the community – developing relationships that will raise the quality of life.

◊ *Consider the following questions and record your answers in your working notes.*

1. Why is it so important for the church to mix with society?
2. How do **schmoozers** mix with people in their circles?
3. How do **machers** mix with people in their circles?
4. What are you already doing that could be called **schmoozing**?
5. What are you already doing that could be called **maching**?
6. How could you do more **schmoozing** in your circles?
7. How could you do more **maching** in your circles?

3.3. Changing our Model of Church

50 minutes

I was brought up to try to be "a *great* man of God." As William Carey, a famous Baptist missionary, said:

> To *expect* great things *from* God; *attempt* great things *for* God.

Hence, I was always looking for something *great* to do. One day, however, I was confronted with the example of Jesus. Jesus' approach was not *great*. To the contrary, he consciously set aside any aspirations that he may have had to greatness. In addition, Paul says that those of us who would follow the example of Jesus need to empty ourselves of our ambition to do *big* things – so we can do *little* things with a lot of love over the long haul – as little brothers and sisters of Jesus.[8]

Paul unpacks the implications of Jesus' example of practical compassion for us when he writes:

> Each of you should look not only to your own interests, but also to the interests of others.

> Your attitude should be the same as that of Christ Jesus:

> Who, being in very nature God, did not consider equality with God something to be grasped, but made himself nothing, taking the very nature of a servant, being made in human likeness. And being found in appearance as a man, he humbled himself and became obedient to death – even death on a cross! (Phil. 2:4–8)

---

[8] Adapted from D. Andrews, *Not Religion, but Love* (Oxford: Lion, 2001).

Paul points out that Jesus moved in alongside us, as one of us. He did not try to be different. He lived the same life that other people lived, experiencing the same hassles and the same hardships as everybody else. Jesus wasn't full of himself. Rather, emptying himself, he immersed himself in the lives of others, allowing their concerns to fill his consciousness. In the midst of their common struggle, Jesus made himself available to the people as their servant, seeking in all he said and did to set them free to live their lives to the full. When it came to the crunch, Jesus did not cut and run. He was prepared to pay the price for his commitment to people – in blood, sweat and tears.

Paul says that practising compassion means taking the approach Jesus took. It is not something we can do vicariously through others. It is something we must do ourselves. There is a role for organizations. They may provide a useful framework for the work we want to do in the community.

And there is also a role for professionals. They may provide extra insight, knowledge and skills that are useful for increasing the effectiveness of the work we want to do. But there is simply no substitute for our face-to-face, hands-on, grass-roots involvement. If we're going to follow Jesus' example of involvement, we've got to step out into the community and get our hands dirty too.

Step one – move into the locality

We must be willing to set aside our concerns for security and status. We must be willing to forego the comforts that privilege and position bring, in order to meet people, many of whom are profoundly disadvantaged and distressed, on their territory and on their terms.

Step two – remember our humanity

We must not try to be different from the people around us. Rather, we must discover the similarities we share in the humanity that runs as blood through our veins. We all get sick. We all get tired. We all grow old. Nevertheless, we all want to love and be loved. And we all want to live life to the full before we die. We can share these common struggles with our brothers and sisters in the community – even if our economics, politics, culture and religion are poles apart.

Step three – empty ourselves

We must empty ourselves of our preoccupation with our own thoughts and feelings so that we can immerse ourselves in the lives of others and allow their joy and their anguish to fill our lives.

Step four – serve others

We must enter into people's struggles with them and, in the context of that struggle, serve them as a servant – not like a public servant, but like a personal servant. Our relationships with people should be marked by an uncommon quality of care, a quality of life that reflects the love of Christ who came "not to be served, but to serve, and to give his life as the price he was willing to pay" to bring life to people in the community.

Step five – embrace suffering

If we are going to have any hope of bringing life to people in our communities, we too must be willing to pay the price – by dying to ourselves in the midst of the inevitable frustrations, tensions, difficulties and conflicts that work in the community always entails. There is no easy option. If there had been, Jesus would have taken it. He was a Messiah, not a masochist.

Jesus took the hard path because it was the only path that led to the practise of compassion. And, for those of us who would follow in his footsteps, there is no other way than to open our hearts and risk the heartache and the heartbreak of real involvement in people's lives. Compassion comes from the Latin words *com*, meaning "with," and *passion*, meaning "suffering." So to practise "com-passion" means "being willing to suffer with others" – like Christ did.

The third step above is the central one. I know of no step more difficult to take in our society than emptying ourselves and making time and space for others.

The first thing we need to empty ourselves of is seeking success

As part of the great consumer generation, we all tend to be more preoccupied with materialistic rather than non-materialistic values – like appearance, finances and success. Radicals have as many difficulties with these things as conservatives do; we are just preoccupied with different versions of the same thing. We want to be like Mother Teresa rather than Princess Di – or Mahatma Gandhi rather than Winston Churchill. But we all tend to be preoccupied – positive or negatively – with body image, private property and public recognition. We need to empty ourselves of our preoccupation with materialism and make time and space for the Spirit.

The second thing we need to empty ourselves of is game playing

We may try to empty ourselves of materialistic values and embrace more non-materialistic values – like personal development, social responsibility and communal contributions. However, we are often still so influenced by the materialistic perspective of our materialistic culture that we tend to give our spiritual acceptance, relationships and connections a heavy-handed materialistic twist.

A materialistic perspective leads to the "objectification" of people – turning our relationships with "people" into relationships with "things" (what Martin Buber describes as "I-Thou" to "I-It" relationships). A materialistic perspective leads to the "utilization" of people – using "people" as we would use "things" as means to attain our ends. Materialistic people tend to develop "instrumental friendships" which are characterized by a low degree of empathy, a high degree of manipulation and a willingness to disclose truth only when it is useful.[9]

This leads to a lot of game playing. We all know the rules. Keep the conversation shallow, but pretend it is deep. Talk about yourself, but tune out when others talk about themselves. Use meaningful jargon, but avoid a genuine meeting of souls. Two of the favourite games conservative Christians play are the "piety game" and the "proselytization game." And two of the favourite games radical Christians play are the "ideology game" and the "indoctrination game."

The object of both the "piety game" and the "ideology game" is to convince others and ourselves of our virtue. In both the "piety game" and the "ideology game" we judge people on the basis of our pet issues. We are not concerned about meeting people at their points of need. In these games we use their needs to make them look bad – and to make

---

[9] T. Kasser, *The High Price of Materialism* (London: The MIT Press, 2002), pp. 67–70.

us look good by comparison. All of this prevents a genuine encounter in which we can come to terms with our common needs together.

The object of both the "proselytization game" and the "indoctrination game" is to convince as many people as possible to join our cause. In both the "proselytization game" and the "indoctrination game," we treat people as faceless commodities – potential trophies for us to win.

We do not treat people as people. If we meet people's needs, it is not so much to help them win, but to help us win them over. Both the "proselytization game" and the "indoctrination game" may promote encounters with people, but they subvert the possibility of developing relationships of mutual acceptance and respect.

Jesus refused to play games. He criticized people who played "piety" and "ideology games" (Matt. 23:23). He also criticized people who played "proselytization" and "indoctrination games" (Matt. 23:15). He condemned those who pretended to be concerned for the welfare of others when their only concern was for themselves (Matt. 23:25). He consistently called for a genuine concern for others. Hence, Jesus calls us to empty ourselves of everything – everything but love.

The third thing we need to empty ourselves of is wasting time

If we want to relate to people in our locality we need to *live* in our locality. We need to empty ourselves of our tendency to live our lives everywhere else but where we are located.

If we want to relate to people in our locality we need to not only *live* in our locality, but also *stay* in our locality.

People who expect to move in five years are 25% less likely to get involved in their locality.[10] If we want to get more involved, we need to stay around for more than five years. To do that, we need to empty ourselves of our tendency to keep on the move.

If we want to relate to people in our locality we need to spend less time at church and more time in our locality. If we reduce involvement in church to three meetings per week – a large celebratory gathering, a small nurture group and a small action group – then we will have more time for locality. To do that, we will need to empty ourselves of our preoccupation with church.

---

[10] Putnam, *Bowling Alone*, p. 205.

If we want to relate to people in our locality we need to spend less time at *work* and more time in our locality. Two-career, full-time working households are less likely to be involved in their community, but both men and women in part-time work are more likely to have opportunities for community involvement. To increase our involvement, we will need to empty ourselves of our preoccupation with career-orientated, full-time work.

If we want to relate to people in our locality, we need to spend less time *commuting* and more time *communicating*. Every ten minutes not spent in commuting increases the possibility of community involvement by 10% – not only of the commuters, but those associated with them.

If we want to spend more time communicating, we need to stop watching *Neighbours* and start relating to our neighbours. Those who watch the news on television, however, are more likely to be involved in the community than those who do not. Those who watch talk shows, game shows and soap operas are less likely to be involved in the community.[11] There are three reasons for this.

1. TV takes time. On average, people now watch television four hours per day.
2. TV induces passivity. The more people watch TV, the more likely they are to want to rest and/or sleep.
3. TV provides a sense of pseudo-community (for example, through soap operas like *Neighbours*). Each extra hour a day spent watching TV reduces community involvement by 10%.[12] The easiest way to make more time for our community is to turn off the television.

So we turn off the TV. But where do we start? The answer is – start wherever you are!

Hugh Mackay says the trick is to remember that it's "not about *where* you live," but "*how* you live *wherever* you are."[13]

> If communities are going to be regenerated, people need to reconnect face-to-face. Once that happens, the rest will follow. All over suburbs, you can still see people "popping next-door" to do some babysitting or to borrow the stereotypical cup of sugar." The challenge is to make it happen more![14]

---

[11] Putnam, *Bowling Alone*, p. 243.

[12] Putnam, *Bowling Alone*, p. 228.

[13] Hugh Mackay, *Turning Point* (Sydney: Macmillan, 1999), p. 268.

[14] Mackay, *Turning Point*, p. 268.

◊ Consider the following questions and record your answers in your working notes.

1. Why are so many of us obsessed with the idea of greatness?
2. What does it mean to be little brothers and sisters of Jesus?
3. What are the five steps we are to take to step into our communities?
4. Which step would you find easiest to take? Why?
5. Which step would you find hardest to take? Why?
6. What is the "central" step in the process? Why is it so crucial?
7. Which part of "emptying yourself" is most difficult for you?
8. What is the next step you need to take into community?
9. What help do you need in order to take that next step?

4.   CONCLUSION

The follow-up reading for this session is:
*   *Not Religion, but Love*, pp. 26–51/9–35.[15]

The set community tasks for this session are:

◊ Talk with two or three people outside your church this week about their view of the locality in which you live. Find out about their experience of the locality as a community.

1. If it is not too intrusive or threatening for them, gently inquire if they feel at home in the community. If they do, ask them to tell you some stories that illustrate why they feel at home in the community.
2. If they don't, ask them what would have to change in order to make them feel more at home in the community.

◊ Meet with your learning partner and discuss how your findings compare or contrast with the material in this session and the reading from *Not Religion, but Love*.

◊ *Record your actions, reflections and conclusions in your working notes.*

---

[15] The page numbers after the "/" refers to numbers in the 2005 Tafina Press editions published in Australia, The Lion (UK) and Pilgrim Press (USA) editions page numbers are the same and these precede the "/".

THE STRATEGIES OF COMMUNITY DEVELOPMENT

1. PREPARATION

1.1. Objectives

- To review your understanding of the dominant ideas, images and models of the church, and how they impact the church's potential to be an agent of community development
- To review your understanding of what issues those ideas, images and models of church raise for you
- To introduce Christ-like community development strategies – the principle of justice and the processes of relief, education, confrontation, formation and transformation

2. REVIEW

15 minutes

Review your work from the previous session.

Review the issues raised in Session 3, demonstrating your ability to distinguish between different kinds of community and your understanding of the church as a kind of "intentional", "testamental" community with the potential to become an effective catalyst for "integral" community development.

Review the reading:

Not Religion, but Love (Oxford: Lion, 2001/Cleveland: Pilgrim Press), pp. 26–51/(Armidale: Tafina), pp. 9–35.

Review the tasks:

1. What was the most important thing you learned while doing the community tasks for the last session?

2. How was your discussion with your learning partner about how your findings compare or contrast with the course material and the reading in **Not Religion, but Love**?

Finish your review with a consideration of three of the questions raised in the reading:

1. How do you respond to the way Christ related to people on the periphery?

2. How can you become more sympathetic towards others?

3. What does the practice of true compassion mean to you?

◊ *Record your reflections in your working notes.*

3. THE FOCUS OF CHRIST-LIKE COMMUNITY DEVELOPMENT

45 minutes

3.1. The Sheep and the Goats

Read the Parable of the sheep and the goats as told by Jesus:

> *When the Human One comes, all the nations will be gathered before him, and he will separate the people one from another as a shepherd separates the sheep from the goats. He will put the sheep – who have done right – on his right, and the goats – who haven't – on his left. Then the True Leader will say to those on his right, "Come, join the party. For I was hungry and you gave me food. I was thirsty and you gave me a drink. I just arrived in town and you took me into your home. My clothes were in tatters and you gave me your own outfit. I was sick in bed and you came and spent time with me. I was stuck in prison and you were there for me and my family." Stunned, the people on the right will say to him, "When on earth did we see you hungry and give you a feed, or thirsty and give you a drink? When did we meet you after you had just arrived in town and give you a bed for the night? When were you sick in bed and we spent time with you? When were you stuck in prison and we were there for you and*

your family?" The True Leader will say, "Whenever you did the right thing by those whom most consider least, you did the right thing by me!" Then, turning to those that are left, the True Leader will say, "Get out. You can go to hell with everyone else who has made life hell for others. I was hungry and you never gave me a feed; thirsty and you never gave me a drink; lonely, without a friend, and you walked by; half-naked and you didn't give me any clothes; sick in bed, and stuck in jail, and you didn't even visit." And those who are left will be bewildered, and say, "When did we see you hungry or thirsty? When did we see you without a friend or without clothes? When did we see you sick in bed or stuck in prison?" And the True Leader will say to them, "Whenever you did not do the right thing by those whom most consider least, you did not do the right thing by me!" (Matt. 25:31–46 [author's version])

1. Why do you think both the "sheep" and the "goats" were so surprised by the connection Jesus made between the way they had treated those "whom most consider least" and the "True Leader"?

2. What are your reactions to Jesus' suggestion that, on Judgment Day, we will all be judged by the way that we have treated "the least"?

3. What is the principle by which we will all be judged?

4. Who are those "that most consider least" in our society?

5. How can we treat "the least" so that we do them justice?

6. In what ways are we most likely not to do the right thing by those in the community that most of us consider "least"?

7. What excuses do you usually use to rationalize your failures?

8. What do you imagine God's response will be to our rationalizations?

9. How can we make sure we succeed more often than we fail in doing the right thing by those in the community "that most consider least"?

10. If we focus on doing the right thing by those in the community "that most consider least," what difference will that make in how we do community work?

◊ *Record your answers to these questions in your working notes.*

4.   STRATEGIES FOR CHRIST-LIKE COMMUNITY DEVELOPMENT

45 minutes

Jesus used a comprehensive range of strategies to help people.

Community relief

- Precept – You help people yourself
- Proverb – "You give them a fish!"

Community education

- Precept – You train people to help themselves
- Proverb – "You teach them to fish themselves!"

Community confrontation

- Precept – You challenge groups who won't help
- Proverb – "You protest industries polluting the fishing grounds!"

Community formation

- Precept – You develop a way of helping one another
- Proverb – "You develop a little fishing co-operative!"

Community transformation

- Precept – People adopt that way as their way of life
- Proverb – "The fishing community becomes co-operative!"

4.1. Community Relief

Jesus took it upon himself to meet the needs of others.

Jesus and his disciples gave regular gifts of money to people so that their immediate needs could be met (Jn. 12:4–6; 13:29).

The emergency relief that Jesus and his disciples provided was a simple transfer – in cash or kind, with no strings attached – to anyone in need who asked for help. In the most famous example of this, Jesus was approached to provide food for a crowd of more than five thousand people who were desperately hungry because they had not eaten for three days. Though his disciples were daunted by the size of the request, Jesus didn't hesitate. Refusing to send the crowd away hungry, Jesus simply asked for donations of food, then began to distribute the bits of bread and pieces of fish that he was given, with a prayer on his lips that there would be enough to go around and – miraculously – there was more than enough for everyone (Mk. 6:37–44).

4.2. Community Education

Jesus also taught the community to meet their own needs.

The teaching of Jesus, as seen in the Sermon on the Mount, took the form of non-formal education. He taught people that there would never be enough resources in the world to gratify anyone's greed, but that there are more than enough resources in the world – if shared – to satisfy everyone's need.

The classic example of this is Jesus' encounter with Zacchaeus, the notorious tax collector. Over a meal together, Jesus talked to Zacchaeus about the possibility of a community meeting its own needs and the importance of people in the community, like him, playing their part in the process. Jesus encouraged Zacchaeus to renounce his greed, to redistribute his riches to the poor so as to meet their needs and to make restitution to the community for the extortion he had committed (Lk. 19:1–10).

4.3. Community Confrontation

Jesus challenged all community groups to meet the needs in their communities, and he confronted organizations that refused to play their part in meeting needs in their communities.

Jesus turned the process of direct, public, non-violent, political confrontation into an art form. The most famous of these confrontations was Jesus' attack on the temple in Jerusalem. One day, when Jesus was in the temple, he observed that the Court of the Gentiles was so crowded with temple officials and their flunkies that no Gentiles could get in. And what were these temple officials and their flunkies doing? They were flogging off temple sacrifices at vastly inflated, monopoly prices – exploiting the vulnerability of the worshippers, who came from afar to offer their sacrifices of thanksgiving to God at the great temple in the Holy City.

As he watched what was happening, Jesus became more and more angry. Here was exploitation of the worst kind – the religious authorities ripping off innocent believers in the name of God. So Jesus overturned the tables of the merchants and drove them out of the temple, with a rebuke ringing in their ears.

> *This temple was meant to be a place of prayer for people, but you and your henchmen have turned it into the home cave of Ali Baba's forty thieves!* (Lk. 19:45–46 [author's version])

4.4. Community Formation

Jesus developed an alternative model of community which was in contrast to the dominant mode of operating in society that he denounced.

It was not good enough for him to criticize the injustice of the system. He felt he needed to demonstrate a process of community formation, showing how to structure a political economy that would do justice to the poor.

The original model was the "common purse." Jesus and his large band of at least seventy disciples shared a "common purse." People contributed to the common fund as much as they could afford, and took from the common fund as much as they needed. After the expenses of the group were paid, the excess was shared with the poor. This was a revolutionary way of restructuring the political economy of a community which, if adopted by society, had the potential to meet the needs of everybody in the community, including people on the margins (Jn. 12).

4.5. Community Transformation

Jesus encouraged a movement of people in society who would take the alternatives that he had developed with his disciples and implement these principles, practices and processes in their lives, individually and collectively, without hesitation or reserve.

His prayer was for a process of total transformation of society. He not only prayed for this himself, he also taught his disciples to pray earnestly for the day when God's will would be "done, on earth, as it is in heaven," the day when all debts would be cancelled, all wage slaves would be set free, and all men and all women would be able to meet all the basic human needs of their families.

In those early years, the church was a movement of people who took the alternatives that Jesus had developed with his disciples and began to implement these principles, practices and processes in their communities.

Not without hesitation or reservation, but haltingly, and falteringly, these people opened themselves to the Spirit of Christ and to the incredible possibility Christ espoused, that they – as ordinary people – could actually transform society.

They took the co-operative approach of the "common purse" and applied it to a whole range of personal, social and economic issues in their communities. They "devoted themselves to relationships, to sharing meals with each other, and to praying for one another." They were all together with "sincere hearts." They "had everything in common." Even their possessions were held in trust for one another. Whenever it was necessary, "people would sell their possessions," and "give to anyone as they had need," so there "wasn't anyone with an unmet need" (Acts 2:43–45; 4:32–34).

◊ *Record your answers to the following questions in your working notes.*

1. Rate the strategies above from 1 to 5, where 5 stands for the strategy you think church groups and organizations actually use *most,* and 1 stands for the strategy you think church groups and organizations use *least.*

2. Do you think any one of these strategies is more important than another? If so, why? If not, why not?

3. In general, which of these strategies do church people tend to use *more*?

4. In general, which of these strategies do church people tend to use *less*?

Usually, most people will rate "community relief" as 5, "community education" as 4, "community confrontation" as 3, "community development" as 2, and "community transformation" as 1. That is probably a reasonably accurate rating.

In fact, however, no one strategy is more important than another. What is really important is not a particular strategy but the appropriate use of a particular strategy.

We need, then, to consider the following questions.

1. Why do churches tend to use a community relief strategy most?

2. Why do churches tend to use a community transformation strategy least?

There are a whole heap of reasons that are given. Like – "time," "effort," "speed," "ease," "specificity," and so on. However, the most critical reason of all is "control."

1. Why do we tend to use strategies that we can control more?

2. What is the strength of using strategies we can control more?

3. What is the weakness of using strategies we can control more?

4. Where does the power for community transformation come from?

5. Which strategies have the potential to undermine community transformation? How?

6. Which strategies have the potential to undergird community transformation? How?

We need to learn what strategies are most appropriate in a given situation, and how to develop an integrated response that combines all of the appropriate strategies needed to address the given situation systematically.

◊ Choose an issue that your church is confronting, and consider what strategy you could use to deal with it. All five strategies have their time and place. Therefore, you will need to think carefully about which of the processes is most appropriate for addressing any particular issue. It may be that a combination of strategies needs to be adopted in order to try to solve the presenting problems.

◊ Take some time to evaluate the strengths and weaknesses of your proposals.

5.   CONCLUSION

The follow-up reading for this session is:
*   *Not Religion, but Love*, pp. 52–72/36–56.

The set community tasks for this session are:

◊ With your learning partner, organize an informal meeting with a few friends, colleagues and/or neighbours from the community with whom you would like to get more involved. Over a cup of tea or coffee, ask them to talk about the issues they think need to be addressed in the community.

1. The issues you want to address may be in the church community itself.

2. There may be a need for more support for older members, or the need for more options for younger members.

3. The issues you want to address may involve a part of the church community, such as a home group, ministry group or mission group.

4. The issues you want to address may involve the relationship between the church and the locality, such as the church's involvement in its neighbourhood.

5. The issues you want to address may be in the local community itself, such as street violence.

These issues – and many more like them – are possible topics for discussion in your group.

◊ Without putting people under pressure, try to get everyone to prioritize the issues – by putting them in the order that you think they need to be dealt with.

◊ Later, get together with your learning partner and discuss which of the issues you listed as priority you feel you would like to deal with. Talk about the possible responses you could make and the combination of strategies you could use to address the issue(s).

◊ Record your actions, reflections and conclusions in your working notes.

THE SPIRIT OF COMMUNITY DEVELOPMENT

1.   PREPARATION

1.1. Objectives

- To review your understanding of Christ-like community development strategies – including the principle of justice, and the processes of relief, education, confrontation, formation and transformation

- To introduce you to an understanding of Christ-like community development structures – including an understanding of the nature of power, the power of the *Spirit*, the power *within* people, and the power *with* people

2.   REVIEW

Review your work from the previous session.

Review the issues raised in Session 4, particularly the principle of justice, and the processes of relief, education, confrontation, formation and transformation in development.

Review the reading:

Not Religion, but Love, pp. 52–72/36–56.

Review the tasks:

1. How did you find trying to organize an informal meeting with a few friends, colleagues and/or neighbours from the community?

2. What was the most important thing you learned while doing the community tasks for the last session?

◊ *Record your reflections in your working notes.*

3. THE SPIRIT OF CHRIST-LIKE COMMUNITY DEVELOPMENT

30 minutes

In order to understand the inner workings of power, let's begin with a few questions:[16]

- Who do you think is powerful?
- Why do you think this person is powerful?

There are two kinds of power:
1. *Access:* the ability to develop connections, make telephone calls, write letters, talk to people and get invited to meetings at which decisions are made.
2. *Influence:* the ability not only to get to the table, but also to get issues on the table – not only to speak, but also to be heard.

Influence is the kind of power that the Bible says the Spirit of God seeks to instil in his people. Peter says in Acts:

> *In the last days, God says,*
> *I will pour out my Spirit on all people.*
> *Your sons and daughters will prophesy,*
> *your young people will see visions,*
> *your old people will dream dreams.*
> *Even on my servants, both men and women,*
> *I will pour out my Spirit in those days.* (Acts 2:17–18)

There are three kinds of influence:

a) Sanctions

The use of punishments or threats, or the proverbial "stick," to influence an outcome. This is "coercive" power – getting people to do what you want them to do, based on what you can do to them if they don't do it.

1. When are you most tempted to be coercive?
2. What fears provoke this reaction?
3. What fears do you invoke in others?
4. What are the outcomes you achieve that cause you to continue?
5. What are the dangers associated with continuing to be coercive?

Jesus discouraged the use of sanctions.

---

[16] Adapted from B. Lee, *The Power Principle* (New York: Simon & Schuster, 1997).

Jesus called them together and said, "You know that the rulers of the Gentiles lord it over them, and their high officials exercise authority over them. Not so with you. Instead, whoever wants to become great among you must be your servant, and whoever wants to be first must be your slave – just as the Son of Man did not come to be served, but to serve, and to give his life as a ransom for many." (Matt. 20:25–28)

b) Bargains

The use of inducements or rewards – the proverbial "carrot" – to influence an outcome. This is "collaborative" power – getting people to do what you want them to do, based on what you can do for them if they do it for you. Christians often use bargaining. We need to recognize its use, and the limit of it use.

1. What do you offer to people in exchange for doing you favours?

2. How do you try to improve your bargaining power in negotiations?

3. What are some of the limits to your bargaining power?

4. What are some of the limits to bargaining as a means of influence?

Jesus also discouraged the use of bargains:

You have heard that it was said, "Eye for eye, and tooth for tooth." But I tell you . . . If someone strikes you on the right cheek, turn to him the other also. And if someone wants to sue you and take your tunic, let him have your cloak as well. If someone forces you to go one mile, go with him two miles. Give to the one who asks you, and do not turn away from the one who wants to borrow from you. . . . Love your enemies and pray for those who persecute you, that you may be sons of your Father in heaven. He causes his sun to rise on the evil and the good, and sends rain on the righteous and the unrighteous. . . . Be perfect, therefore, as your heavenly Father is perfect. (Matt. 5:38–42, 44–45, 48)

c) Persuasion

Influencing an outcome while preserving the dignity, integrity and credibility of the truth. This is "co-operative" power – getting people to do what needs to be done, in the best way they can, by simply working things out with each other.

Note that Jesus *encouraged* the use of persuasion:

> *On my account you will be brought before governors and kings as*
> *witnesses to them and to the Gentiles. But when they arrest you, do*
> *not worry about what to say or how to say it. At that time you will*
> *be given what to say, for it will not be you speaking, but the Spirit of*
> *your Father speaking through you.* (Matt. 10:18–20)

◊ Think of a person who has influenced you for the better – not through any threats or rewards, but by the inspiriting example that he or she set for you.

◊ Reflect on the influence this person has had on your life and consider how you might become more like him or her.

◊ After reflecting, read this passage of Scripture again:

> *On my account you will be brought before governors and kings as*
> *witnesses to them and to the Gentiles. But when they arrest you, do*
> *not worry about what to say or how to say it. At that time you will*
> *be given what to say, for it will not be you speaking, but the Spirit of*
> *your Father speaking through you.* (Matt. 10:18–20)

◊ Now answer the following question:

What is the source of this power of persuasion that you need?

And, of course, the answer to the question is – "the Spirit." But that answer only leads to another question:

What in the world is the power of the Spirit all about?

4.   THE POWER OF THE SPIRIT

45 minutes

Practising compassion as Jesus did involves developing power that is strong, but gentle, with people. Power that is strong but gentle *with* people is not exercised *over* people. Rather, it is *power that people exercise over themselves.* The power that is strong but gentle *with* people essentially comes from *within* a person or a group of persons.

Yet nearly every time I talk with people about developing a project in their community, the conversation quickly turns away from *internal* sources to focus on *external* sources of power. If people want to organize a welfare program, they talk about funds. "Where can we get the funds we need to run the program?" they enquire. If people want to organize a protest movement, they talk about numbers. "How can we get the numbers we need to get a major social movement on a roll?" they ask. These reactions reveal that people, both on the right and on the left of the political spectrum, believe that external resources matter more than internal sources of power. They believe that we can only do significant work in our communities if we have access to either lots of cash or large crowds, or both. It's essentially all about fund-raising and number-crunching.

Because so many communities frame their problems and the solutions to their problems in terms of access to resources – which, by definition, are beyond their control – they disempower themselves. If they can't get access to the resources they require in order to act, they simply do not act. If they do get the resources they require they may act, but only according to the terms and conditions that have been set for them by those providing the support. Either way, they abrogate their power to solve their own problems; they project the power to solve their problems onto others; and, in so doing, they render themselves powerless.

Jesus challenged people's dependence on external resources for community work. On two occasions he sent his disciples out into various villages to do community work. On the first occasion he forbade them to take any money at all. According to Jesus, money was *not* essential for community work. Money was merely a note promising to share a certain amount of commodities or services. What mattered to Jesus was not that his disciples carried a note that held the promise of help, but that his disciples actually helped the people they met out of their own *internal* resources.

On the second occasion that Jesus sent his disciples out into the community, he allowed them to take a little money – but not much. According to Jesus, money was never to be considered a *primary source*, but rather a *secondary resource*. External resources like money can be helpful as a secondary resource for community work. But if external resources ever become a substitute for internal resources and money becomes a primary, rather than secondary, consideration then, Jesus warned us, that money will destroy not only our work, but also our community. After all, "the love of money is a root of all kinds of evil" (1 Tim. 6:10).

On both occasions that Jesus sent his disciples out to do community work, he didn't send them out in big numbers – and he didn't expect them to get big numbers involved. It was not a mass movement but more a micro movement. He didn't send his disciples out in their hundreds or thousands, but in twos. He didn't expect them to get hundreds or thousands involved, but one here and one there. As far as Jesus was concerned, two meeting one and forming a group of three was a big enough crowd to begin to overthrow the order of the day.

For Jesus, a "trinity" was not so much a theological abstraction as it was a theological strategy for developing true community in society. A group of three could create, within themselves, the stability and security necessary for any development. "A cord of three strands is not quickly broken" (Eccl. 4:12). A group of three could create, within themselves, the subjectivity and objectivity necessary for community development. Let "every matter . . . be established by the testimony of two or three witnesses" (Matt. 18:16). And a group of three could create, within themselves, the time and space necessary for Christ-like community development. "For where two or three come together in my name," Jesus said, "there am I with them" (Matt. 18:20).

According to Jesus, a small, apparently insignificant, group of just three people can actually have all the internal resources they need to create a significant movement in society towards community.

Most attempts to bring about change in society haven't come unstuck because the groups involved lacked the funds or the numbers. Most have fallen apart because of power struggles that caused the groups to self-destruct. The people involved lacked the power to change themselves, let alone their society. Hence, Jesus taught that the most important single issue in bringing about change was for groups to discover the power to be able to manage their affairs in a way that gave everyone a fair go. This power would enable them to transcend their selfishness, resolve their conflicts and deal with their issues in a way that does justice to everybody involved. Without that strong but gentle power, Jesus said that we should not even try to start working for change, lest we end up destroying the world that we are trying to create (Lk. 24:49).

Once we have that strong but gentle power, however, Jesus said that nothing on earth can stop us from building a better world – neither lack of funds nor lack of numbers – nothing (Matt. 17:20)! So, when Jesus sent his disciples out to build a better world, he imparted to them what he called the power of the Spirit (Jn. 20:21–22).

The Holy Spirit is not "a spirit of timidity, but a spirit of power," characterized by self-discipline and compassion for others (2 Tim. 1:7). So, as they received the Spirit, it produced in them the strong but gentle power to control themselves and to love others as they loved themselves.

Most people who have been involved in trying to bring about change in the world would find it easy to accept Jesus' idea – that power is the single most important issue in the process. But many would find it more difficult to accept the kind of power – "the power of the Spirit" – that Jesus advocated. This is not merely because of the spiritual language Jesus used to describe this power, but also because of the substantial difference between the dominant notion of power to which many of us subscribe and the power of the Holy Spirit.

Traditionally, people have defined power as *the ability to control other people.* The emphasis is on bringing about change through *coercion* – trying to make others change to fit our agendas. While according to this traditional definition power means *taking control of our lives by taking control of others,* Jesus' radical alternative says that power means *taking control of ourselves.*

Jesus emphasizes *bringing change by conversion.* Instead of trying to make others change, we try to change ourselves, individually and collectively, in the light of a glorious agenda for justice. This power breaks the control that others have over us and liberates us from our desire to control others. The traditional notion of power is popular because it often brings quick, dramatic results. But the cost of short-term gains for some is long-term losses for everyone else. Every violent revolution has – sooner or later – betrayed the people in whose name the bloody war of liberation was fought. Jesus' notion of power is unpopular because it usually involves a slow, unspectacular process. But Jesus' approach is the only way for groups to transcend their selfishness, resolve their conflicts and manage their affairs in a way that does justice for everyone.

The essential problem in any situation of injustice is that one human being is exercising control over another and exploiting the relationship of dominance.

The solution to the problem is not simply to reverse roles in the hope that, once the roles have been reversed, the manipulation will discontinue. The solution is, rather, for people to stop trying to control each other. All of us, to one degree or another, exploit the opportunity if we have control over another person's life.

Commonsense, therefore, dictates that the traditional approach to power will not solve the problem of exploitation. The solution is in the alternative – the strong but gentle approach – which emphasizes controlling ourselves, individually and collectively, through self-managed processes and structures.

Some of us sincerely believe that, if we are to help people, particularly the oppressed, we need to manage their affairs for them. But, regardless of how we try to rationalize it, controlling others always empowers us and disempowers those we seek to help. The only way people, and particularly the oppressed, can be helped is for them to be empowered to take control of their own lives. This is why Jesus explicitly forbade his followers to take control over others, no matter how dire the circumstances. Their job was not to seek control, but to enable others to take control over their own lives (Matt. 20:25–28). It is a pity that many of us who claim to follow Christ have not followed his advice. We could have been saved the Crusades and the Inquisition.

It's interesting to note that Jesus and his disciples used organic images to describe how "the power of the Spirit" – the secret of *swaraj*, or self-rule[17] – actually operates in our lives. Self-management is described as the "fruit of the Spirit" (Gal. 5:22). The capacity to manage ourselves develops quite unobtrusively

---

[17] *'Swaraj'* is a Hindi term used in India for independence.

– indeed, as quietly as fruit growing on a tree. Although it develops unobtrusively, however, it is far more significant than we might imagine. Like a tiny seed so small it seems like it could never amount to anything great, the "power of the Spirit" seems embarrassingly insignificant at first. And yet it grows to be of tremendous significance (Matt. 13:31–32).

This capacity to control our own lives does not develop without opposition but, like a plant growing in the midst of weeds, "the power of the Spirit" grows strong in an environment that could easily destroy it (Matt. 13:24–30). How the seeds of transformation that bear the "fruit of the Spirit" grow in a community always was, and always will be, a mystery (Mk. 4:26–29). However, it is no secret that the seeds of transformation that bear this fruit of the Spirit will not grow in a community unless those of us whose lives constitute those seeds bury ourselves in the life of our community. "Unless a grain of wheat falls to the ground and dies, it remains only a single seed. But if it dies, it produces many seeds" (Jn. 12:24). (From *Not Religion, but Love*, pp. 73–78/57–62.)

This suggests that Jesus had in mind not only a particular spirit, but also a particular personal, relational and organizational structure for the community work he wanted his disciples to do.

◊ *Consider the following questions and record your answers in your working notes.*

1. What is the difference between internal and external sources of power?

2. What sources of external power do we usually rely on?

3. What are the problems associated with relying on external power?

4. What kind of internal power does Jesus say we should rely on?

5. What do you think it means to have power **within** you? Give a few examples.

6. What does it mean to have power **with**, rather than power **over**, people?

7. How can we encourage people to change without trying to control them?

8. How can we encourage people to learn to take control of their own lives?

5.   THE DYNAMICS OF COMMUNITY DEVELOPMENT

10 minutes

At the heart of Paul's "charter for healthy community" is his concern for people to co-operate with the *Spirit of community*.

> *Make sure you don't lack in enthusiasm, but maintain your spiritual passion, serving the Lord. Be joyful in hope, patient in affliction, faithful in prayer. Be careful to do what is right in the eyes of everybody.* (Rom. 12:11–13 [author's version])

A healthy community is first and foremost a work of the Spirit. It doesn't begin or end with us. It begins and ends with the Spirit – whether other people recognize it as the work of the Spirit or not. The church community in Acts that we considered above is a classic example.

> *When the day of Pentecost came, they were all together in one place. Suddenly a sound like the blowing of a violent wind came from heaven and filled the whole house where they were sitting. They saw what seemed to be tongues of fire that separated and came to rest on each of them. All of them were filled with the Holy Spirit and began to speak in other tongues as the Spirit enabled them.*

> *Now there were staying in Jerusalem God-fearing Jews from every nation under heaven. When they heard this sound, a crowd came together in bewilderment, because each one heard them speaking in his own language. Utterly amazed, they asked: "Are not all these men who are speaking Galileans? Then how is it that each of us hears them in his own native language? Parthians, Medes and Elamites; residents of Mesopotamia, Judea and Cappadocia, Pontus and Asia, Phrygia and Pamphylia, Egypt and the parts of Libya near Cyrene; visitors from Rome (both Jews and converts to Judaism); Cretans and Arabs – we hear them declaring the wonders of God in our own tongues!" Amazed and perplexed, they asked one another, "What does this mean?"*

> *And Peter answered them:*

> *"In the last days, God says, I will pour out my Spirit on all people. Your sons and daughters will prophesy, your young people will see visions, your old people will dream dreams. Even on my servants, both men and women, I will pour out my Spirit in those days."* (Acts 2:1–12, 17–18)

Any time we see a glimpse of healthy community – a meaningful moment of real reciprocal communication and co-operation in a world with so little regard "to do what is right in the eyes of everybody" – it is a miracle.

But we need to remember that these miracles occur not only in the extraordinary events that happen, but also in the course of our everyday lives.

◊ Reflect on the following questions to identify some of these miracles in your own experience:

1. What characterized the best times you've had with the people in your church?

2. When did you feel most at home with people in your church at church?

3. When did you feel most at home with people in your church outside of church?

◊ *Record your reflections in your working notes.*

We need to not only recognize these moments of camaraderie, but also celebrate these moments as ordinary, everyday miracles.

As psycho-social researchers David Cooperrider and Suresh Srivasta say, "there are simply no theories that can account for the life-giving essence of co-operative existence. *Co-operative human interaction is a miracle.*"[18]

But to say that a healthy community is first and foremost a work of the Spirit that doesn't begin or end with us but with the Spirit does not mean that the role you and I can play in developing a healthy community is insignificant. In fact, the contrary is true.

We can either nurture the spirit of community or hinder the spirit of community. If we are unco-operative, we can actually squash or stifle the Spirit's initiatives. Therefore, we are urged in Scripture to not quench the Spirit (1 Thess. 5:19).

---

[18] David Cooperrider and Suresh Srivasta, "Appreciative Inquiry in Organizational Life," in *Research in Organizational Change and Development*, I (Greenwich, CT: JAI Press, 1987), pp. 129ff.

6.   THE INDICATORS OF HEALTHY COMMUNITY DEVELOPMENT

10 minutes

The following constitute Paul's "indicators of a healthy community" (2 Cor. 3:17; Gal. 5:22–23).

> *The fruit of the Spirit (in a community) is love, joy, peace, patience, kindness, goodness, faithfulness, tolerance and self-control . . .*

At a personal level there is:

> *love – passion and compassion*
>
> *joy – awareness and appreciation*
>
> *peace – trust and tranquillity*

At a relational level there is:

> *patience – persistence*
>
> *kindness – sweetness, not bitterness*

At a social level there is:

> *goodness – generosity*
>
> *faithfulness – fidelity*

At a political level there is:

> *gentleness – and non-violence*
>
> *self-control – and self-management. Against such things there is no law.* (Gal. 5:22–23)

Note that a healthy community must be assessed at all of these different levels: personal, relational, social and political.

◊ Unpack some of the practical implications of these indicators for the development of a healthy community by asking the following questions:

1. What signs of love, joy and peace would you look for as indicators that people within a community are healthy?

2. How can you encourage people to be more loving, joyful and peaceful?

3. What signs of patience and kindness would you look for as indicators of a community being healthy relationally?

4. How can you encourage people to be kinder with each other?

5. What signs of goodness and faithfulness would you look for as indicators of a community being healthy socially?

6. How can you encourage people to treat each other better?

7. What signs of tolerance and self-control would you look for as indicators of community being healthy politically?

8. How can you encourage people to be more self-managed as a group?

9. Why do you think Paul insists that a key indicator of a healthy community is that, within it, there is "no law against these things"?

◊ *Record your conclusions in your working notes.*

7.   CONCLUSION

The follow-up reading for this session is:
* *Not Religion, but Love*, pp. 73–83/57–68.

The set community tasks for this session are:

◊ With your learning partner, try to identify at least one person in the community who might be interested in joining you and doing some work in the community with you. Meet over a cup of tea or coffee and talk about the possibility of forming a small informal group that could act as a community development support group for the work that you would like to do in the community.

◊ Discuss the issues you talked about last week with your friends, the issues you listed as priority issues and the possible strategies you could use to address the issue(s).

◊ Decide on an issue you would like to deal with together. Talk about the kinds of things you would like to do. Then discuss the kinds of things you would need to do *before* you would be able to tackle the issue.

◊ Record your actions, reflections and conclusions in your working notes.

BREAKING THROUGH THE BARRIER OF FUTILITY

1. PREPARATION

1.1. Objectives

- To review your understanding of Christ-like community development structures
- To consider barriers that might block the progress you would like to make towards community development – beginning with your sense of hopelessness about being able to bring about change

2. REVIEW

Review your work from the previous session.

Review the issues raised in Session 5, particularly Christ-like community development structures – including an understanding of the nature of power, the power of the *Spirit*, the power *within* people, and the power *with* people, as well as Trinitarian structures that create the space for the development of that power.

Review the reading:

Not Religion, but Love, pp. 73–83/57–68.

Review the tasks:

1. How did your meeting with your learning partner go?

2. What was the most important thing you learned while doing the community tasks for the last session?

Finish with a detailed reflection on the kinds of things you would need to do *before* you could tackle the issue.

◊ *Record your reflections in your working notes.*

3.   **ANY ANXIETIES?**[19]

30 minutes

Reflect for a moment and try to articulate any anxieties that the course has raised so far. Have you felt challenged to the point of being a bit uncomfortable with any of the course material or set community tasks? Have you left your comfort zone at all?

We are all anxious now and again – especially when we are trying to do something we have never done before, or when we are trying to do something we have done before but in a new way. At the very beginning of his ministry, Jesus was anxious.

Read the following reflection, slowly and thoughtfully.

> *The scene is barren,*
> *Jesus has journeyed into the wilderness*
> *to a place the Jews call Jeshimmon,*
>   *"the place of devastation."*
> *He finds himself*
> *amidst blasted hills and broken valleys,*
> *in a bare land strewn with hard boulders,*
>   *where only the slow dust speaks.*
> *It is the ruin of a land;*
> *the resting place of many a dream.*
> *Where the realities of life and death*
> *take on stark contrasting shapes and colours.*
> *The Desert's breath is stale and still,*
>   *the air thick with the weariness of time.*
> *It is a quiet place, without the confusion*
> *of a more so-called civilized situation.*
>
> *Here he stops and sits and reflects,*
> *inhaling the quietness, listening to his heart.*
> *This is a place of rumination;*
> *a place where the muddy water clears*
>   *and the spirit plumbs its depths.*
> *Jesus contemplates.*
> *He thinks of his encounter with John*
> *the man they call "The Baptist."*
> *The skies tearing open,*
> *the fluttering of wings,*
>   *the sound of the Voice.*

---

[19] Adapted from D. Andrews, et al., *Building Better Communities* (Brisbane: Praxis, 2000).

A seeing and a hearing,
a glimpsing of the unseen and the unspoken,
       a grasping of a vision and a vocation.
Earth and heaven bursting with a new beginning,
       and his own unbearable, undeniable, calling;
to hold the dream, and to not rest until it be born
       to bear the pain of bringing it to birth.
He considers John.
John, the prophet and the preacher,
       the wild man calling for wild changes.
Longing for the will of God,
       aching for love and justice in the land,
insisting the impossible is possible,
       and, not just possible, but imperative!
Jesus feels the echo of the message
       resounding in his own soul,
smells the fragrance of the spirit
       wafting through the air.
Oh, to be a part of the movement;
       to bring the dream into being.
Fleshing out faith,
       speaking grace, practising equality.
"Filling every valley, levelling every hill,
       making the crooked paths straight,
       making the rough paths smooth,
ensuring every man and woman
       knows the awesome salvation of God."

Jesus feels his imagination soaring
       like an eagle in the empty sky.
And beneath it, far below it,
       the sobering landscape of reality.
How to bring heaven to earth
       without destroying the synergy?
How to take a soul, grown bone weary,
       and make it sing and dance again?
How to take a half-forgotten step,
       and make it a whole-hearted movement?
       How to bring about genuine change in a world,
       where love is bought and sold,
       justice goes to the highest bidder,

and freedom is a faint memory carried by the wind?
Unsummoned, the memory serves him a warning:
a roadside lined with impaled bodies on bloody crosses –
Revolutionaries hung out, and left to dry,
for the treason of trying to fight for freedom.
Here, in the wilderness, without food or water,
Jesus waits and weighs up his options.

A thought comes to him –
"If you are who you claim to be;
if you have the potential
that you are supposed to have, prove it!
That's it – just prove it!"
"Then people will be with you.
And you will be unstoppable."
Jesus turns his head and scans the horizon.
There is nothing to see save the desert;
The wilderness scattered
with boulders, rocks and stones.
And the thought comes to him –
"If you turned these stones into bread
then the masses would be behind you."

Jesus remembers the masses
gathering daily at dawn at the temple;
waiting for the sunrise, and the signal
from the priests in the tower, to begin a new day.

And the thought comes to him –
"If you climbed that tower, and leapt down,
and landed safely in the midst of that crowd,
the masses would be with you all the way."

Jesus remembers the masses
of the twisted, tortured frames of rebels.
Who had gone "all the way" to change the world,
but ended up hanging, ignominiously,
on crosses at the side of the road
like scarecrows in the sun.
Is this the fate of all dreamers and their dreams?
Nailed to history as a lesson in futility?
Are there no other options?

And the thought comes to him –
"If you were prepared to compromise,
accept the system, respect the status quo,
and work for change, gradually, incrementally,
then, maybe,
you could succeed, where others failed!"
Jesus feels these thoughts
worming their way into his heart.

And he begins to wrestle
with the issues that they raise.
Didn't he need to prove himself?
How else could he expect them to risk all
for a penniless carpenter from Nazareth?
Bet on an uneducated seer from Galilee
with nothing more than a pipe dream?
To ask a lot, you have to give a lot,
a sample, if you like, of what's possible.
It's only sensible. Only reasonable. Only practical.
And what better way to show what's possible
than to provide the people
with more of the things that they want
and display your power in the process?
That would impress the people – wouldn't it?
That would ensure the support of the masses.
And that would mean a better deal,
when he came to terms with the system.
Jesus feels the rush of this logic
sweeping him inexorably downstream.
And he might have been carried away by it
except for a small stubborn rock of doubt.
How could a person, obsessed
with having to prove himself,
ever hope to lead a movement
dedicated to the service of others?
That would be impossible. Absolutely impossible.
So Jesus lets the wave of desire to prove himself
that is washing over him, simply come and go.
Where does that leave the idea of providing people
with the things that they wanted
and displaying his power, spectacularly?

It might assure him of support – but for what?
Spectacular events and free provisions!
And, dishing out what people want,
        might distract them from what they need.
Bread and circuses may be fun –
        but they don't bring transformation.
Miracles fade into memory,
        and bellies, once filled, are soon empty again.
Jesus knows full well that
        the only way hungry people will be fed
        is if people create a culture of love and justice
        where they care, and share, with one another.
So.
        No side shows. No free lunches.
Where does that leave the idea of negotiating?
Some kind of new deal with the system?
Jesus knows that, in the furnace of his soul,
        the answer to that question is already forged.

The middle ground is occupied territory,
        "negotiation," but another name for "capitulation."
Brokering some kind of deal with the system
        might provide him with safety and security himself.
But he knows that the system is always willing
        to sacrifice the poor on the altar of expediency.
And, when it comes to the crunch,
        Jesus cannot – and will not –
        collaborate with such an iniquitous system.
                Regardless of the consequences.
He does not have a death wish.
        He has no desire to die a martyr's death.
But, if death is the price he has to pay
        for fighting for life and liberty, he'll pay it.
Jesus is committed.
        There will be no compromise.
No taking a backward step.
        And no turning back.[20]

1. Which of the temptations of Jesus can you relate to most?
2. What anxieties did these temptations raise for you?

---

[20] D. Andrews, *Christi-Anarchy*, pp. 118–26.

◊ *Be sure to record your reflections in your working notes.*

Jesus was able to work through these anxieties and move on, but he was only able to move on by being able to work through his anxieties.

4.   "MY BIGGEST ANXIETY IS . . . BECAUSE . . ."[21]

30 minutes

◊ Spend a few minutes brainstorming and jot down all of the anxieties that might prevent you from attempting the community work you'd like to do – or that might dampen your enthusiasm about doing this work.

◊ Draw a picture of a large brick wall, with at least twenty bricks, on a piece of paper. Write each anxiety in one of the bricks.

◊ After you have named as many bricks in the wall as you can, sit back and look at the bricks in the wall in front of you. Then circle the anxiety you see as the biggest barrier and name it by saying out loud "my biggest anxiety is . . . because . . ."

◊ Beginning now and over the next few sessions, the course material will try to help you find a way through the wall – or over it, or around it.

◊ Set up two chairs facing each other. Imagine it is an interview situation, and you are interviewing yourself. Sit in one chair, facing the other, and ask the following questions, one by one. After you ask a question, move to sit in the "hot seat" and answer the question. After you have answered the question as fully and as frankly as you can, go back to the interviewer's chair and ask another question, then move to the other chair to answer it, and so on until you have gone through all of the questions.

1. Why do you think you might have this anxiety?

2. How have you overcome this anxiety in the past?

3. What would be the best way for you to overcome this anxiety in the future?

4. What help would you need?

5. Where could you get the help?

---

[21] Adapted from Andrews, et al., *Building.*

◊ After you have finished this "interview," record the details in your working notes and consider the following insights.[22]

Mahatma Gandhi said:

> Almost anything you do will seem insignificant, but it is very important that you do it anyway.

We must not be put off by the scoffers who say it is impossible. As Lois Brandeus says:

> Most of the things worth doing in the world had been declared impossible before they were done.

It doesn't matter how small a group we are, or how big the opposition is. As Margaret Mead says:

> A small group of thoughtful, committed citizens can change the world. Indeed, it's the only thing that ever has!

◊ *Record your reflections on these observations in your working notes.*

5.   CIRCLES OF INFLUENCE AND CIRCLES OF CONCERN

20 minutes

Let's consider the concept of circles of influence and circles of concern as developed by Stephen Covey.[23]

◊ Draw a large circle on a piece of paper. This is your "circle of concern."

---

[22] Adapted from K. Shields, *In the Tiger's Mouth* (Newtown: Millennium, 1991).

[23] Adapted from S. Covey, *The Seven Habits of Highly Effective People* (Melbourne: The Business Library, 1989) pp. 81–83.

No Concern

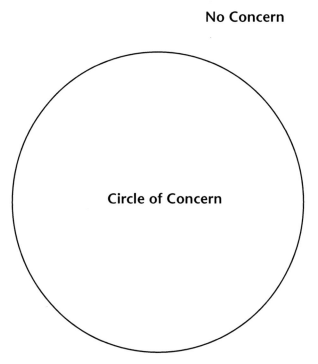

Figure 9. Circle of concern

What are all the things you would like to see changed in the world that you would like to include in your "circle of concern"?

Write those things in the big circle, leaving some space in the middle.

◊ Draw a small circle in that space. This is your "circle of influence."

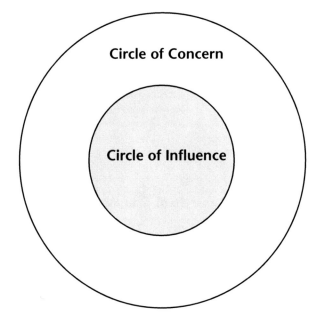

Figure 10. Circle of concern + circle of influence

What are all the things you think you could actually change in the world, things you could include in your "circle of influence"?

Write those things in the small circle.

◊ What would happen if you concentrated on your "circle of concern" rather than your "circle of influence" and focused on the enormous difference between the size of your "circle of concern" and the size of your "circle of influence"?

That's right – in all likelihood you would probably disempower yourself!

When was the last time you did that?

How do you feel about that?

Hold the feelings. But let's move on.

◊ What would happen if you concentrated on your "circle of influence" rather than your "circle of concern" and focused on slowly, but surely, increasing the size of your "circle of influence"?

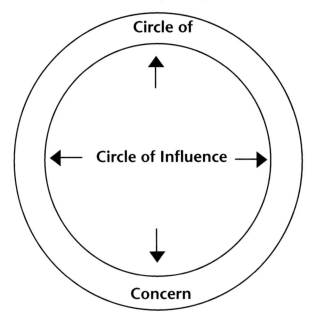

Figure 11. Developing a proactive focus

That's right – chances are that you would actually empower yourself!

So, the challenge is to be *conscious* of your "circle of concern," but to *concentrate* on your "circle of influence."

Let's go on to a reflective exercise that can help you to focus on your God-given capacity to influence the world and so overcome your sense of futility.

6.   REFLECTION ON YOUR CAPACITY FOR INFLUENCE[24]

15 minutes

Although you may never have done an exercise like this, try to stay focused as you go through each step of the process. Read through all of the instructions for this exercise before you begin.

◊ Get into a relaxed position. Close your eyes and pray for God to bring to your mind a time when you were able to say or do something that made a positive difference to a situation in which you found yourself.

---

[24] Adapted from Shields, *In the Tiger's Mouth*.

◊ Remember that time. Reconnect with the scene. Play it over and over again in slow motion. Recall the thoughts and the feelings you had at the time. Then ask yourself the following questions:

1. What did it feel like to be able to make a positive difference in that situation?

2. What factors enabled you to make a positive difference in this situation?

3. What lessons can you learn from this reflection on your God-given capacity to influence the world?

◊ Hold those thoughts and feelings and turn them into a prayer.

◊ Thank God for what happened in this particular situation and pray that, through the power of God's Spirit, you may be able to say and do things that make a positive difference more often. Ask God to help you to focus on what you can say or do, rather than on what you can't!

◊ *Be sure to record these reflections in your working notes.*

7. CONCLUSION

The follow-up reading for this session is:
*   *Not Religion, but Love*, pp. 86–91/70–75.

The set community tasks for this session are:

◊ Meet with your learning partner and your community development support group.

◊ During this meeting, map out the potential within this group. Fold a large piece of paper into four. When you unfold it, write "Experiences" at the top of one quadrant, "Qualities" in another, "Skills" in another, and "Resources" in the last one. Then spend some time filling in this "map" together.[25]

1. Under "Experiences," write in any experience that any of you have that could contribute to your community work (such as living with a family, working as a volunteer, etc.).

2. Under "Qualities," write down any qualities that you have that could contribute to your community work (such as easygoing, hard-working, etc.).

---

[25] Adapted from Shields, *In the Tiger's Mouth.*

3. Under "Skills," list any skills that you have that could contribute to your community work (such as listening, talking, etc.).

4. Under "Resources," write down any resources that you have that could contribute to your community work (such as a car, a phone, etc.).

◊ Circle the things you'd love to do.

◊ Then ask yourselves the question: *What does this say about what we have to offer as a group to our community?*

◊ *Record your actions, reflections and conclusions in your working notes.*

BREAKING THROUGH THE BARRIER OF SELFISHNESS

1. PREPARATION

1.1. Objectives

- To review your understanding of the first barrier that might block progress towards community development – hopelessness
- To consider another barrier that might block progress towards community development – preoccupation with ourselves, at the expense of others, which mitigates against significant change

2. REVIEW

15 minutes

Review your work from the previous session.

Review the issues raised in Session 6, particularly your understanding of how hopelessness might block community development.

Review the reading:

Not Religion, but Love, pp. 86–91/70–75.

Review the tasks:

1. How did your meeting with your learning partner and your community development support group go?

2. What was the most important thing you learned while doing the community tasks for the last session?

◊ *Record your reflections in your working notes.*

3.   VALUES INVENTORY

15 minutes

◊ Read carefully through the following "Values Inventory."[26]

1. Salvation – a restored life
2. Adventure – an exciting life
3. Involvement – a useful life
4. Security – a sheltered life
5. Love – a sacrificial life
6. Prosperity – a comfortable life
7. Pleasure – an enjoyable life
8. Creativity – a productive life
9. Fame – a celebrated life
10. Service – a helpful life
11. Family – a connected life
12. Friends – a sociable life
13. Freedom – an unfettered life
14. Any other

◊ Select your top five life values and rank them in order of importance.

◊ After you have completed selecting and ranking your life values, write down your answers to the following three questions in your working notes:

1. What three things do you feel you value most in life?

2. Why do you think you value those three things most?

3. What evidence do you have that you really value these things so much?

We'll come back to the "Values Inventory" a little later on.

4.   SELF-INTEREST AND SELF-CENTREDNESS

15 minutes

Self-interest is not bad. Self-interest is good – so good that Jesus called us "to love others as we love ourselves." What is bad is not self-interest, but self-centredness. Our proclivity is to "love ourselves at the expense of others." Our culture celebrates selfishness. "I've got to look after number one," we say. "If I don't look after myself, no-one else will!"

---

[26] Adapted from J. Staley, *People in Development* (Bangalore: SEARCH, 1982), pp. 121, 124.

Our philosophy can be summed up best by the popular slogans that are doing the rounds of the cocktail party circuit. "Greed is good!" "If you want it, get it!" "Buy now, pay later!"

Our political economy is a capitalist economy based on capital as the means of production, and on consumption of goods and services. Money is the currency required to purchase these goods and services, and the market is the mechanism for distributing the goods and services that are purchased.

Those with a lot of money get lots of goods and services. Those with little money get few goods and services. Those with no money get nothing. We say we believe in charity, but that "charity begins at home." That being so, charity seldom extends much beyond our own families.

◊ Consider the following incident:

> Christians profess to be different, but often display the
> same self-centredness. Some time back, I was talking to
> a young lady from a trendy, suburban church. She was
> extraordinarily animated. What amazed me was that she oozed
> with enthusiasm for life. But what worried me was that her
> enthusiasm was focussed entirely on her own life. She was
> completely preoccupied with herself – her business and her
> success in her business. Unfortunately, this young woman
> typifies the self-involved spirituality that is rampant in far too
> many trendy, suburban churches, a spirituality that prays for
> a parking space, but drives past poor people stranded in the
> rain. I tried to talk to this young woman about her self-involved
> spirituality. But she got mad at me, stormed out of the room,
> and sped off in her brand new BMW.[27]

1. How common do you think this kind of self-centred spirituality is?

2. To what degree do you feel you and your church are guilty of practicing this kind of spirituality?

◊ After reflecting on this question, consider the following facts that the National Church Life Survey uncovered in their research (NB: people were given the opportunity to list multiple reasons):

- 50% of Christians are involved with their church because it gives them the chance to share the Lord's Supper.

---

[27] D. Andrews, *Can You Hear the Heartbeat?* (Manila: OMF, 1995), p. 45.

- 33% of Christians are involved with their church because they get good teaching or preaching.
- 28% of Christians are involved with their church because they enjoy traditional worship.
- 21% of Christians are involved with their church because they enjoy contemporary worship.

Note that only 20% of Christians are involved with church because they are concerned with care for one another, and only 12% of Christians are involved in a church because they want to care for people outside the church.[28]

What does this National Church Life Survey research reveal about the so-called "self-involved spirituality" of many churches?

5. VALUES INVENTORY REVISITED

30 minutes

◊ Take out your personal "Values Inventory" and, in light of your reflections about self-interest and self-centredness, reflect on what you have written.[29]

◊ Look again at the answers to the questions you wrote in your working notes.

1. Why do you value these five things most in life?

2. What evidence do you have that you really do value these things as much as you think you do?

◊ Set up two chairs facing each other. Imagine it is an interview situation, and you are interviewing yourself. Sit in one, facing the other, and ask the following questions, one by one. After you ask a question, go and sit in the hot seat, and answer the question the best you can. After you have answered the question as fully and as frankly as you can, go back to the interviewer's chair and ask the interviewee another question. And so on.

1. Is what you say what you really value – or not?

2. Is what you really value based on self-interest or self-centredness?

◊ After you have finished the interview with yourself, record details of the conversation in your working notes.

---

[28] P. Kaldor, *Initial Impressions* (Adelaide: Open Book, 2002), p. 24.

[29] Adapted from Staley, *People in Development*, p. 124.

Note that we can test whether our choices are self-interested or self-centred by asking ourselves:

1. Is what I am choosing to do with others, or by myself?
2. Is what I am choosing to do for others, or for myself?

6.   LEADING DOUBLE LIVES

15 minutes

We need to acknowledge that many of us lead "double lives."[30] We say that we "love others as we love ourselves." However, in practice we often do not actually love others as we love ourselves.

◊ What are the dilemmas associated with leading "double lives"? What is in the gap between what we say we believe in and how we really live our lives? To answer these questions, try to focus on times when you are most aware of leading a double life.

◊ Set up two chairs facing each other. Imagine it is an interview situation, and you are interviewing yourself. Sit in one, facing the other, and ask the following questions, one by one. After you ask a question, go and sit in the hot seat, and answer the question the best you can. After you have answered the question as fully and as frankly as you can, go back to the interviewer's chair and ask the "interviewee" another question. After you ask the question, go and sit in the hot seat again. After you have answered the question as fully and as frankly as you can, go back to the interviewer's chair and ask the interviewee another question. And so on.

1. When was the last time you were conscious of acting contrary to your professed values?
2. What are the core issues involved for you in leading a "double life"? (A desire for approval? A reluctance to deal with an underlying issue? An addiction of some kind? Or?)
3. How do you feel about these dilemmas?
4. What would you like to do about them?

◊ After you have finished the interview, record details of the conversation in your working notes.

---

[30] Adapted from Shields, *In the Tiger's Mouth*, p. 8.

7. WILLING ONE WILL

20 minutes

Remember that Jesus and his disciples struggled with similar issues.

◊ Read the following reflection meditatively:

> *Jesus has just discovered his mission in life.*
> *He has decided not only to be involved,*
> > *but also to take a lead in the movement.*
> *He is determined to lead by personal example,*
> > *by embodying the ideals of the movement.*
> *He is determined to be loving, and to be just,*
> > *and to give himself freely in service of others.*
> *"The Spirit of God has gripped me," he says,*
> > *"and has singled me out for a special task:*
> > *'To share good news with the poor,*
> > *to free the prisoners,*
> > *to help the handicapped,*
> > *and to break the shackles of the oppressed.'"*
> > *"I must let the people know*
> > > *that the day of God's grace is upon us!"*
>
> *For Jesus, this is not rhetoric; this is reality –*
> > *the reality he eats and drinks,*
> > *the reality he works for every day.*
> > *Every day*
> > *he makes time and space for the Spirit of God,*
> > *and he opens his soul to the Spirit of God;*
> > *his gut is ignited by the passion of God,*
> > *his bowels on fire with the compassion of God.*
> > *For him, empathy is not a superficial emotion*
> > *but a deep gut-wrenching bowel-twisting sensation.*
> > *A visceral response*
> > > *to the tears he sees and the cries he hears,*
> > > *and the suffering of others*
> > > *that he feels, as if it were his very own.*
> > *He feels particularly anxious*
> > *about seeing desperately vulnerable people,*
> > > *"Sheep, without a shepherd,"*
> > > *with nobody there to protect them.*
> > *And he feels especially angry*
> > *hearing about totally unscrupulous people,*

"Wolves, in sheep's clothing,"
    taking advantage of that vulnerability.

"My grief is beyond healing,
    My heart is sickened within me."
"Because of the plight of the daughter of my people,
    from the length and breadth of the land."
"For the wound
    of the daughter of my people
    is my heart wounded.
    I mourn, and dismay has taken hold of me."
"Can a woman forget
    a baby she has borne?
    Can a mother refuse to care for
            the child at her breast?"
"Perhaps," he says. "Even these may forget."
    "But, I will never forget you."
    "Come to me," he calls,
            beseeching the crowds;
            the broken men,
            the battered women,
            the abused children.
    "Come to me, all you who are weary;
            crushed by carrying the burden of living.
    Come to me, and I will offer you a place of rest,
            an oasis to restore your soul for the journey."
    "Abide in me," he tells them, and I'll abide with you.
    Together we'll be friends, you and I.
    "You can ask of me whatever you like,
            and I'll do it because of my love for you.
    "I want you to know my joy in you,
            and I want your joy in life to be full."

And they do come,
these lonely wanderers,
these broken,
        battered
                bruised.
A man dripping with leprosy,
        his body rank with running sores,
        his soul hungry for belonging.
Jesus reaches out to enfold him,

to embrace him with love,
to heal him with touch.
A woman, bleeding for twelve years,
a dozen winters of rejection,
her self-respect haemorrhaging.
Reaching out one last time,
she finds Jesus and relief
in the same beautiful moment.
"Go in peace," he tells them,
"your faith has made you whole."
They come, and they keep coming,
this troubled tribe of outcasts.
He tries to keep a lid on it, to keep it quiet.
Cautions them to mute their enthusiasm
lest acts of kindness become circus acts.

But the winds blow,
and the stories grow
and the crowds gather.
The all-consuming masses, pushing and shoving,
jostling like moths battering a single light.
They want this and they want that;
they want to see a miracle
and they want to see more.
Jesus, at the centre of the chaos,
is giving all he has to give,
and still it is not enough.
He often feels he is on a highway to nothing.
He wants to help people,
but the more he does,
the more they want him to do.
It is never ending.
But when he tells his disciples about it,
and they try to help him,
they just make matters worse.
When some parents bring their children to him,
to ask him to bless them,
The disciples push them away,
to prevent them from pestering him.
Jesus is incensed, and says,
"Hey. Let the little children come to me."

He takes the eager children,
>>*lifts them on to his lap, gives them a hug,*
>>*and blesses each of them, one by one.*
Then, he turns to his disciples, and says,
>*"What are you doing?*
>*This is what my work is all about!*
>*The worst disease in the world is not leprosy –*
>*it's being unacknowledged, being unwanted!"*

But they take their toll,
>*these ravenous throngs.*
Frustration clouds his compassion.
How to be pressed and yet patient;
>*how to be tired and yet care?*

To dwell in the whirlwind,
>*in the midst of confusion and conflict,*
>*without losing his vision,*
>>*Jesus knows he needs a quiet centre.*
And he finds that still place
>*where he can be at peace with himself*
>>*in the eye of the cyclone,*
>>>*face to face with God.*
Jesus nurtures the hideout in the canyon of his heart,
>*harbouring in it and lingering in its shelter.*
It is a cave in the midst of the commotion,
>*a quiet retreat in the midst of the action.*
Here he enters and listens;
>*and hears the still small Voice once again.*
>*"You are my Beloved.*
>*In you I am well pleased."*
Fragrant, unconditional, limitless love,
>*running down, like thick olive oil,*
>>*into the recesses of his wounded soul.*
Refreshing, renewing, reforming, redeeming grace.
>*Filling the void with the joy*
>*of being loved and being able to love.*
A balm for frustration,
>*healing the deep hurt.*
A wellspring of passion,
>*bubbling with compassion.*

In it Jesus finds his strength, his stamina,
>> *for the endless rounds*
>>>> *of giving and forgiving.*
He learns the craft of caring,
>> *the hard task of loving*
>> *friend and foe regardless.*
Jesus realizes that it is important
>>>> *for him to learn to care, himself, on his own,*
>>>> *regardless of whether anyone else does or not.*
But he also recognizes that caring is essentially
>>>> *a communal, rather than individual, activity,*
>>>> *and that even he simply cannot do it alone.*
So he invites others to join him on the job,
>>>> *reviving the lost art of community care.*
He is painfully aware
>>>> *of his friends' strengths and weaknesses,*
>>>> *their gifts, and their frailties.*
He knows
>>>> *he can't pin his hopes on them*
>>>> *because, sooner or later, all of them*
>>>> *will, one way or another, let him down.*
But he also knows
>>>> *that they can be good company,*
>>>> *and, in their own inept, but well-intended way,*
>>>> *will be a great vanguard of love and justice.*
In sharing their company, Jesus feels stronger.
>>>> *They reflect and reaffirm his personal struggle.*
In watching their faltering, clumsy, stumbling,
>>>> *often very funny, little attempts*
>>>>>> *to advance their great cause,*
Jesus gets a lot of encouragement,
>>>> *just to keep on going himself.*
"Together," he tells them, wryly,
>>>> *"we can change the world."*
Change, he knows, is not so much in a strategy
>>>> *as it is in the ability of people, like them,*
>>>> *to convert every interruption*
>>>> *into an opportunity to care,*
>>>>>> *as constructively and productively*
>>>>>> *as possible.*

> *Thus the movement*
> *deepens and widens;*
> *the faltering ripple of hope*
> *begins to extend outwards.*[31]

1. Which of the issues Jesus struggled with can you relate to most?

2. What can you learn from how Jesus approached these difficulties?

◊ *Be sure to record your reflections in your working notes.*

Note that:

- We need to deal with these issues like Jesus did.
- We need to learn to live at peace with ourselves.
- We need to find a still point in our turning world, a quiet centre in the noisy vortex of our activities, and affirm others and act with equanimity.
- We need to learn to live in companionship with others.
- We need to find a network of relationships, a community of family and friends, in the midst of the multitudes, where we can be at home, open our hearts, let down our hair, put our feet up and be ourselves. In so doing, we need to draw on the strength of the group so that we can keep going, in spite of the difficulties along the way.
- We need to learn to turn our interruptions into opportunities.
- We need to find a way of developing the art of embracing each difficult problem that we come across, every difficult person that we meet, each and every frustration that we encounter, as wonderful opportunities to express the spirit of compassion, the power of love and the possibility of justice.

8. CONCLUSION

The follow-up reading for this session is:
- *Not Religion, but Love*, pp. 92–96/76–80.

The set community tasks for this session are:

◊ Meet with your learning partner and your community development support group.

◊ Review the "map" of the potential within your group that you created in the last session and what it says about what your group has to offer to your community. Then decide what you are going to do about it.

---

[31] Andrews, *Christi-Anarchy*, pp. 131–39.

◊ Share what you learned in this session about leading a "double life" – saying one thing and doing another – and about the need to "will one will," to "love others as we love ourselves."

◊ Read an excerpt from the reading from *Not Religion, but Love*:

> The best way (for me) to deal with the selfishness is not by trying to conquer my self in an epic struggle, but by simply trying to become more conscious of others in the midst of my daily life.
>
> I have found it very useful to start the day with a time of prayer. When I pray, I often find myself automatically going through a list of personal requests. Which is okay. It's as good a place as any to start. But it's not a good place for me to end up.
>
> So, having gone through the items on my list of the things that I'd like God to do for me, I tear it up and toss it in the bin. Then I take a blank piece of paper and, in the quiet, I start writing down a list of things that I believe God would like me to do around the place.
>
> Sometimes the ideas that come to mind are the obvious. But the issue for me is not whether the idea is obvious or not, but whether it is something I ought to do or not.[32]

Praying over a piece of paper might be a way to go.

However, if praying over a blank piece of paper is too daunting, you could start with praying over your "map." Everyone could take a copy home and review it. Under "Experience," review any experience that you have that could contribute to your community work. Under "Qualities," review any qualities that you have that could contribute to your community work. Under "Skills," review any skills that you have that could contribute to your community work. In addition, under "Resources," review any resources that you have that could contribute to your community work. (Under "Resources" make sure you also review the time you could contribute regularly to your community work.)

◊ Look over your "map" and tick off the areas you *really* want to work on. (If you use a red pen, these ideas will stand out more clearly.)

◊ *Record your actions, reflections and conclusions in the working notes.*

---

[32] Andrews, *Not Religion*, p. 94.

BREAKING THROUGH THE BARRIER OF FEAR

1. PREPARATION

1.1. Objectives

- To review your understanding of the second barrier that might block progress towards community development – our preoccupation with ourselves
- To consider another barrier that might block progress towards community development – particularly our paranoia

2. REVIEW

15 minutes

Review your work from the previous session.

Review the issues raised in Session 7, particularly your understanding of the barrier of selfishness that might block progress towards community development.

Review the reading:

Not Religion, but Love, pp. 92–96/76–80.

With your working notes handy, review the tasks:

1. What was the most important thing you learned while doing the community tasks for the last session?

2. How helpful did you find it to pray about what you should do?

Finish with a careful reflection on what you have decided you want to commit to your community work before the end of the course.

Record your reflections in your working notes.

2.   FEAR

15 minutes

Read the following excerpt on fear:

> Some time back I spent a number of weeks talking to a church about becoming involved in their community. Discussions had gone well and the congregation had quickly identified a range of isolated people in their community that they could get involved with. However, when it came to putting their plan into operation, their enthusiasm suddenly evaporated.
>
> "Why?" I asked them in astonishment. "Because we are scared," they replied. "If we visit those people, chances are they will visit us. Then we'll never get rid of them. They'll just keep hanging around the house like a bad smell." They wanted to get involved, but they were afraid.
>
> Fear of the unknown. Fear of others. Fear of ourselves. Fear of success. Fear of failure. Fear of risking private space. Fear of losing personal security. Fear of fear itself. We are all full of fears. And each and every fear stands like a street corner bully ready to take us apart if we dare to cross the line and actually get involved in the community.[33]

1. Do you identify with any of these fearful people? In what way(s)?
2. In what situations are you most afraid?
3. How could that fear affect your involvement in the community?

3.   JESUS WAS NO STRANGER TO FEAR

20 minutes

There were many times in his ministry that Jesus was afraid.

◊ Slowly read the following reflection:

> *Jesus was no stranger to fear,*
> *When large crowds surrounded him,*
> > *he knew the threat they could be to him.*
> *He had no illusions about a fickle public.*
> > *John says that Christ didn't trust the crowds*
> > *because he knew what was in their hearts.*

---

[33] Andrews, *Not Religion*, p. 97.

He knew how they could use him and abuse him.
He knew that eventually
        they would turn against him
        and would stab him in the back
        as soon as pat him on the shoulder.
But
        although there were times
                Christ didn't trust people,
        there was never a time he didn't care for them.
Christ looked beyond the threat
                and saw their need.
        Instead of recoiling in fear,
          he reached out and embraced them –
        even the people whom he knew would betray him.
Christ overcame his fear by
        developing a compassion for people
                that was more powerful
        than his concern for himself or his own safety.
When confronted by a man
        with a sickening case of leprosy,
        Mark says, Christ "was moved with compassion,
        reached out his hand, and literally touched him."
He touched a man
        that everyone else in his society
                was too scared to touch.
It was Christ's sense of compassion
        that compelled him to overcome his fear
        and impelled him to reach out his hand
        and touch the man that no-one else would touch.
The compassion
        that helped him overcome his fear
        was inspired by listening as a child
        to the beat of his Father's throbbing heart.

He knew
        how much his Father was pained
        by the suffering of his children,
        and he was willing to risk his life
        to relieve that pain.
But his compassion
        was not only inspired by divine passion.

It was also inspired by human experience
       of the needs of the people around about him.
John says Christ "became flesh and dwelt among us."
       Not only did he choose to live among us,
                      he chose to live like us.
Paul says, "though he was rich, yet he became poor."
                      He made our poverty his own.
And, as a pauper,
       he experienced the same hassles
              and the same hardships as everybody else.
So Christ overcame much of his fear
       of involvement with people
              through prayer on the one hand
                      and empathy on the other.
But, in the end,
       Christ overcame his fear by
              being more afraid of what would happen
                      if he didn't get involved than if he did.
For him,
       to watch the suffering of the poor
              from a safe distance
                      and not lift a finger to help them
       was a far more terrifying scenario,
              than joining them in their struggle
                      and sharing in their suffering.
To compromise his commitment to fight for justice
       was far more frightening to him
              than being killed for his core values.
The death of his soul if he did nothing
       was a much more appalling prospect
       than the death of his body, for doing something.[34]

◊ Reflect on these thoughts and then consider the following questions.
Be sure to record your reflections in your working notes.

---

[34] Andrews, *Not Religion*, pp. 97–98.

1. What were Christ's fears?

2. Can you identify with any of Christ's fears? Which ones?

3. How do you normally deal with your fears?

4. How does that compare with the way Jesus dealt with his fears?

5. What can you learn from the way Jesus dealt with his fears?

4.   FACING OUR FEAR

30 minutes

Jesus dealt with his fear of involvement, and so can we.[35]

Many of our fears are fears of the unknown. They are based on ignorance or prejudice rather than reality. Simply coming to terms with the facts can help to dispel these fears. Usually, simply getting to know our neighbours can dispel our fear of getting involved with them.

> A little while ago, a friend of mine wanted to get involved with a person in the community with a disability. But he was afraid of getting involved because he felt awkward around people with disabilities. He didn't know anybody with a disability and he didn't know how to relate to anybody with a disability.
>
> He was embarrassed to admit it, but he was actually quite scared. However, after I was able to introduce him to a neighbour with a disability and they were able to spend some time together, he discovered, to his delight, that his neighbour with a disability was pretty much like him. His fear, based on ignorance, totally disappeared in the light of his discovery of their common humanity.

◊ Think of two or three examples of fears that you have had (or that your friends have had) that were dispelled by coming to terms with the facts.

◊ Consider those examples for a while, exploring any connections between these fears you experienced in the past and any fears you anticipate you may have in the future.

---

[35] Adapted from Andrews, *Not Religion*, pp. 98–101.

We can deal with some of our fears pretty easily by knowing the facts. But we cannot deal with all of our fears so simply.

Some fears have no basis in reality, but others do. Simply coming to terms with the facts can't dispel these fears – because the facts themselves are very frightening.

The more you know about these kinds of situations, the more scared you become. These fears shouldn't necessarily stop us from getting involved – because there may be people who need our help – but these fears should slow us down and make us much more careful about how we get involved. Read the following story:

> One night I was walking down the street and came across a man being attacked by a couple of hoods who were stabbing him with the jagged shards of a broken bottle. His face was already covered in blood and the hands he used to protect his face were already badly cut and bleeding.
>
> I thought, "If someone doesn't do something soon, this chap could be cut to pieces."
>
> I looked up and down the street. But no-one else was around.
>
> I knew it was up to me to do something but, I must confess, I was tempted to just walk on by pretending I hadn't seen anything warranting my attention, let alone my intervention. I was afraid, terribly afraid, and my fear was well founded. It had a strong basis in fact. There were two men across the road trying to kill someone and, if I tried to help him, chances were that I could be killed too. After all, there were two of them and only one of me. They looked like street fighters and I looked like the wimp that I was. I had no weapon and wouldn't know how to use one even if I had one and they had shards of sharp glass that they wielded as wickedly as the grim reaper himself might have swung his scythe.
>
> Fears such as these should not be dismissed, because fears based in fact act as a basic reality test for our intentions. Believe it or not, on a number of occasions, when confronted with people who wanted to kill him, even Christ decided that it was better for him to run away and fight another day than to die for nothing at all (Lk. 4:29–30). And sometimes there are situations it might be better for us to run away from, too – the faster the better!

However, this was not one of those times. This time, someone's life was at stake. Christ would not have run away on this occasion. And neither – really – could I. So I wrapped the tattered rags of my makeshift courage around me and, with trembling hands, wobbly knees and a heart ringing like an alarm bell, crossed the road to intervene in the fight. I didn't rush over and try to crash tackle the assailants. That only ever works in the movies – and even then it doesn't work all the time.

I simply walked to within ten metres of the melee, stopped, and said from a safe distance the most inoffensive thing I could think of at the time, which was, "G'day." The antagonists immediately turned in my direction. Now I had their attention, I tried to distract them from further hurting their victim. But the trick was to do it without them harming me instead. So, I said to them in as friendly a tone as I could muster, "Can I help you?"

The aggressors looked at one another, then at me, and laughed. They thought it was a big bloody joke. "Does it look like we need any help?" they asked facetiously. "No," I said very carefully. "It doesn't look like you need any help. But it looks like he might need some help. What do you reckon?"

By now they had stopped stabbing their prey and, in answer to my question, they shrugged their shoulders, and said, "Well you help him then!" And, with that, they walked off and left me to care for the mutilated man on the side of the road. He was seriously injured, but at least he was still alive. And so was I.

I've intervened in many violent situations in my life. Sometimes I've been beaten up so badly I've had to be hospitalized. One time I had to be rushed in for emergency surgery. But that was when I was younger and intervened more aggressively, thereby unconsciously escalating the spiral of violence in the situation. Now that I'm older, I'm a little wiser.

These days I am very wary about intervening. And, when I do, I am very careful to do it as peacefully as I possibly can. My fear doesn't usually stop me, but it does usually slow me down. This is exactly what fear ought to do. Not stop us, but slow us down. And make us more careful about the way we go about the task of getting involved with people.

Have you heard any stories, read any reports, or seen any incidents yourself in which people have been able to intervene successfully in a fearful situation?

◊ If you can think of your own such story, then use that for your reflection. If not, use the story above as the basis for your consideration of the following questions.

1. What was the cause of fear in the situation?
2. What was the effect of fear in the situation?
3. How did the people in the situation deal with their fear?
4. How did the people deal with the situation in spite of their fear?
5. What lessons can you learn from this story?

◊ *Be sure to record your reflections in your working notes.*

5. CONFRONTING OUR CRITIC

30 minutes

We may have great discussions abut "facing our fears" and we may make a sincere commitment to act with greater courage in the future, but, sooner or later, most of us hear a little voice inside telling us that we will never have all the poise and competence we need to deal with the situations we will inevitably confront.

To have this poise and the competence, we have to confront not only our *external circumstances*, but also our *internal critics*.[36]

◊ Take a piece of paper and draw a picture of your internal critic – the internalized self-critic whose criticism you fear most. Make this image of your internal critic as clear as you can. Take a little time to characterize, exaggerate and caricature it the best that you can. It may look like a demon, a priest, a police officer, your mum or your dad, your partner – or even yourself! Once you have the image in your mind, draw it right in the middle of your piece of paper, leaving plenty of space around the edges.

◊ In the space around the edges, write in half a dozen cartoon speech bubbles coming from the mouth of the internal critic, saying some of the scary things that your internal critic often says to you. For instance:

---

[36] Adapted from Shields, *In the Tiger's Mouth*, pp. 19–20.

- "You're useless!"
- "You'll never get it together!"
- "When it comes to the crunch, you're just a scaredy cat!"
- "You'll never do any good! (Scaredy cat! Scaredy cat!)"

◊ Once you have completed your picture of your internal critic, spend a little time just looking at it. Then say the words out loud that your internal critic usually says to you.

◊ Repeat what your internal critic says to you out loud – with feeling! As you listen to what your internal critic says to you, reflect on how the words affect you. Pause for a moment.

◊ Think about what you'd like to say in defence of yourself to your internal critic. Say what you would like to say in defence of yourself out loud. Then repeat what you would like to say out loud, as honestly and as authentically as you can. As you listen to what you say to your internal critic, reflect on how your own words make you feel.

◊ Respond, loudly and clearly, to all of the criticisms that your internal critic makes.

Note that internal critics seldom "speak the truth, the whole truth and nothing but the truth." The things they say are half-truths – or total lies.

So, by speaking out the truth about yourself – as a person made in the image of God, destined to become like Jesus – you can free yourself from the tyranny of these half-truths and total lies.

> "I am *not* 'useless'!"
>
> "I may have a long way to go, but it's *not* true to say I'll 'never get it together.'"
>
> "When it 'comes to the crunch,' everyone is 'a scaredy cat.'" "But 'a scaredy cat' is only a part of who I am – it's the truth, but not the whole truth. Even the biggest 'scaredy cat' has the courage of a wild tiger somewhere deep inside them."
>
> "To say I can 'never do any good' is a lie. The truth is that 'I can do all things through Christ who strengthens me! I can think of plenty of examples of good, helpful things I have done just in the past few days, such as . . .'"

After you have spoken out against your internal critic, take a little time to reflect on the words that you have spoken.

Write down a couple of phrases you spoke out which encapsulate the core truth at the heart of the responses you made.

Write down these phrases in your working notes and make them your motto.

Read the following reflection on risk:

Only one who risks is free![37]

To laugh is to risk appearing the fool.

To weep is to risk appearing sentimental.

To reach out is to risk involvement.

To disclose feelings is to risk disclosing your true self.

To place your dreams before the crowd is to risk their love.

To live is to risk dying.

To hope is to risk despair.

To try is to risk failure.

But the greatest hazard in life is to risk nothing.

The one who risks nothing does nothing and has nothing – and finally is nothing.

He (or she) may avoid sufferings and sorrow, but simply cannot learn, feel, change, grow or love.

Only one who risks is free!

6.   Conclusion

The follow-up reading for this session is:
*   *Not Religion, but Love*, pp. 97–101/81–85.

The set community tasks for this session are:

◊ Collect as many stories as you can of local incidents in which local people acted courageously and creatively in fearful situations.

◊ Meet with your learning partner and your community development support group.

---

[37] A. and W. Howard, *Exploring the Road Less Travelled* (Melbourne: Rider, 1985), p. 80.

◊ Review what you said about what you decided to do in terms of community involvement. Try to identify which parts of what you plan to do you are most scared about.

◊ Share what you learned in this session about facing your fears and confronting your critics and relate it to this situation, discussing how you can still do what you are scared of doing.

◊ Then share the stories you collected of incidents in which local people acted courageously and creatively in fearful situations. And discuss what you can learn from them about particular fears in your community and how to deal with them.

◊ Pray for the courage to live life to the full like the people in these stories.

◊ *Record your actions, reflections and conclusions in your working notes.*

BREAKING THROUGH THE BARRIER OF SPITEFULNESS

1. PREPARATION

1.1. Objectives

- To review your understanding of the third barrier that might block progress towards community development – our proclivity to paranoia
- To consider another barrier that might block progress towards community development – particularly a propensity for "payback"

2. REVIEW

15 minutes

Review your work from the previous session.

Review the issues raised in Session 8, particularly your understanding of how paranoia might block your progress towards community development.

Review the reading:

Not Religion, but Love, pp. 97–101/81–85.

Review the tasks:

1. What was the most important thing you learned while doing the community tasks for the last session?

2. You were asked to talk about some of these stories that you collected of local incidents. What did you learn from those stories yourself?

Finish with a careful reflection on how you can do what you're scared of doing.

◊ *Don't forget to record your reflections in your working notes.*

3.   BEYOND "TIT-FOR-TAT"[38]

10 minutes

Most of us function according to a policy of reciprocity or retaliation – a "tit-for-tat" approach. We are told to "treat others just like they treat us." If they do us a good turn, then we should do them a good turn. "You scratch my back, I'll scratch yours." If they give us any trouble, then we have a right to give as good as we get. "An eye for an eye, and a tooth for a tooth." Vengeance is smart; mercy is stupid; and a smack on the jaw for someone who's crazy enough to try to insult us is nothing but pure "poetic justice."

There's no bigger barrier to creative involvement in a community than the cycles of *action* and *reaction* that the payback approach sets in motion. I can remember one pastor saying to me, "Unless the people in the community cross the threshold of our sanctuary, I'm not prepared to waste my time on them." A priest once told me, "We don't mind those people using our church facilities, but if they break anything we'll kick them out quick smart." Another minister once took me aside and declared, "We are assessing the cost-effectiveness of our community programs. Those that have not produced enough converts over the last twelve months will have to be axed." All of these comments by clergy indicate a willingness for the church to get involved with people on certain terms. What are those terms? There must be a payback of some kind or other – and involvement. That's the way things work. It's "good for good," and "evil for evil."

Doing "good for good" and "evil for evil" may sound sensible enough. As soon as someone makes a mistake, however, the payback approach sets in motion vengeful cycles of *action* and *reaction* that destroy community. It is only as we break with the payback approach and try to be *proactive*, rather than *reactive*, as we return "good for evil" rather than "evil for evil," that we can be free to build and rebuild community in spite of the mistakes that we make.

If we are to play a constructive, rather than destructive, role in our communities, we cannot afford to be *reactionary* conservatives – treating others as they treat us. We need to be *proactive* revolutionaries – treating others like we would like to be treated ourselves. Jesus said, "Do to others as you would have them do to you" (Lk. 6:31). He said,

---

[38] Adapted from Andrews, *Not Religion*, Lion, pp. 102–103/Tafina, pp. 86–87.

"Love your neighbour as yourself" (Lk. 10:27). "Love your enemies" (Lk. 6:27). He said, "Love your enemies and pray for those who persecute you" (Matt. 5:44). He told us to do good not just to people who do good to us, but to all people – regardless of what they do, or do not do, to us (Lk. 6:32–35).

4.   "What's That?"

40 minutes

◊ Read the following "revolutionary principles" Jesus spelled out in Luke 6:27–31.

> *Love those who hate you*
> *and be kind to those who would like to kill you.*
> *Bless those who curse you*
> *and pray for the welfare of those who frustrate you.*
> *Even if they beat you up, embrace them.*
> *Even if they rip you off, help them out.*
>
> *If someone needs something, give it to them.*
> *Don't try to get back anything they take.*
> *Treat others just as you would like them to treat you.*

1. What is the difference between the reactive way we usually act and the proactive way that Jesus suggests we ought to act?

2. How do you feel about Jesus' proactive approach?

3. What difference do you think it would make to your community if people practised this proactive approach?

4. What principle is the proactive approach based on? (Not "treat others as they treat you," but "treat others just as ...")

◊ *Be sure to record your reflections in your working notes.*

Note that all of the major religions advocate the principle of the "Golden Rule".

> In Taoism, the call is *descriptive*. "Regard your neighbour's loss or gain as your own loss or gain." In Jainism the call is *instructive*. "One who neglects existence disregards their own existence." In Hinduism, Buddhism, Zoroastrianism, Confucianism, Judaism and Baha'i, the call is *imperative* and framed in *negative terms*. "Never do to others what would pain you." "Hurt not others with that which hurts yourself." "What is hateful to you do not do

to your neighbour." "Do not impose on others what you do not
yourself desire." "Desire not for anyone the things you would not
desire for yourself." While in Christianity, Islam and Sikhism the
call is *imperative* and framed in *positive terms*. "Do unto others
as you would have them do unto you." "Do unto all people as
you would they should do to you." "Treat others as you would be
treated yourself."[39]

The **Golden Rule**	Hinduism	Buddhism	Zoroastrianism
	"Never do to others what would pain you." *(Panchatantra 3.104)*	"Hurt not others with that which hurts yourself." *(Udana 5.18)*	"Do not to others what is not well for oneself." *(Shayast-na-shayast 13.29)*
Jainism	**Confucianism**	**Taoism**	**Baha'i**
"One who neglects existence disregards their own existence." *(Mahavira)*	"Do not impose on others what you do not yourself desire." *(Analects 12.2)*	"Regard your neighbour's loss or gain as your own loss or gain." *(Tai Shang Kan Ying Pien)*	"Desire not for anyone the things you would not desire for yourself." *(Baha'Ullah 66)*
Judaism	**Christianity**	**Islam**	**Sikhism**
"What is hateful to you do not do to your neighbour." *(Talmud, Shabbat, 31a)*	"Do unto others as you would have them do unto you." (Matthew 7:12)	"Do unto all people as you would they should do to you." *(Mishkat-el-Masabih)*	"Treat others as you would be treated yourself." *(Adi Granth)*

Figure 12. The Golden Rule in the world's religions

---

[39] Adapted from D. Andrews, *In-Situ Community Education* (Brisbane: Frank Communications, 2000), pp. 12–13.

People of all religions, all over the world, know this truth – there are no short cuts, no quick fixes, and we cannot hope to develop community unless we "do unto others as we would have them do unto us." Jesus, too, insisted that his disciples practise this principle religiously.

Luke 6:32–36 says:

> *If you love those who love you – big deal!*
> *Everybody does that.*
> *If you do good to those who do good to you,*
> *where's the grace in that?*
> *Everybody acts that way already.*
> *If you give*
> *with the expectation*
> *of getting something back,*
> *you're just doing business as usual.*
> *Love those who hate you.*
> *Do good to those who are bad to you.*
> *Give yourself*
> *fully and freely*
> *without any expectations*
> *of getting anything back.*
> *Then you'll have something*
> *to be really pleased about.*
> *Our actions will reflect the character of God*
> *because God is kind to all,*
> *the grateful and the ungrateful, saint and sinner alike.* (Lk. 6:32–36
> [author's version])

◊ Now consider the following questions.

1. Why does Jesus dismiss our usual efforts to be nice as being of no real consequence?

2. What does Jesus suggest is the only way we can make a significant difference in our community?

3. What is the divine principle on which this proactive approach is based? ("Do good to those who are bad to you – because God is ..."

◊ *Be sure to record your answers and reflections in your working notes.*

Note that in Jesus this principle takes on a whole new dimension.

> The old commandment had been that you "love your neighbour
> as you love yourself." But Jesus said, "A *new* commandment I
> give to you: that you love one another as I have loved you!" (Jn.
> 13:34). Now the big difference that there is between the old
> commandment and the new commandment is simply the way
> in which we are called to love one another. According to the old
> commandment we find in all religions, we are expected to "love
> our neighbour as we have loved ourselves." But according to
> the *new commandment* we find alone in Jesus, we are expected
> to *"love our neighbour as Christ has loved us."* And it is loving one
> another, *"as God in Christ has loved us,"* that is the quintessential
> characteristic of the new covenant inaugurated by Christ on the
> cross.[40]

So, we are called to:

> *"Treat others just as you would like them to treat you."*

Moreover, we are also called to:

> *"Treat others just as God – in Christ – has treated you."*

> 1. How should this radically-responsive, proactive principle be
> translated into the way we treat one another in our community?
> 2. How could you start to put this principle into practice more
> conscientiously in your own church community?
> 3. What impact do you imagine it might have? What would it look
> like?

◊ *Be sure to record your reflections in your working notes.*

Many say that the ultimate expression of this principle in community
is our *embrace* of one another – of friend and foe alike.

Miroslav Volf, a Croatian Christian whose family was brutally
driven out of the former Yugoslavia, says:

> A refusal to embrace the other, in her otherness, and a desire
> to purge her from ones' world by ostracism or oppression,
> deportation or liquidation is . . . an exclusion of God; for our
> God "is a God who loves strangers"!

---

[40] Adapted from *The Crux* (Fitzroy Zadok, 2001), p. 44.

Volf says that some people say "too much blood has been shed for us to live together." In contrast, Christ calls us to embrace the other because the "only way to peace is through embrace."

An embrace always involves "a double movement," Volf says, "of *aperture* and *closure*. I open my arms to create space in myself for the other. The open arms are a sign of discontent at being myself only and of a desire to include the other. They are an invitation to the other to come in and feel at home with me, to belong to me."

> In an embrace I close my arms around the other – not tightly, so as to crush her, or assimilate her forcefully into myself; but gently, so as to tell her that I do not want to be without her in her otherness. An embrace is a microcosm of the new creation.[41]

For Volf, an embrace is not just a *hug*, but "a sign of discontent at being myself only and of a desire to include the other" – gently – as the other.

◊ What do you think he means by "the embrace of one another"? What do you think that "the embrace of one another" might mean for you in your community?

◊ *Be sure to record your reflections in your working notes.*

4.   DOING GOOD FOR EVIL

5 minutes

Our broken communities can never be rebuilt unless we develop a "good" approach to a person, which does not depend on receiving "good" in return for our investment and is not diminished by having "evil" returned for "good."

Thus, Jesus urged his disciples to become good like God, who "causes his sun to rise on the evil and the good" (Matt. 5:45).

Remember that:

- To "do evil for good" is *demonic*.
- To "do evil for evil" is *human*.
- To "do good for evil" is *divine*.

So, in order for us to be able to do "good for evil" we must exorcise our *demonic tendency* to vent our frustrations on others. We must transcend our normal human reaction to want to avenge any violation

---

[41] Adapted from Andrews, *Christi-Anarchy*, p. 191.

against us and call on God for divine inspiration to help us renounce evil and channel the energy released by outrage – when evil is done to us – into good, constructive acts of tough, but tender, love.

5.   RAGING AGAINST OUR "ENEMIES" IN PRAYER

15 minutes

One way we can exorcise our demonic tendency to vent our frustrations on others is to *rage against our "enemies" in prayer*. This is a great biblical tradition practised by the psalmists. Take Psalm 70, for example, in which David says:

> *Hasten, O God, to save me;*
> *O LORD, come quickly to help me.*
> *May those who seek my life*
> *be put to shame and confusion;*
> *may all who desire my ruin*
> *be turned back in disgrace.*
> *May those who say to me, "Aha! Aha!"*
> *turn back because of their shame.*
> *But may all who seek you*
> *rejoice and be glad in you;*
> *may those who love your salvation*
> *always say*
> *"Let God be exalted!"*
> *Yet I am poor and needy;*
> *come quickly to me, O God.*
> *You are my help and my deliverer;*
> *O LORD, do not delay.*

Note how David uses prayer as an opportunity to vent his rage.

> *May those who seek my life*
> *be put to shame and confusion;*
> *may all who desire my ruin*
> *be turned back in disgrace.*
> *May those who say to me, "Aha! Aha!"*
> *turn back because of their shame.*

According to the Bible, prayer is the *only* place that we should ever ventilate uncensored rage, because God is the *only* one who can take and transform it.

Try the following exercise:

◊ Place a metal bowl on a table. Take out a piece of paper and a pen. Think of a person with whom you have an ongoing disagreement or unresolved conflict. Envisage their face and the kinds of things they say or do that make you angry. Feel your anger then write a prayer, like Psalm 70, venting your anger towards them to God.

◊ After you have written it out, pray the prayer you have written once or twice out loud – passionately, from the heart.

◊ Place the paper on which you have inscribed your rage in an old metal bowl on the floor and burn it as an offering to God.

◊ After you have done this, reflect on the experience.

1. How did you feel envisaging your "enemy"?

2. How did you feel praying your prayer against them?

3. How did you feel burning your prayer against them?

4. How do you feel now that you have offered your rage to God?

◊ *Be sure to record your reflections in your working notes.*

6.   BLESSING, NOT CURSING, OUR "ENEMIES"

15 minutes

One way we can transcend our normal human reaction to want to avenge any violation against us is by blessing, not cursing, our "enemies."

Jesus said that we should pray *for* them rather than *against* them. He says:

> Bless those who curse you, pray for those who ill-treat you. (Lk. 6:28)

◊ Take out a pen and another piece of paper. Think of the person whom you don't like, and/or who doesn't like you that you wrote a prayer against.

◊ Set aside the way you see them and try to see them through the eyes of Christ. Envisage their face and the kinds of things they say or do that make Christ pleased with them. Feel Christ's joy in them and write a prayer *for* them, *blessing* them.

◊ After you have written this prayer light a candle and, while the candle flickers, pray your prayer of blessing that you have written for your enemy, from your heart – out loud – as passionately as you can.

◊ After you have done this, reflect on the experience.

1. How did you feel envisaging your "enemy" through Christ's eyes?

2. How did you feel writing a prayer for them rather than against them?

3. How did you feel writing your prayer of blessing for them silently?

4. How did you feel praying your prayer of blessing for them out loud?

5. How do you feel now that you have offered your prayer to God?

◊ *Be sure to record your reflections in your working notes.*

7. TREATING OUR "ENEMIES" WITH RESPECT

15 minutes

One way we can call on God to help us renounce evil and channel the energy released by outrage into good, constructive acts of tough, but tender, love is by treating our "enemies" with respect. We need to remember that, although our "enemies" are people we don't like and/or don't like us, they are in fact people just like us. As such, we need to treat them with respect, in spite of any real or perceived grievances that we may have against one another.

◊ Take out a pen and another piece of paper. Think of the person you nominated as your "enemy" and the grievances that you may have against one another.

◊ Define an issue of grievance with a short, neutral title (one that would be acceptable to all sides) and write it in the middle of the piece of paper.

◊ Identify all of the parties in the dispute, including your enemy and yourself, and allocate them each a section on the paper around the issue in the middle.

◊ Then list the significant *needs* of each party involved in the dispute, including those of your enemy and your own, in each section of the paper.

◊ Also list the significant *fears* of each party involved in the dispute, including those of your enemy and your own, in each section of the paper.

◊ Then look for common ground, common needs and/or common fears that you may share with others – including your enemy.

◊ Keep on looking until you find at least one thing that you have in common with your enemy. Once you've found it, hold it close to your heart.

◊ Treat any common ground you have with your enemy as holy ground. Take off your big boots, walk in your bare feet and tread very carefully.

◊ Draw up a list of three things that you need to do in order to tread carefully on the holy ground you share with your enemy. Write this list as three "I shall . . ." statements.[42]

◊ Pray each statement, concluding "So help me, God."

8.   CONCLUSION

The follow-up reading for this session is:
- *Not Religion, but Love*, pp. 102–106/86–90.

The set community tasks for this session are:

◊ Talk to people in your community who have a reputation for being respectful. Ask them how they do it – especially under pressure.

◊ Meet with your learning partner and your community development support group.

◊ Share what you learned in this session about "treating others as you would like to be treated," rather than "treating others as they (might, or might not) treat you." Also explain to them about raging against your enemies in prayer, blessing, not cursing, your enemies, and treating your enemies with respect. Share what you learned from talking to some of the respectful people in your community.

◊ *Record your actions, reflections and conclusions in your working notes.*

---

[42] Adapted from Shields, *In the Tiger's Mouth*, pp. 66–67.

BUILDING BRIDGES TO PEOPLE

1. PREPARATION

1.1. Objectives

- To review your understanding of the fourth barrier that might block progress towards community development – our propensity for "payback"
- To introduce the art of building community networks, considering the "times," "levels" and "phases" of building bridges to people

2. REVIEW

15 minutes

Review your work from the previous session.

Review the issues raised in Session 9, particularly your understanding of how a desire for "payback" might block your progress towards community development.

Review the reading:

Not Religion, but Love, pp. 102–106/86–90.

Review the tasks:

1. How did you find talking to people in your community who have a reputation for being respectful?

2. What was the most important thing you learned while doing the community tasks for the last session?

Finish with a careful reflection on what you learned from talking to some of the respectful people in your community.

◊ *Don't forget to record your reflections in your working notes.*

3.   THE ART OF NETWORKING

15 minutes

Networking can be defined as "the art of developing networks of reciprocal relationships" – those relationships that are the foundation of all community development. Developing these networks of reciprocal relationships is an age-old art. Jesus himself recognized the importance of this process. For thirty of his thirty-three years – 90% of his time here on earth – Jesus was just the "boy next door" in the small village of Nazareth. There he grew, so the records say, "in favour with God, and his neighbours," developing a credible local identity as "Jesus of Nazareth." Even when he began his public ministry, he deliberately played down his superstar status as "the Messiah," preferring to refer to himself as a "Son of Man." He wanted to remain the boy next door so people would not be put off by the stories that the press gave out (Mk. 1:28, 43–44; 8:29–30).

Some people say that Jesus *didn't do* anything in the first thirty years of his life. However, I would like to suggest that it was what he was doing in the first thirty years that gave him the credibility to do what he did in the last three years. During these last three years he addressed the needs of the community, but it was the first thirty – when he learned the language and the culture, developed his connections, picked up the stories around town and truly listened to the people who were hurting – that gave him the right to speak about the issues that affected the community.[43]

Paul, who was an apostle of Christ, worked from Jesus' example and developed networking into an art form. He was a Jew who understood Greek culture, Roman law, Gentile society and pagan religions:

> *I made myself a Jew to the Jews, to win Jews, and a Gentile to the Gentiles, to win Gentiles. I made myself all things to all people in order to save some at any price.* (1 Cor. 9:20–22 [author's version])

His first visit in any city would be to the local Jewish synagogue or church. He would speak to the people there in Hebrew, illustrating his talks from the Bible. Then, afterwards, he would go to places where Gentiles gathered. He would speak to them in Greek, quoting local poets and philosophers.[44]

---

[43] Adapted from Andrews, *Not Religion*, pp. 108–109.

[44] Adapted from R. Linthicum, *Empowering the Poor* (Monrovia, CA: MARC, 1991), p. 52.

Note that there is no substitute for the process of building a credible, local identity. It is the foundation for any bridges we might want to build in our communities. We lay this foundation when we introduce ourselves – emphasizing what we have in common with our neighbours can help to lay a strong foundation.

If we want to work in a traditional church community, then we need to introduce ourselves in terms of our experience of, and our appreciation for, traditional church community. If we want to work in a contemporary church community, then we need to introduce ourselves in terms of our experience of, and our appreciation for, contemporary church community. With Catholics, we need to "talk Catholic." With Baptists, we need to "talk Baptist." With Pentecostals, we need to "talk Pentecostal and walk Pentecostal, and to sing Pentecostal and dance Pentecostal." In addition, we need to be able to do it sincerely. "'Cause if ain't sincere, it won't work!"

If we want to work for the wider local community, then we need to introduce ourselves in terms of our experience of, and our appreciation for, the local community. We need to be able to do that in the language, terms, tenor and style that people in the local community are most comfortable with. Therfore, even though I am a member of a Baptist church, I never introduce myself to anyone as a Baptist unless I know that person is also a Baptist. With Catholics, I identify myself as a follower of Christ. With Muslims, I identify myself as a fellow believer in God. With agnostics and atheists, I usually identify myself as a fellow seeker of Truth. When I don't know where people in my neighbourhood are coming from, I simply introduce myself as their neighbour. Moreover, I make sure that I never use any Christian clichés!

This may seem obvious enough, but many of us don't do it. We often emphasize those things that separate us rather than those things that unite us. And, consequently, we blow up the bridges we are trying to build.

Remember that the object of this ancient art of networking is, as Paul says, to be "all things to all people" in order to be able "to save some."

1. What is the community that you want to get (more) involved with?

2. How do the people in that community understand their identity?

3. Which aspects of that culture do you identify with most strongly?

4. How could you identify with that culture more closely?

5. What would you need to change in order to be "one of them"?

◊ *Be sure to record your reflections in your working notes.*

4.   NETWORKING HERE AND NOW

10 minutes

Establishing a credible local identity involves far more than introducing myself as a neighbour. It means *being* a neighbour. That takes a lot of time – time many of us don't seem to have. For me, it is a constant struggle to make sure I'm not too busy to be neighbourly. I have to make the time.

If we want to relate to people in our church community, we need to *be* in our church community. If we want to relate to people in our local community, we need to *be* in our local community.

If we want to relate to people in our community, we need to *be there* – not just for a short while, but over the long haul. People who move a lot are less likely to get involved – and others are much less likely to get involved with them. If we want to get more involved, we need to make a commitment to stay around.

If we want to relate to people in our church community, we need to spend less time at work and more time in the community there. Part-time work may give us more time to spend with the church community. If we want to relate to people in our local community, we need to spend less time at *church* and more time in that local community. However, we need to make sure we still spend enough time at church. Three meetings a week is manageable – attending, for example, one large celebratory gathering, one small nurture group and one small mission group. Then we will still have time for involvement in our local community.

Remember that, if we want to relate to people in our community, we need to spend less time *commuting* and more time *communicating*. Every ten minutes not spent commuting increases the possibility of community involvement by 10% (the likelihood of interaction increases for the commuter as well as for those with whom they will interact).[45]

Don't forget, either, that if we want to spend more time *communicating* we need to stop watching *Neighbours* and start relating to neighbours. Each extra hour a day spent watching TV reduces community involvement by 10%. So the easiest way for us to make more time for our community is to throw out – or at least turn off – the TV!

1. How can you make time for networking next week?
2. How can you make more time for networking next month?
3. How can you make more time for networking next year?

◊ *Be sure to record your reflections in your working notes.*

5.   "KAIROS" MOMENTS IN COMMUNITY NETWORKING

30 minutes

There are two kinds of time that we can use for building bridges to people in our community[46] – "scheduled time" and "casual time."

Scheduled time involves
*   Planned meetings,
*   which are dominated by the *clock*
*   and are usually *formal.*

Casual time involves
*   Opportune moments,
*   which are oriented to the *event*
*   and are usually *informal.*

Both kinds of contact are essential for building bridges in the community.

Formal contacts connect us with representatives of groups we might not normally have access to and may give us access to the resources of that group. Through *informal* contacts we can turn our connections into friendships that enable us to relate to one another not in terms of

---

[45] Putnam, *Bowling Alone*, pp. 212–13.
[46] Adapted from Andrews, *Not Religion*, pp. 110–14.

our respective roles, but as real people. Actually, many formal meetings build barriers rather than bridges. The very formality of proceedings often keeps people apart. People relate to each other on the basis of their official roles, not as long-lost relatives in the human family. If formal meetings are to build bridges between people as people, the proceedings need to be interspersed with enough informality that people can relate to each other authentically as brothers and sisters.

We may live in a modern society characterized by formal meetings rather than a traditional society characterized by informal gatherings, but all of us are aware that it is in our informal encounters that the real business of relationship building takes place.

Tragically, many of us in community organizations – including church organizations – are often so preoccupied with our programs that we cannot respond to opportunities to develop community as they arise with the ebb and flow of daily life.

The Bible warns us not to be so preoccupied with what it calls the *chronos,* or "the time," that we miss what it calls the *kairos,* or "the moments," when people are more *open* than *closed* and we have opportunities to develop significant *relationships* with one another.

These *kairos* moments often pass as quickly as they come. So it is important that we grasp these moments when they come our way – otherwise we risk losing the opportunities they present forever.

In order to grasp these moments, we must either schedule in time for these events or throw out our schedules altogether!

Some significant *kairos* moments include changes, cycles, conflicts, celebrations and chance encounters. These are the times when even the most closed people in our society are open to relationships; and they represent our best opportunities to build bridges to people in the community who would usually be suspicious of anyone approaching them.

5.1. 'Kairos' Moment Number One – a Time for Change

When there is a change, people are suspicious; they are also curious.

More often than not – at least for a little while – their curiosity exceeds their suspicion, and that time presents us with a window of opportunity to introduce ourselves to people. The window of opportunity created by change may last a day or a week – but once a person becomes used to the change, their interest subsides. They tend to close off again and the moment of openness passes.

1. Give a few examples of times of change that could be *kairos* moments.

2. What are some of the ways in which you can make the most of such moments to connect with people?

◊ *Record your reflections in your working notes.*

5.2. 'Kairos' Moment Number Two – A Stage in the Life Cycle

Different stages in the life cycle also bring opportunities for new or renewed relationships. At significant moments in the life cycle – such as births, marriages and deaths – we are reminded of our common humanity and remember the similarities that transcend our differences.

Everyone loves to show off a new baby. You can stop a total stranger in church and chat with them about their toddler. When the kids first start school, it's not hard to make contact with the other parents dropping off their children at the gate. When they leave school, it's natural to talk to other parents about their concerns for the future of their kids. Weddings provide plenty of opportunities to get acquainted or reacquainted with people with whom we have not had contact. Funerals can bring people together again who have not seen or even spoken with one another for years.

Think of someone you know of in your community who is going through a significant life-cycle change. How could you reach out to connect with him or her?

◊ *Record your reflections in your working notes.*

5.3. 'Kairos' Moment Number Three – Open Crowd Conflicts

In community there is a phenomenon known as an "open crowd." An open crowd is when people get together in a way that naturally draws other people in. It's the complete opposite of a "closed meeting" – it's an "open gathering." The indicators of an open crowd are colour and movement – and lots of noise. If the colour and movement don't attract the crowd, then the noise usually will.

Conflicts are often "open crowds." There is nothing like a fight in the church, in the factory, or in the office, to bring people together. Ironically, conflicts can often break down the walls of alienation. Having to resolve a conflict can build bridges between people who never had to relate to each other before – as long as those who join in relate to people respectfully.

We noted above that the indicators of an open crowd are colour, movement and lots of noise. Not only conflicts, but also celebrations are often open crowds.

> How do you usually respond to conflict? How would you need to approach conflict differently so that you can make the most of conflict as a *kairos* moment?

5.4. 'Kairos' Moment Number Four – Open Crowd Celebrations

At celebrations, people are often as happy to talk to a new person as to talk to an old friend. A church potluck dinner – where everybody in the congregation is invited to bring food to share with everybody else – is a classic example of a celebration that is an open crowd with great opportunities to connect with one another. Christmas and Easter celebrations can also open up the crowd at church for others.

> Think of a celebration which you attended recently. Were you able to make the most of this moment to connect? How might you make more of such an opportunity next time?

◊ *Record your reflections in your working notes.*

5.5. 'Kairos' Moment Number Five – Chance Encounters

Some people will never respond to an invitation, no matter how many times we invite them. The only way we may ever meet them is by chance.

Some people only feel safe relating to others if they meet them by accident. It's the only way they can be sure that they are not being set up. An accidental meeting is – by definition – unpremeditated.

It may be that we arrive late at church and the only seat left is next to somebody we have never met before. It may be that we are scheduled on a cleaning roster with a team of people we meet only just before we get to work. It might be that we have a minor collision with another car driven by a stranger on the way out of the parking lot. We need to readjust our perspective and expectations so that we are always ready to make the most of such "accidents" as opportunities to connect!

Be on the look-out today for a chance encounter that is an opportunity to connect. Be sure to record how you made the most of this opportunity in your working notes.

6.   CRITICAL LEVELS IN COMMUNITY NETWORKING

20 minutes

There are four levels at which we can build bridges to people.[47]

Critical level one – at the level of our feet

Where we stand – in our locality . . .

As *compatriots* – with a sense of *shared history*.

Critical level two – at the level of our hands

What we do – in our activity . . .

As *colleagues* – with a sense of *shared industry*.

Critical level three – at the level of our heads

How we think – in our ideology . . .

As *comrades* – with a sense of *shared solidarity*.

Critical level four – at the level of our hearts

How we feel – in our personality . . .

As *companions* – with a sense of *shared intimacy*.

- Jesus' *compatriots* were the crowds.
- Jesus' *colleagues* were the disciples.
- Jesus' *comrades* were Peter, James and John.
- Jesus' *companion* was John, "the disciple Jesus loved."

---

[47] Adapted from Andrews, et al., *Building*, p. 10.

1. Who do you think are, or could be, your compatriots?

2. Who do you think are, or could be, your colleagues?

3. Who do you think are, or could be, your comrades?

4. Who do you think is, or could be, your companion?

Record your reflections in your working notes.

We need to recognize these four different levels of relationships and relate to people accordingly.

- We can expect *acceptance* from our level-one *compatriots*.
- We can expect *help* from our level-two *colleagues*.
- We can expect *support* from our level-three *comrades*.
- We can expect *sympathy* from our level-four *companion(s)*.

Problems arise when we expect too little or too much from people.

Like Jesus, we will probably be able to build bridges with hundreds of people at level one (the crowds), scores of people at level two (the disciples), a dozen people at level three (Peter, James and John) and one person at level four (John). This means that, at best, we can expect some degree of acceptance from hundreds of people, some degree of support from scores of people, some degree of help from a dozen or so people, and some degree of sympathy from one or two along the way.

For Jesus, it was enough to start his own do-it-yourself community revolution.

1. Why is it unreasonable to expect *intimacy* with everybody?

2. List a few of your compatriots. What is it reasonable to expect of them in terms of *acceptance?*

3. List a few of your colleagues. What is it reasonable to expect of them in terms of *help?*

4. List a few of your comrades. What is it reasonable to expect of them in terms of *support?*

5. List one or two of your companions. What is it reasonable to expect of them in terms of *sympathy?*

◊ *Record your reflections in your working notes.*

7.   CRUCIAL PHASES IN COMMUNITY NETWORKING

20 minutes

Most groups involved in this long, slow process of community networking find that they go through four very distinct phases.

Not every group, however, will go through these phases in exactly the same way. Your group may skip one or two phases entirely or go forward a couple of steps and then go back one before making any progress. The following phases are typical of the experience of most churches that try to *mix* with their communities.

Crucial phase one – the "angel phase"

During the "angel phase," connection with people is so *superficial* that everyone seems like an "angel." People reach out but keep one another at arm's length. They are very pleasant, very polite and very superficial. As long as this phase lasts, therefore, the dream of real connectedness remains an unrealized dream. This phase lasts for as long as people can repress their real thoughts and feelings. Once our deeply held thoughts and feelings erupt, we move to the next phase.

Crucial phase two – the "devil phase"

The "devil phase" usually involves a *critical disconnection* from people. The ones who acted like angels start to act like "devils." People are no longer so superficial. They act from deep within and the reality emerges or, rather, erupts. Discussions turn into disputes and arguments into fights. The cosy dream of connectedness becomes a scary nightmare.

This phase lasts as long as people can cope with the crisis that has erupted. Once we decide we can't cope with the crisis any longer, we can end the relationship, impose law and order on the situation or explore the issues in terms of love and understanding.

If we opt to impose law and order on the situation to deal with the chaos, chances are that the relationships we have built will move back to the previous phase of *superficial – but comfortable – connection*. If we opt to explore love and understanding of the situation as a way to deal with the chaos, we can move on to the next phase.

Crucial phase three – the "human phase"

The "human phase" usually involves *careful reconnection* as people realize that others are neither angels nor devils, but human beings –

with good points and bad points – just like themselves. In this phase, therefore, people no longer keep one another at a distance but embrace one another, sharing their hopes and their despair – including the despair they share about not being able to make their dreams of real human connectedness come true. This phase lasts as long as people can cope with the discomfort associated with affirming those with whom we have unresolved conflict without resolving the conflict.

Once we decide we can't cope with this discomfort any longer, we will end the relationship, resume the conflict or resolve the conflict. If we decide to resume the conflict, people will either give up and go home or move back to *superficial – but comfortable – connection*. If we decide to resolve the conflict, we can move on to the next phase.

Crucial phase four – the "family phase"

The "family phase" involves *meaningful connection* with people in the light of the realization that they are family! Regardless of whether they are friends or enemies, people accept that they are beautiful, but fallible, brothers and sisters who need one another and who need to resolve their conflicts with one another in order to meet one another's needs. Only then can their dreams of real human connectedness come true.

When we think through these stages, it's not surprising many churches end up with superficial rather than meaningful connections. Few are willing to endure the chaos and extend the care that is required to develop meaningful mutual connections with people.

If we are to create meaningful, rather than superficial, connections, then we need to encourage one another to endure the chaos and extend the care that is required. For there is no other way that we can ever hope to make our dream of community come true.

1. What are the four crucial phases in building bridges to people?
2. Which phase do you think you are at in your community now?
3. What is the evidence that you are in this particular phase?
4. If you are not in the final phase, how can you progress towards it? If you are in this final phase, how can you strengthen and deepen the relationships?

Record your reflections in your working notes.

8.   CONCLUSION

The follow-up reading for this session is:
* *Not Religion, but Love*, pp. 108–15/92–99.

The set community tasks for this session are:

◊ Meet with your learning partner and your community development support group.

◊ Discuss how each person in your group can connect with two other people in the community you want to be involved with. Share what you learned in this session about the art of networking, networking here and now, *kairos* moments, the critical levels and the crucial phases. Plan how you can put all of this knowledge into practice in your community.

◊ Each person in your group should have a go at making a connection with two other people in your community. Then meet again as a group to discuss how this went. Talk about what worked best and what you would need to do in order to network better in your community.

◊ *Record your actions, reflections and conclusions in your working notes.*

BUILDING BRIDGES ON RELATIONSHIPS

1. PREPARATION

1.1. Objectives

- To review your understanding of the art of building community networks, the *kairos* moments, the critical levels and the crucial phases of building bridges to people
- To consider the "protocols" on which relationships are built

2. REVIEW

15 minutes

Review your work from the previous session.

Review the issues raised in Session 10, particularly your understanding of the art of building community networks, the *kairos* moments, the critical levels and the crucial phases of building bridges to people.

Review the reading:

Not Religion, but Love, pp. 108–15/92–99.

Review the tasks:

1. How did your meeting with your learning partner and your community development support group go?

2. What was the most important thing you learned while doing the community tasks for the last session?

Finish with a careful reflection on what you have learned about building community networks.

◊ *Don't forget to record your reflections in your working notes.*

3.   BEYOND GAME PLAYING

15 minutes

Most people in our society have superficial relationships. We ostensibly build bridges of friendship to each other, but we actually want little or no involvement with each other. Instead, we play games. We all know the rules. Keep the conversation shallow, but pretend it is deep. Talk about ourselves, but tune out when others talk about themselves. Use meaningful jargon, but avoid a genuine meeting of souls.

Religious people have their own variations on these games. As a friend of mine, a migrant who has stopped going to his local church says, "Religious people love to play a game called 'church.' We all dress up and go through our paces in the service together and whoever looks the most religious wins. The prize for the winners is approval. No-one gives a damn about really being involved in one another's lives." After church the people go home, convinced they have had meaningful contact with one another – and that they have shown significant concern for their friends. After all, they did pass the peace as part of the liturgy. My friend feels that, even though he made an effort to meet people, the encounters he had were superficial. The banal chatter bore no relevance to the loneliness of the single room in the boarding house.

The object of the "piety game" is to convince ourselves and others of our virtue. In this game, people judge others on the basis of petty issues.

Players are not concerned about meeting people at their points of need. This game is about using the needs of others to make them look "bad" – and to make us look "good" by comparison. The piety game prevents a genuine encounter in which we can come to terms with our common needs together.

The object of the "proselytization game" is to convince as many people as possible to join our cause. In the proselytization game we treat people as faceless commodities, potential trophies for us to win. We do not treat people as people.

If we meet people's needs, it is not so much to help them win, but to help us win them over. The proselytization game may promote encounters with people, but it subverts the possibility of developing relationships of mutual acceptance and respect.

Many of us, recognizing the destructiveness of these games, give up playing religious games. But few of us give up playing games altogether. Many of us who give up playing religious games take up secular games instead!

One of the secular games religious people play is the "welfare game." The object of this game is to appear as if you are involved with the needs of the community without actually getting too involved. If you play the game well, you can get a lot of credit without paying the price of costly involvement. The game begins when a group is challenged about being involved in their community. The group can't say "no," because they would be denying the voice of their conscience. Nevertheless, they find it hard to say "yes," because of the cost it would involve. To resolve the dilemma, they appoint a committee to do the job for them. The committee appoints a professional to do the job on their behalf. The welfare game has a number of variations, but the aim is always the same: to get the credit for being involved in the needs of others without actually getting involved.

1. What is the difference between playing church and being church?

2. What is the difference between being righteous and playing the piety game?

3. What is the difference between being evangelistic and playing the proselytization game?

4. What is the welfare game?

◊ Record your reflections in your working notes.

4.   PLAYING IT STRAIGHT

20 minutes

Jesus refused to play games. He sought to live out his own life, but he criticized people who played piety games (Matt. 23:23). He sought to share his faith with others, but he criticized people who played proselytization games (Matt. 23:15). He condemned those who pretended to be concerned about the welfare of others when their only concern was for themselves (Matt. 23:25). He consistently called for a *real* concern for others. (See Session 5.)

The story he told about the Good Samaritan perhaps best illustrates his attitude:

*According to the story, a badly beaten traveller lay bleeding by
the side of the road when a priest passed by. It was the perfect
opportunity for him to practise what he preached about compassion.
However, the priest didn't stop to help. The priest was too
preoccupied with his religious activities to spare the time to care
for his neighbour. Then a Samaritan, whom the priest would have
considered a "pagan," passed by. Unlike the priest, this "pagan" was
not so preoccupied with religious duties that he couldn't spare the
time to care for his neighbour. He practised what the priest preached.*

*He stopped and helped the traveller. In doing so, the Samaritan
took a grave risk – at great cost. The Samaritan exposed himself to
possible danger from the bandits who had beaten up the traveller and
who, for all he knew, were still lurking somewhere nearby waiting to
beat up anyone so incautious as to stop and help the traveller lying
by the side of the road. The bandits, as it turned out, did not rob the
Samaritan. But what the bandits didn't take, the doctors did. The
Samaritan went to quite considerable personal expense to pay the bill
the hospital presented him with, to care for the penniless traveller.
When he had finished the story, Christ turned to the crowd and told
them to stop playing games like the priest and start caring for people
authentically like the Good Samaritan did.* (Adapted from Lk.
10:25–37)

1. What game was the priest playing?
2. Who were the winners and losers in this game?
3. What are the equivalent games that we play today?

◊ *Record your reflections in your working notes.*

Christ developed a "non-game-playing way of relating" – a way of
relating committed to no-one winning at the expense of anyone else
and committed to finding solutions to problems that would ensure
either everyone won or would share in the loss. His non-game-playing
way of relating brought together the very people that the game playing
way of relating kept apart. As a result of his way of relating he built
good bridges – genuine relationships with people.

The story of the woman at the well is the classic example of how
Jesus built bridges to people.

When the woman met Christ at the well, she seemed intent on only discussing mundane matters – like the water in the well. However, Christ seemed intent on making the conversation much more meaningful. He was happy to start with a discussion about physical water, but he wanted to move on to spiritual water – and talk with her about the "water of life," that could sustain her in her struggle. The woman tried to avoid the discussion by turning it into a religious debate. She tried to start an argument over the merits of different types of worship in different types of groups. But Christ refused to buy into the debate. He neatly sidestepped the argument and gently moved the conversation towards a genuine meeting of their souls. The bridge that Christ built, bit by bit, developed an authentic heart-to-heart connection that carried an uninhibited exchange of heart-to-heart communication. The woman shared with him her heartache. And he took her heartache to heart. (Jn. 4:4–26)

1. What is the difference between a "game playing" and a "non-game-playing" approach to relationships with people?

2. How do you see Jesus' "non-game-playing" approach in the story of his encounter with the woman at the well?

3. If we are to relate to people in a "non-game-playing" way, what do we need to ensure we practise in our approach?

◊ *Record your reflections in your working notes.*

Note that a non-game-playing approach is characterized by:

- The actual practice of compassion
- A genuine concern for the other person
- An authentic heart-to-heart communication
- A commitment to seek a win-win resolution of problems
- A determination not to win at the expense of anyone else
- Should anyone lose, everyone should share the loss.

We must approach relationships not only with great sincerity, but also with great sensitivity. As Stephen Covey says, "to touch the soul of another . . . is to walk on holy ground."[48]

---

[48] Covey, *Seven Habits*, p. 258.

5.   THE PRACTICE OF CIVILITY

15 minutes

An important consideration in building bridges to people reverentially is the practice of civility to others.

Civility is more than politeness. It is acting appropriately with people in a relationship. It includes honesty and integrity, acceptance and respect, modesty and commitment, humility and confession.

All relationships with people depend on the practice of *honesty* and *integrity*. Honesty is saying what we mean. Integrity is meaning what we say. If we practise honesty and integrity in our dealings with people – all people, without exception, all the time – then the people we are relating to will have reason to trust us, because they can trust our word. They will know that our word is our bond.

All relationships with people also depend on the practice of *acceptance* and *respect*. Acceptance means recognizing people as people just as they are. Respect means regarding people just as they are. Practising acceptance and respect doesn't mean we will always agree with what people say or how people act. However, it does mean we will always express our recognition and our regard for them as people – consistently, publicly and privately, whether we agree with them or not. Our trust may need to be conditional, but our love should be unconditional.

All relationships with people depend on the practice of *modesty* and *commitment*. Modesty is the opposite of extravagance. It means promising people only what we are sure we can deliver, and commitment means delivering whatever we promise. If we practise modesty and commitment with people we won't attract the big crowds, but they will be able to count on us.

All relationships with people depend on the practice of *humility* and *confession*. Humility is the opposite of arrogance. It means owning responsibility for any instance where we over-promise and under-deliver. Confession means owning up, and making up, for any promises we break, by under-promising and over-delivering in the future. If we practise humility and confession, we will create a context for people to count on us even when we make mistakes. In so doing, we open up the potential for developing the relationship.

◊ Write down the following eight qualities that contribute to the practice of *civility* on a piece of paper:

1.   Honesty
2.   Integrity
3.   Acceptance
4.   Respect
5.   Modesty
6.   Commitment
7.   Humility
8.   Confession

◊ Go through the list and make sure you understand the qualities of civility by thinking of a few examples of each of the qualities.

◊ After you have gone through the list and understand each quality, rate yourself on a scale of 1 to 3, with 1 being "I always practise this," 2 being "I sometimes practise this," and 3 being "I never, or rarely, practise this."

◊ Finish by answering the question:

Identify one area of civility in which you really need to improve. What will you do today to start working on that area?

◊ *Record your reflections in your working notes.*

6.   THE PRACTICE OF COMPASSION

20 minutes

Another important consideration in building bridges to people reverentially is the practice of compassion for others.

Compassion is more than civility. It's more than sympathy. It's more than empathy. It is actually interacting with people in such a way as to be able to transact their pain. It includes attending and reflecting, listening and speaking, grieving and forgiving, singing and dancing.

All relationships with people where we can transact our pain depend on the practice of *attending* and *reflecting*. Attending means not pretending but truly concentrating on the other. Reflecting means not only understanding, but also communicating that understanding of the other in terms they can understand. If we practise attending and reflecting, we will be able to create a space that is safe for listening and speaking.

All relationships with people where we can transact our pain depend on the practice of *listening* and *speaking*. Listening means not hearing superficially, but deeply, the pain of the other. Speaking means not only talking about the pain of the other but also, after talking about their pain, talking about our own pain too – in so far as it relates to the pain of the other. If we practise listening and speaking, we will be able to create a period that is free for grieving and forgiving.

All relationships with people where we can transact our pain depend on the practice of *grieving* and *forgiving*. Grieving means not struggling with our anguish alone, but working through the agony of the pain together. Forgiving means not holding onto the rage, but letting go of the resentment and starting all over again – in spite of the pain. If we practise grieving and forgiving, we will be able to create the possibility, believe it or not, for singing and dancing once more.

◊ Write down the following eight qualities that describe *compassion* on a piece of paper:
   1.   Attending
   2.   Reflecting
   3.   Listening
   4.   Speaking
   5.   Grieving
   6.   Forgiving
   7.   Singing
   8.   Dancing

◊ Go through the list and make sure you understand the qualities of compassion by thinking of a few examples of each of the qualities.

◊ After you have gone through the list and understand each quality, rate yourself on a scale of 1 to 3, with 1 being "I always practise this," 2 being "I sometimes practise this," and 3 being "I never, or rarely, practise this."

◊ Then, when you have rated your own practice, think of how another person might rate your practice of compassion. Think of someone close to you who knows the truth about who you really are, and who would not be afraid to tell you the truth, and imagine how they would rate you in terms of your practice of compassion.

◊ Cover the ratings you gave yourself with a piece of paper, and write down how you imagine they would rate you from 1, or "I always practise this," to 3, "I never, or rarely, practise this."

◊ Then compare the ratings you gave yourself and what you imagine they would give you.

1. How similar or different are the ratings?
2. What are the similarities?
3. What are the differences?
4. What do the similarities in ratings signify?
5. What do the differences in ratings signify?

◊ Finish by answering the question:

Identify one area of compassion in which you really need to improve. What will you do today to start working on that area?

◊ *Be sure to record your reflections in your working notes.*

7.   THE PRACTICE OF CO-OPERATION

25 minutes

Yet another important consideration in building bridges to people reverentially is the practice of co-operation with others.

Co-operation is more than compassion. It's more than coincidence. It's more than concurrence. It is actually interacting with people in such a way as to be able to transact their hopes. It includes communication and collaboration, trusting and risking, giving and receiving – and, if not consensus, at least consent.

All relationships with people, where we can transact our hopes, depend on the practice of *communication* and *collaboration*. Communication is a dialogue in which all the people concerned can speak and can also be heard. Collaboration is some sort of ongoing negotiation that takes into account the hopes of all the people concerned. If we practise communication and collaboration, it is possible to start to transact our aspirations.

All relationships with people where we can transact our hopes depend on the practice of *trusting* and *risking*. Trusting means believing there is a chance to do something about our hopes together. And risking means taking the chance when it arises to do something about our hopes together. We all know there are great dangers associated with trusting and risking. We should never trust anyone more than we have reason to. And we should never risk anything more than we are prepared to lose, in the short term, for a long-term gain. But the dangers associated with *not* trusting and *not* risking are even greater.

It is only as we practise trusting and risking that we are free to explore our aspirations together.

All relationships with people where we can transact our hopes depend on the practice of *giving* and *receiving*. Giving means sharing something of ourselves in order to do something about our hopes together. And receiving means welcoming something of others, apart from ourselves, in order to do something about our hopes together. We all know that it is better to give than to receive, but if we only give, without ever receiving, it doesn't do anyone any good. Why? Because we never give anyone else the chance to give. Receiving without giving constitutes exploitation. Giving without receiving constitutes manipulation. Both experiences are dehumanizing. It is only as we practise giving and receiving that we are free to explore our aspirations together as fully functioning human beings.

All relationships with people where we can transact our hopes depend on the practice of at least *consent, if not consensus*. Consensus means finding a way forward together which we can all agree without any underlying reservations. Consent means finding a way forward together, in spite of our reservations, that is consistent with our aspirations. Consent constitutes a group decision (which some members may not feel is the best decision, but which they can all live with and commit themselves not to undermine). This decision is arrived at without voting, through a process whereby the issues are fully aired such that all members feel they have been adequately heard. Everyone involved in the decision has equal power and responsibility. Different degrees of influence, by virtue of individual stubbornness or charisma, are avoided so that all are satisfied with the decision-making process.

The process requires the members to be emotionally present and engaged; frank in a loving, mutually respectful manner; sensitive to each other; selfless, dispassionate, and capable of emptying themselves. Group members must also possess a paradoxical awareness of the value of both people and time (including knowing when the solution is satisfactory and that it is time to stop and not re-open the discussion until such time as the group determines a need for revision).[49]

◊ Write down the following eight qualities that are key in *co-operation* on a piece of paper:

---

[49] S. Peck, *A World Waiting to Be Born*, pp. 290–91.

1. Communication
2. Collaboration
3. Trusting
4. Risking
5. Giving
6. Receiving
7. Consensus
8. Consent

◊ Go through the list and make sure you understand the qualities of co-operation by thinking of a few examples of each of the qualities.

◊ When you have gone through the list and understand each quality, rate your community development support group, as a group, so far, on a scale of 1 to 3, with 1 being "we always practise this," 2 being "we sometimes practise this," and 3 being "we never, or rarely, practise this."

◊ When you have rated the group's practice, give your learning partner a phone call and ask him/her how he/she would rate your group in terms of co-operation.

◊ Then discuss your ratings.

1. How similar or different are the ratings you and your learning partner gave?

2. What are the similarities?

3. What are the differences?

4. What do the similarities in ratings signify?

5. What do the differences in ratings signify?

◊ Before concluding the conversation, try to come to some agreement – consent, if not consensus – in answering the following questions.

1. What are we already doing really well?

2. How can we celebrate that in the group?

3. What do we need to work on most?

4. How can we address that in the group?

◊ Finish by answering the question:

How co-operative were you in the conversation with your learning partner?

◊ *Record your reflections in your working notes.*

8.   CONCLUSION

The follow-up reading for this session is:
*   *Not Religion, but Love*, pp. 116–23/100–107.

The set community tasks for this session are:

◊ Meet with your learning partner and your community development support group.

◊ Talk about how it went for each person in your group last week as they connected with two other people in the community.

◊ Share what you learned in this session about getting beyond game playing, playing it straight, extending civility to others, expressing compassion for others and developing co-operation with others.

◊ Talk about what you already do really well as a group and celebrate it. Then talk about what you need to work on most, and how you can address that in your relationships inside the group, and also outside the group – especially with the two other people with whom each one of you has started to connect.

◊ Encourage each person in the group to connect again with the two other people in the community they connected with last week, but with a greater degree of civility, compassion and co-operation this time. Agree that you will discuss how this went at your next meeting.

◊ *Record your actions, reflections and conclusions in the working notes.*

BUILDING BRIDGES THROUGH GROUPS

1. PREPARATION

1.1. Objectives

- To review your understanding of the "protocols" on which relationships with people are built – civility to others, compassion for others and co-operation with others
- To introduce the important part played by groups – both existing groups and starting groups – in community development

2. REVIEW

15 minutes

Review your work from the previous session.

Review the issues raised in Session 11, particularly your understanding of the "protocols" on which relationships with people are built – civility to others, compassion for others and co-operation with others.

Review the reading:

Not Religion, but Love, pp. 116–23/100–107.

Review the tasks:

1. How did you find trying to connect with the two other people in the community you connected with last week, with a greater degree of civility?

2. What was the most important thing you learned while doing the community tasks for the last session?

Finish with a careful reflection on what worked best and what
you would need to do in order to connect with a greater degree
of civility, compassion and co-operation with people in your
community in future.

◊ *Don't forget to record your reflections in your working notes.*

3.   DEPENDENCE, INDEPENDENCE AND INTERDEPENDENCE

15 minutes

In much of the Western world today, independence is considered a
virtue and dependence is considered a vice – so much so, in fact, that
on one famous occasion Margaret Thatcher (the then Prime Minister
of Great Britain) said:

> And, you know, there is no such thing as society. There are
> individual men and women, and there are families.

Even when we talk to each other, an attitude of isolation often still
exists. We may talk about our problems – but we want to solve them
alone. Even if we seek help from others, we are asking for advice on
how we can solve our problems by ourselves. Unfortunately, for far
too many of us:

- *Independence* is healthy.
- *Dependence* is sick.
- Therefore we avoid *interdependence* like the plague.

Even though our insistence on independence appears liberating, it is,
in fact, debilitating. Nothing exists in and of itself. Everything that
is alive is interdependent: and everything that is alive stays alive by
being interdependent. If we act as if we are independent, we are like
branches cut from a tree. We are cut off from the sustenance that flows
from the tree of life and cut off from the sustenance rooted in our
common human life. We cannot blossom.

Not only do we lose the sense of being a part of a community, we
also lose the part of ourselves that can only be fully alive while we are
part of a vibrant community.

Is it any wonder, therefore, that we cannot solve many of our
problems in society? Independence not only causes many of our

problems, it also separates us from access to many of the solutions that can only be discovered (together, interdependently) in community.

Christians are often as blinded by *individualism* as the people in the wider community. Not only have we been shaped by the same cultural values as the rest of society, but many of us have also adopted spiritual values that reinforce our individualism rather than diminish it.

This stress on the individual over against the collective is strongest in churches where an overemphasis on "personal" conversion, "personal" salvation and "personal" sanctification rationalizes a preoccupation with the individual at the expense of the collective. And, as a result, many Christians I know operate very individualistically indeed.

1. What evidence do you see in society that independence is considered a virtue and dependence is considered a vice?

2. How might our emphasis on "personal" conversion, "personal" salvation and "personal" sanctification rationalize a preoccupation with the individual at the expense of the collective?

◊ *Record your reflections in your working notes.*

In contrast, Jesus grew up in a close-knit Jewish village. Groups – in which individuals could draw on the love, strength and wisdom of the collective in order to resolve their problems – were of enormous importance to him. Given this upbringing, it is hardly surprising that Jesus did most of his work with people in groups.

Jesus started with existing groups: ranging from conservative groups like the men in the traditional Hebrew synagogue in Nazareth, his home town, through to radical groups like the charismatic Messianic movement in Jordan led by his cousin John.

Jesus only started his own groups when existing groups could no longer accommodate his vision or carry out his mission – after he was put out of his synagogue and the reform movement fell apart when its leader was put in prison.

When he did start his own groups, Jesus set them up on the edge of existing groups – close enough to maintain relationships with the existing groups, but far enough away to create the space for a degree of experimentation not normally permitted in the existing groups.

In the groups he established, Jesus encouraged a healthy culture of interdependence and empowered people to realize their personal potential in the context of corporate support.

1. Why did Jesus work through groups?
2. Which groups did he start with?
3. Why do you think Jesus started with these particular groups?
4. What groups did Jesus start himself?
5. Why did Jesus start his own groups?
6. Where did he locate his own groups?
7. How did his groups operate?

◊ *Report your reflections in your working notes.*

4.   EXISTING GROUPS

4.1. Surveying Groups

20 minutes

If we want to work *in* our church community, then we need to begin with the groups already established in our church community. Like Jesus did. If we want to work *through* our church community in the local community, we need to look for the formal and informal groups in our church community that are less inward looking and more outward looking.

There are many different kinds of groups in a church community.

- There are *formal organizational groups* like the elders, deacons, pastoral committees and Parish councils.

- There are *formal ministry groups* like music ministry committees, worship teams and church choirs.

- There are *formal mission groups* like evangelistic ministry committees, visitation teams and care services.

- There are *formal nurture groups* like home groups, small groups and support groups.

- There are *formal focus groups* like children's ministries groups, youth work and aged care committees.

- There are also all of the *informal groups* of families and friends that are associated with the church community somehow or other.

◊ With some pens and a large piece of paper, draw a map of all the formal groups that are associated with your church community.

◊ Add any informal groups associated with your church community that you are personally – or potentially could be – involved with.

The diagram of the church below is a generic map of key individual contacts, groups, committees, congregations and community networks, or "grapevines," that link them all together. You might want to use this map as a starting point for developing your own group map – adapting it to your own context and labelling your key individual contacts, the main groups you are (or could be) connected with and community networks that link them.[50]

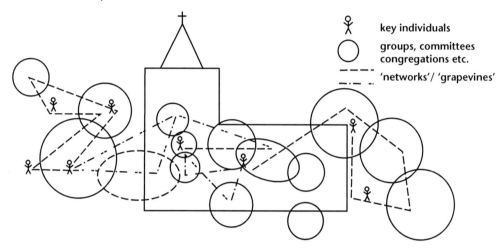

Figure 13. A church "map"

◊ After you have drawn your group map, sit back and have a look at it, and ask yourself:

1. Can you think of any other groups that you haven't included?
2. What group(s), if any, are you part of?
3. What group(s), if any, would you like to be part of? Why?

◊ *Remember to record your reflections in your working notes.*

4.2. Selecting Groups

10 minutes

If you want to get involved in your church community or in your local community through the church community, there are usually plenty

---

[50] G. Lovell, *Human and Religious Factors in Church and Community Work* (Pinner: The Grail, 1982), p. 24.

of groups you can approach. The best groups to start with are dynamic groups, characterized by:

1. An orientation towards the present rather than the past
2. An awareness of problems
3. An acceptance of the importance of problem solving
4. An appreciation of change
5. A perception of change as positive rather than negative
6. An assessment of the pace of change
7. An understanding of the pace of change
8. A concern for people rather than programs
9. A commitment to nurture rather than to maintenance
10. A consideration of accountability, not just accounts
11. A comprehension of the whole rather than the parts
12. A capacity to provide a wide range of knowledge and skills.

1. Which of these criteria are most important to you?

2. What group(s) in your church meet this criteria?

It's often a good idea to talk with people in your church about their groups in order to assess whether they are the kind of groups you might like to join. If a group sounds like it might be a possibility, it's always best to visit the group (and check it out for yourself) before deciding whether to throw your lot in with them.

What else do you need in a group to help you with your community work?

◊ *Record your reflections in your working notes.*

No one group will meet all our needs. Consider being a part of different groups for different purposes.

What group(s) – if any – could help you with your community work?

4.3. Entering Groups

10 minutes

Don't be afraid to consider groups outside the church as well as groups inside the church – informal as well as formal.

If you find the kind of group that you are looking for – that is, for example, concerned for people rather than programs, and with the capacity to provide a wide range of knowledge and skills that you need for the kind of work that you want to do in your community – then you need to think about joining this existing group rather than starting your own.

There are a number of important steps that need to be taken very carefully by those who want to join an existing group successfully.

1)   The first step is to *accept the guidelines of the group* and abide by their requirements as much as possible. If we go along with the group, we have a better chance of getting along with the group.

2)   The second step is to *seek a sponsor in the group* who sympathizes with the work that we want to do and who is willing to give us some space to do it through the group. It doesn't have to be a lot of autonomy. Just a little opportunity can make a lot of difference. It can give us the room we need to do what we want to do.

3)   The third step is to try to *find some supporters in the group* who already share a similar passion for the work we want to do and with whom we can work co-operatively through the group. It doesn't have to be a lot of support. Even a little support can make a lot of difference. It can give us the combined resources we need to do what we want to do together.

1. If you have already joined a group, did you take any of these steps?

2. If not, why not? If so, how did it go?

3. If you are planning to join a group, would you take any of these steps?

4. If not, why not? If so, how would you go about it?

5. Do you think it is possible to succeed in a group without taking these steps? Why or why not?

◊ *Record your reflections in your working notes.*

5.   STARTING GROUPS

Sometimes we can find an *existing* group in our church community that is interested in the community development work that we want to do. In that case, it is just a matter of joining the group and getting on with the job.

As we have seen, Jesus started with existing groups but had to form his own groups when the existing groups could no longer accommodate his vision, or carry out his mission. On occasion, we may need to do the same.

Respected community development worker Alan Twelvetrees says:

> It is probably more difficult to re-orientate an existing group to take up (new) objectives than to work with a new group to that end.[51]

5.1. Initiating Groups

20 minutes

Initiating groups can be both surprisingly easy and infuriatingly difficult.

Jesus suggested it could be as easy as two or three people recognizing a common concern. He suggested that we begin to work out our common concerns for the neighbourhood over meals in one another's homes (Lk. 10:7).

At times, however, the search for people with a common concern can be extremely difficult and frustrating. Search as we may, we just can't seem to find someone whose heart beats in harmony with ours. These are times of quiet desperation that call for quiet determination.

We need to heed the advice of Jesus, who said to his disciples:

> Look, and look, and keep on looking – for, only then, will you find what you are looking for. (Matt. 7:7 [author's version])

We need to look among people we already know who may be interested. We should talk to these people about our concerns. They may think we are crazy. But they may share our concerns. We should also look at existing groups that may be engaging in activities closely related to those we are interested in. When we find two other people and three of us decide to work together, then a group has formed.

You are already involved in a new group – the community development support group with your learning partner and at least one other person from the community. You may need to initiate another new group – including other people – as well.

1. Do you think you need to start another group to help with your work?

2. If so, why? What are the reasons? How valid are those reasons?

◊ *Record your reflections in your working notes.*

---

[51] A. Twelvetrees, *Community Work* (Basingstoke: MacMillan, 1991), p. 58.

To initiate a new group is a powerful process, and it is essentially a political process that needs to be handled diplomatically. New groups should be set up only if it is absolutely necessary.

Why is initiating a new group a political process?

◊ Record your reflections in your working notes.

Why does it need to be handled diplomatically?

Setting up a new group can be perceived as a criticism of existing groups.

There are two strategies we can use to initiate a new group diplomatically – the first is a *formal* strategy, and the second is an *informal* strategy.

We can initiate a new group formally by consulting the leaders of the church and asking for their permission to set up a new group. Or we can initiate a new group informally by simply setting up a new group with a few friends with no official recognition.

Note that Christ decided to set up all his new groups *informally*.

1. Would you set up a new group formally? If so, why?
2. Would you set up a new group informally? If so, why?

◊ Record your reflections in your working notes.

How would you go about the task of setting up a new group?

◊ Record your reflections in your working notes.

6.   MAINTAINING GROUPS

20 minutes

Setting up a new group can be difficult, but *initiating* a group is never as difficult as the task of *maintaining* a group.

Power struggles are the biggest reason that most groups blow up. Jesus suggested that the best way to deal with power struggles is to make sure there are no bosses in a group – that everyone in the group operates not as a boss, but as a servant working for the welfare of everyone else in the group (Matt. 23:8). Of course, all groups need leadership. But Jesus' idea of being a leader had nothing to do with control. For him, being a leader meant being a facilitator. He said that, in support groups, the leader should be the servant (Matt. 23:11) – not controlling the group, but facilitating.

Understanding the development phases that all groups pass through can be helpful for facilitators. The most commonly recognized phases are forming, storming, reforming and performing.

- *Forming* is when a group gathers round a common concern.
- *Storming* is when a group manages some stormy disputes.
- *Reforming* is when a group develops a plan as a way forward.
- *Performing* is when a group carries through an agreed plan.

◊ Give examples of these phases from your own experience in groups.

1. Can you think of a group that is forming? What characterizes this group as one that is forming?

2. Can you think of a group that is storming? What characterizes this group as one that is storming?

3. Can you think of a group that is reforming? What characterizes this group as one that is reforming?

4. Can you think of a group that is performing? What characterizes this group as one that is performing?

◊ *Record your reflections in your working notes.*

All groups pass through these phases, and any dynamic, growing group will pass through these phases again and again. The role of a facilitator is to help the group deal with these phases by:

- *Initiating* when the group is *forming*
- *Conciliating* when the group is *storming*
- *Consolidating* when the group is *reforming*
- *Co-ordinating* when the group is *performing.*

Consider one of the groups that you are involved in when answering the following questions:

1. What phase is your group in at the moment?

2. What does it feel like to be in that phase?

3. What role do you think a facilitator should play in the group right now?

4. If you were to take on that role, what would it involve for you?

◊ *Record your reflections in your working notes.*

7.   FACILITATING GROUPS

20 minutes

Groups must be developed with a lot of care if they are going to help people grow. They must be *open*, not closed; *inclusive,* not exclusive; *co-operative*, not competitive; *big* enough to have a critical mass and creative mix of people; *small* enough for all the people to be able to participate meaningfully; and *dynamic* enough for everyone in the group to be active, not passive, members of the group.

The facilitator is not an expert but an encourager who creates opportunities for everyone in the group to participate in the group and helps the group to wrestle with the issues it confronts as a group.

The facilitator doesn't try to answer all the questions. Instead, the facilitator asks probing questions, helping the group to come up with their own answers.

The facilitator doesn't try to solve all the problems. Instead, the facilitator brings a range of points of view to bear that can help the group manage their many problems more responsibly.

Wherever possible, a facilitator will include others in the facilitation of the group – rotating the role and broadening and deepening the role to include co-facilitating to enhance a sense of ownership of the group by the group.

The facilitator of a group needs to constantly monitor and manage two quite separate, but equally important, dynamics through every phase of the group to ensure the success of the group, namely the *content* of the group and the *process* of the group.

7.1. The Content of the Group

- The *aims and activities* of the group: What do we want this group to do?
- The *process* of the group: How will this group achieve its aims?
- The *affinity and interaction* in the group: How do we want to be in this group?

7.2. The Facilitator's Tasks in the Group

In order to successfully facilitate a group, the facilitator needs to learn to:

- Sit silently
- Talk cautiously
- Listen attentively
- Reflect faithfully
- Clarify carefully
- Summarize clearly
- Re-frame creatively
- Act enthusiastically
- Shift focus subtly, when necessary
- Use verbal and non-verbal signals.

1. What is a facilitator?

2. What does a facilitator need to monitor in a group?

3. How can a facilitator manage the content in a group?

4. How can a facilitator manage the process in a group?

5. What are the skills a group facilitator needs to learn?

6. Which of these skills have you already learned?

7. Which of these skills do you need to learn?

◊ *Record your reflections in your working notes.*

◊ Think of the last time your community development support group met.

1. Who acted as the facilitator(s) in the small group? (Note: If you were the facilitator, you can either answer these questions yourself or ask another member of the group to answer these questions.)

2. What did the facilitator(s) do to manage the content of the group?

3. What did the facilitator(s) do to manage the process of the group?

4. What did the facilitator(s) do well? What do you need to work on a bit more?

◊ *Record your reflections in your working notes.*

8.   CONCLUSION

The follow-up reading for this session is:

* *Not Religion, but Love*, pp. 124–30/108–115.

The set community tasks for this session are:

◊ Meet with your learning partner and your community development support group.

◊ Share what you learned in this session about initiating, maintaining and facilitating a group and talk about how you operate as a group.

◊ Then, talk about the other groups in your community and whether, with the community work you have in mind, you should operate through an existing group or whether you need to start a new group of your own.

◊ Either way, make plans as to how you can work through a group.

◊ *Record your actions, reflections and conclusions in your working notes.*

BUILDING BRIDGES FOR CO-OPERATION

1. PREPARATION

1.1. Objectives

- To review your understanding of the important part groups play in the process of community development
- To consider the importance of co-operation between groups

2. REVIEW

15 minutes

Review your work from the previous session.

Review the issues raised in Session 12, particularly your understanding of the important part groups play in the process of community development and the processes involved in working with existing groups and starting new groups.

Review the reading:

Not Religion, but Love, pp. 124–30/108–115.

Review the tasks:

1. How did your meeting with your community development support group go?

2. What was the most important thing you learned while doing the community tasks for the last session?

Finish with a careful reflection on the plans you have to work as a group.

◊ *Don't forget to record your reflections in your working notes.*

3.   PEACEFUL, HOSPITABLE AND CO-OPERATIVE[52]

20 minutes

It is one thing to get people to co-operate with one another in a group, but quite another to get the group to co-operate with other groups. Miscommunication, suspicion and competition ensure that most groups move in their own circles and keep a safe distance from one another. One might hope that the church, which preaches reconciliation, might be an exception. However, experience shows that the opposite is often the case.

A few years ago, a coalition of local churches sponsored a Christmas celebration. It was a combined, ecumenical, interdenominational, cross-cultural, multi-lingual celebration of the coming of Christ – held in the street – right in the middle of our suburb. Hundreds of people showed up, thoroughly enjoying the candlelight service that was presented in the manifold colours of the multiple religious traditions represented. All the way through – from the Greek kids' chorus to the Anglican parish choir – the music was mesmerising and, in the end, the Tongans blew everybody away with the beauty of their harmonies.

A week later, the local Baptist church that had boycotted the combined event held an event of their own – and it was a big flop. Without the contributions of the other groups, the program they put on was pretty monochromatic and monotonous. Hardly anyone turned up, and even the few people that the organizers brought with them drifted away, as quickly and quietly as they could, into the night.

No-one wanted to be there. It was embarrassing.

What went wrong, who was at fault, and how might it have been handled differently?

◊ *Record your reflections in your working notes.*

Jesus encouraged everyone to co-operate with everyone else, regardless of the group they belonged to. He even encouraged the "orthodox" to support activities promoted by "heretics," as long as those activities were characterized by a concern for love and justice. Once a religious academic asked Jesus for an authoritative definition of a "neighbour." In response, Jesus told the story of the Good Samaritan we saw in Session 11.

---

[52] Adapted from Andrews, *Not Religion*, pp. 131–32.

A man battered by robbers and left to die on the roadside was ignored by a Levite (a representative of the religious establishment), but was helped by a Samaritan (a man regarded by the "orthodox" religious establishment as a "heretic"). Jesus then instructed the religious academic to get beyond being "religious" and start doing some "good," like the Samaritan.

The idea of a good Samaritan was repulsive to the religious academic. For the Jews, the only good Samaritan was a dead Samaritan. Jesus' instruction for the Jew to join the Samaritan in doing good was equivalent to his telling a Christian to work with a Communist for the good of the community – a horrifying thought for many Christians who find it difficult to conceive of working with other Christians, let alone non-Christians!

But Jesus made no apologies for stressing the importance of working together as neighbours – not just with our friends, but also with those that we consider to be our enemies.

When Jesus sent his disciples out to do community work, he suggested that they find others they could work with. He said nothing to the disciples about checking out their religious credentials. There were just two qualities Jesus said his disciples should look for in the people they wanted to work with. They needed to be "peaceful" and "hospitable" – in other words, "co-operative" (Lk. 9:5–6).

When the religious leaders of Jesus' day criticized him for associating with people whose religious beliefs were "dubious," Jesus simply replied that he had come not to call the "religious," but to call the "irreligious" to the challenge of doing God's work in the community (Matt. 9:13). However, even Jesus' own disciples had problems in relating to people in other groups the way Jesus wanted them to.

One day, they stopped a man doing a good job in "their" locality – because, they said, he did not belong to "their" group. Jesus was appalled at their narrow-mindedness, and he reprimanded them for their short-sightedness. "Do not stop him," Jesus instructed them, "for (whether they belong to your group or not) whoever is not against you is for you" (Lk. 9:50).

For Jesus, the possibility of co-operating with people with differing points of view was not a prospect to withdraw from in horror, but rather an opportunity to relate to a wide range of people that should be embraced wholeheartedly. My wife and I have tried to follow Jesus' example in this regard by drawing together groups in the locality who are willing to work together for the welfare of the community. We have consistently tried to develop co-operation between various cliques in our congregation, and between the various congregations in our neighbourhood, by calling people together to consider common concerns.

> 1. What do you think about the kind of co-operation Jesus advocated? Do you agree with the view that "whoever is not against you is for you"?
>
> 2. How do you feel about working with anyone as long as they're co-operative? Do you agree that we can work with "peaceful heretics"?

◊ *Record your reflections in your working notes.*

4.   THE DIFFICULTIES IN CO-OPERATING

20 minutes

Many familiar difficulties arise when people try to co-operate.

◊ Take out a piece of paper and write a list of as many of the difficulties in co-operating as you can think of in 60 seconds.

After you have done this, look over the following. A list of difficulties in co-operating may include:

- A bit of suspicion
- Habits of isolation
- A fear of co-option
- Mistrust of motivation
- Proneness to competition
- Experience of polarization
- Disagreeable personalities
- Differences in language and style
- Conflicts over theology, ecclesiology and missiology.

◊ Think about which of these would be the greatest difficulties for you and your church to overcome in order to co-operate.

◊ Choose one of the difficulties that you nominated as a "great difficulty" for you and your church and spend the next ten minutes thinking about how you would go about trying to overcome this difficulty.

◊ *Record your reflections in your working notes.*

Some of the ways people try to overcome difficulties in co-operating include:

- Making phone calls
- Meeting one another
- Sharing information
- Consulting one another
- Swapping some ideas
- Affirming one another
- Encouraging mutual respect
- Apologizing for past mistakes
- Resolving present problems
- Organizing visits to the group
- Doing a personnel exchange
- Running a joint training program
- Co-hosting a specific one-off event
- Developing guidelines for co-operation.

Note that the best way to overcome the difficulties of co-operating between groups is to create opportunities for people in those groups to meet together to talk informally or to work on a small manageable joint project. That way, people can get to know one another as people and deal personally with the difficulties they have in co-operating with one another as groups.

It is often helpful if one person from each group acts as a contact person to liaise with the other group, to look for opportunities to develop the relationship and to watch for any problems that may arise.

5.   THE BENEFITS OF CO-OPERATING

20 minutes

There are, of course, many benefits that come from co-operating with one another.

◊ Take out a piece of paper and write a list of as many of the benefits of co-operating as you can think of in 60 seconds.

A list of the benefits of co-operating may include:

- Not being alone
- Knowing others
- Widening contacts
- Deepening connections
- Broadening perspectives
- Reducing competition
- Increasing collaboration
- Sharing personnel and resources
- Developing integrated joint strategies.

The practice of co-operating between groups, as well as within groups, unleashes the potential in the whole "body" that is greater than the sum of the parts. Social scientists refer to the hidden dynamics of this explosion of potential as "synergy" and "serendipity."

Consent, as we have seen, involves finding a way forward together, in spite of our conflicts, that we can all affirm is in harmony with the hopes we have. Synergy means actually finding a way to make our differences work for us rather than against us. Serendipity means that what works out could be far greater than any of us would have been able to imagine.

A group may consent to co-operating with another group. The decision may be one which some members may not feel is the best decision, but which they can all live with and commit themselves to support the best that they can.

Such consent releases latent synergy. Synergy is the essence. It catalyses, unifies and unleashes the greatest powers within people.

Simply defined, it means that the whole is greater than the sum of its parts. It means that the relationship that the parts have to each other is a part in and of itself. It is not only a part, but the most catalytic, the most unifying, the most empowering, and the most exciting part.

Synergy is everywhere in nature. If you plant two plants close together, the roots co-mingle and improve the quality of the soil so that both plants will grow better than if they were separated. The challenge is to apply the principles of creative co-operation that we learn from nature in our social interactions.

Family life provides many opportunities to observe synergy and to practise it. The very way that a man and a woman bring a child into the world, for example, is synergistic.

The essence of synergy is to value differences, to respect them, to build on strengths, to compensate for weaknesses.

We obviously value the physical differences between men and women. But what about the social, mental and emotional differences? Could these differences not also be sources for creating new, exciting forms of life – for creating an environment that is truly fulfilling for each person, that nurtures the self-esteem and self-worth of each, that creates opportunities for each to mature into independence and then gradually into interdependence?[53]

Serendipity is latent in synergy. You don't know exactly what's going to happen or where it is going to lead. Synergy is almost as if a group collectively agrees to (scrap) old scripts to write a new one. It is to start all over again.

> Could synergy not create a new script for the next generation
> – one that is more geared to serve and is less selfish; one that is
> more open and is less protective; one that is more loving and is
> less judgmental?[54]

With synergy and serendipity, you just never know. Anything is possible.

Even a Christmas celebration that is a combined, ecumenical, inter-denominational, cross-cultural, multi-lingual celebration of the coming of Christ, held in the street, right in the middle of our own neighbourhood! Where hundreds of people show up, thoroughly enjoying the candlelight service, which is presented in the manifold colours of the multiple religious traditions represented. In addition, all the way through – from the Greek kids' chorus to the Anglican parish choir – the music is mesmerising. In the end, the Tongans blow everybody away with the beauty of their buoyant harmonies!

Think of an example from your own experience in which co-operation led to similar success. Identify the dynamics of synergy and serendipity at work that made the event a success.

◊ Record your reflections in your working notes.

---

[53] Covey, *Seven Habits*, pp. 262–63.
[54] Covey, *Seven Habits*, p. 263.

6.   CO-OPERATING WITH GROUPS IN THE LOCAL COMMUNITY

45 minutes

There are many opportunities for different groups within the church community to co-operate with one another, as well as for diverse groups from the church and the local community to work co-operatively together.

Co-operating with groups in the church community

Methodist minister and community worker George Lovell says that "within each church there are different groups and if the church is to be a community then there may be need for a considerable amount of inter-group work."[55]

◊ Draw a diagram showing *all the groups in your church* that might be interested in the community work that you want to do.

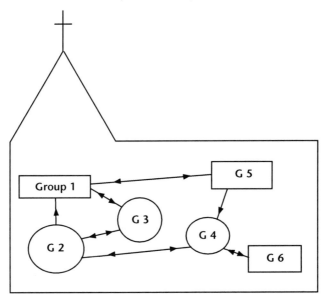

Figure 14. Inter-group relationships in a church[56]
Group 1: Parish Council; Group 2: Pastoral Care; Group 3: Worship Group; Group 4: Discipleship Group; Group 5: Mission Group; Group 6: Home Group

---

[55] G. Lovell, *The Church and Community Development* (Pinner: The Grail, 1972), p. 52.

[56] Lovell, *Church and Community*, p. 53.

◊ Draw a diagram showing *the churches in the locality* that might be interested in the community work that you want to do.

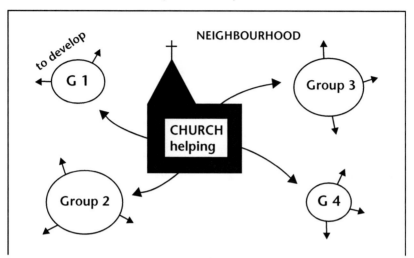

Figure 15. Interchurch relationships in a neighbourhood[57]
Group 1: Meals on Wheels; Group 2: Women's Group; Group 3: Men's Group;
Group 4: Youth Group

George Lovell says that, these days, "churches are coming together in various relationships across previous ecclesiastical boundaries. At every level of inter-church life, people need to learn how to work with each other."[58]

[57] Lovell, *Church and Community*, p. 43.
[58] Lovell, *Church and Community*, p. 53.

◊ Draw a diagram showing *any inter-church group(s) in the area* that might be interested in the community work that you want to do.

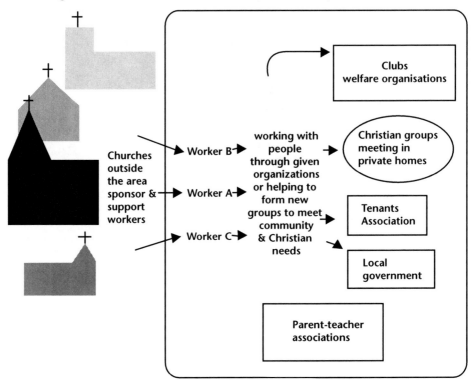

Figure 16. Co-operation with churches outside the neighbourhood[59]

[59] Lovell, *Church and Community*, p. 55.

Co-operating with groups in the local community

Not only is it possible but, in many cases, it is desirable that groups in the church community and groups in the local community work on joint community development projects.

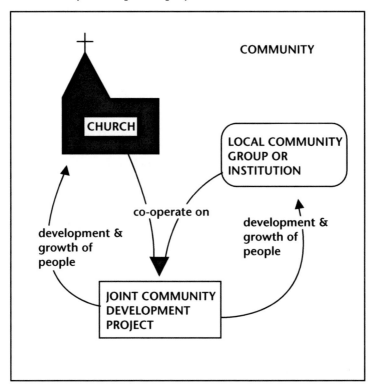

Figure 17. Joint projects with non-church local groups [60]

---

[60] Lovell, *Church and Community*, p. 34.

◊ Think about some of the following possibilities for co-operating:

1)   Churches can allow other groups to use their premises.

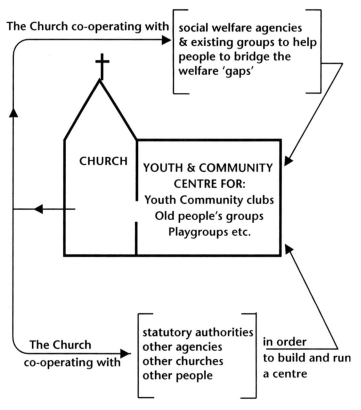

Figure 18. Local co-operation through shared premises[61]

For example, St. Francis, one of the Catholic churches in our area, has allowed an alternative school for local Aboriginal children to use its facilities. Both the church and the school have benefited from this arrangement. The Aboriginal community are able to use a facility that was much needed but that was otherwise overprotected and underutilized. The church has had the opportunity to get to know the Aboriginal community as no other church in the neighbourhood has been able to. In this case, a relationship and the potential for further co-operation grew out of the rental agreement.

But it is possible for churches to allow other groups to use their premises and still have virtually no contact with the group at all – until

---

[61] Lovell, *Church and Community*, p. 42.

it comes time to collect the rent or pay for damages. Allowing others to use our premises may be the place for us to start to co-operate with other groups, but it should never be the place that we stop. We need to be willing to move on from just sharing property to putting our time, energy, expertise and our whole congregational infrastructure at the service of other groups.

2)   We can help administer a program with an already established community association that needs support.

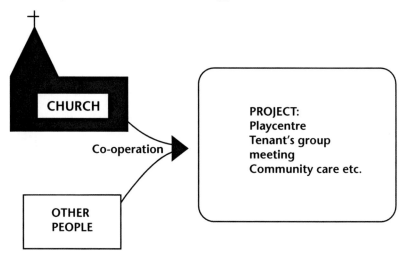

Figure 19. Local co-operation through existing program support[62]

One of our local churches, for instance, helps to run a "Meals on Wheels" group which distributes healthy midday meals, at minimal cost, to frail, elderly people in our community. Besides offering its premises as a base for this program, a number of people in the congregation are personally involved in the day-to-day operations – from preparing the "meals" to providing the "wheels."

3)   We can help initiate or participate in establishing a local community association to provide a needed service.

---

[62] Lovell, *Church and Community*, p. 45.

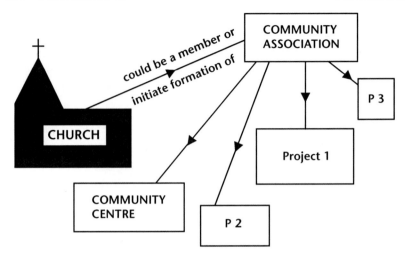

Figure 20. Local co-operation through service provision[63]

For instance, one of our local churches has set up "Family Care Services," which provides assistance for families needing support through a local community centre they established. Besides providing a space where people can just drop in, the centre also includes a base where playgroups can meet, informational resources can be shared, educational courses can be run, counselling services can be offered and community development activities can be organized.

The church initiated and set up "Family Care Services," but it has also continued to participate in the provision of the services by being involved in the committee that co-ordinates the services at the centre.

4)   We can help personalize services of impersonal service agencies.

[63] Lovell, *Church and Community*, p. 45.

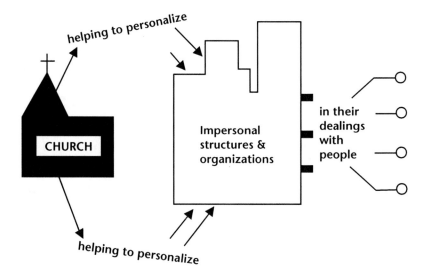

Figure 21. The church as provider of personalized community services[64]

Another of our local churches, for instance, realized that many people in the parish who were entitled to claim social security benefits were afraid to do so because they found the hoops they were expected to jump through quite daunting and demeaning. So the church decided to encourage members of the congregation to get alongside these people and accompany them on their visit to "Centrelink." The fact that only four or five people out of a congregation of 40–50 had jobs meant that the church had lots of people with lots of experience to provide this personal service – and they did it with a vengeance!

5)   We can help advocate for vulnerable people in situations of serious disadvantage.

---

[64] Lovell, *Church and Community*, p. 47.

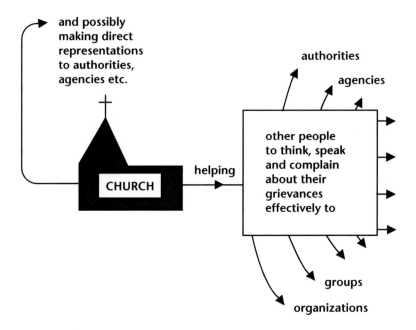

Figure 22. The church as advocate for vulnerable people[65]

For instance, one of our local churches monitors the accommodation problems of particularly vulnerable groups of people in our neighbourhood. When there is a complaint, members of the congregation investigate the matter and, where necessary, make vigorous representations to landlords on behalf of vexed tenants. This group even managed to secure a successful settlement in a notorious "potty" case in which a recently released psychiatric patient was threatened with eviction – and an immediate return to the psychiatric facility that he had just left – due to his accidentally knocking over a "potty" in his flat (its contents seeped through the floor, which was the landlord's ceiling, and the urine dripped onto the head of the unhappy landlord below). How anybody was able to settle that dispute happily, I'll never know. But they did. The "potty" was evicted and the tenant got to stay – on the condition that he used the toilet in future!

6)   The church can actually become a catalyst in the local community for co-operation in community development.

[65] Lovell, *Church and Community*, p. 48.

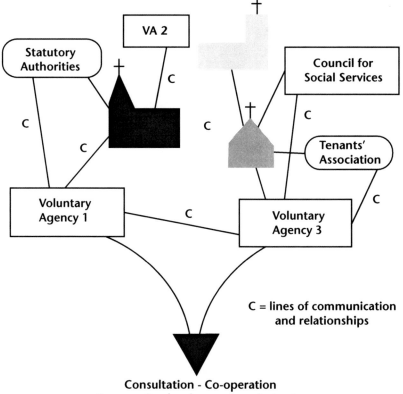

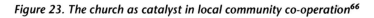

C = lines of communication
and relationships

Consultation - Co-operation
Community development projects etc.

Figure 23. The church as catalyst in local community co-operation[66]

As George Lovell reminds us, "community development means working for the growth of each individual, group and organization, and for the establishment of healthy, interdependent relationships between them."[67]

◊ Think of some examples of co-operation between church groups and local groups in the community, then draw a diagram of *all the joint community projects in the area* that might be interested in the community work that you want to do.

◊ *Don't forget to keep copies of these maps in your working notes.*

---

[66] Lovell, *Church and Community*, p. 51.
[67] Lovell, *Church and Community*, p. 52.

7.   CONCLUSION

The follow-up reading for this session is:
*   *Not Religion, but Love*, pp. 131–136/116–121.

The set community tasks for this session are:

◊ Meet with your learning partner and your community development support group.

◊ Share what you have learned in this session about co-operating with other groups in the church community and in the local community.

◊ Look at the map of all the groups in your church community and in your local community that you have made. See if there are any other groups other people may want to add to the map. Nominate the groups that you need to co-operate with, and arrange to visit them to explore the possibilities for collaboration.

Remember, usually there are government rules and regulations that you will need to take into account in your community work (e.g., child protection guidelines, food safety regulations, building and transport insurance, etc.).

You may need to talk with politicians, police, practitioners, ministers, academics, consultants, teachers, social workers and community workers.

Government agencies, welfare organizations and voluntary groups, universities, colleges and libraries are all groups that you may need to consult.

National departments of surveys and statistics provide valuable information on population, health, education, economics, employment, religion and ethnicity for most localities.

Groups like the National Church Life Survey (NCLS) provide excellent up-to-date data for churches in some countries.

◊ *Record your actions, reflections and conclusions in your working notes.*

BRINGING ABOUT PERSONAL HOPE

1. PREPARATION

1.1. Objectives

- To review your understanding of the importance of co-operation between groups within the church community and between church and community groups

- To consider the importance of imparting hope – and the role that prayer can play in promoting hope

2. REVIEW

15 minutes

Review your work from Session 13. This will include a review of your appreciation of the issues raised in the course notes and clarified in the follow-up readings and your experience of your set community tasks.

Review the issues raised in the previous session, particularly your understanding of the importance of co-operation between groups within the church community and between church and community groups.

Review the reading:

Not Religion, but Love, pp. 131–36/116–121.

Review the tasks:

1. How did your meeting with your learning partner and your community development support group go?

2. What was the most important thing you learned while doing the community tasks for the last session?

Finish with some careful reflection on the plans you have to co-
operate with other groups in your community.

◊ *Be sure to record your reflections in your working notes.*

3. The Importance of Hope

30 minutes

3.1. The Importance of Hope

If we want to try to facilitate transformation in our communities, then
sooner or later we are sure to be confronted by the hopelessness that
completely incapacitates most people in most communities.

I teach courses on transformation in many communities and,
at first glance, most of the people who come to these courses seem
hopeful enough. But when we begin to talk about the possibility of
individual and collective transformation, it doesn't take very long for
the discussions to get bogged down in despair. And those who seem to
know the most about themselves and their society seem to be those
most stuck in despair.

Without hope, there is no motivation for growth or change. It
doesn't matter how many courses people go to, how many skills they
acquire, how many certificates they accumulate. In order for any
personal growth or social change to occur, it is absolutely crucial that
people experience hope in the midst of their hopelessness.

But how? How do you impart hope to the woman contemplating
suicide because the man she loves is having an affair with a younger
woman? How do you impart hope to a man who was abused by his
father as a child and now finds himself doing the same to his own
children? How do you impart hope to grieving parents whose only
son has been killed by a runaway truck? How do you impart hope to
a whole community of people whose homes are to be demolished to
make way for a freeway?

There are many ways to impart hope. "Hope is natural. We all possess
it. It needs only to be *uncovered*, not *dis*covered,"[68] says counsellor
Maurice Lamm. He suggests that the best way for us to impart hope is
to encourage people.

---

[68] M. Lamm, *The Power of Hope* (New York: Rawson Associates, 1995), p. 23.

- "Not to trust statistics – the ones you see quoted may not apply to you."
- "Not to waste energy denying there is a problem. Use it to find a solution."
- "Not to look for approval of absolutely everything you do – you won't get it."
- "To see yourself as others see you – your strengths as well as weaknesses."
- "To learn from the past, set your sights on the future, but live in the present."
- "Not look at the world around for answers – but look inside yourself instead."
- "To link up with God and put love in your life where fear used to be."[69]

1. Do you agree or disagree with the idea of "uncovering" hope? Why?

2. Have you ever tried any of the strategies suggested above? If so, what has worked for you?

◊ Record your reflections in your working notes.

3.2. The Example of Jesus

Jesus found prayer to be the most effective process that he could use to *introduce hope into hopeless situations.*

> One day Jesus got an urgent message from two close friends, Mary and Martha. Their brother Lazarus was dying. By the time Jesus made the long journey to their village, the situation was hopeless. Lazarus was dead. In fact, Jesus had even missed the funeral and Lazarus had already been laid to rest in a sepulchre.
>
> Jesus was overcome with grief. He wept openly, grieving with Mary and Martha. Going to the graveyard with them, he began to pray out loud. He deliberately prayed out loud so he could give voice to Mary and Martha's inner anguish, and in so doing, remind them that God was grieving with them. As he prayed, the family gradually became aware that no matter how hopeless the situation was, there was still hope. There was still hope because, even in the midst of the hopelessness of death, a source of life still existed that had the power

---

[69] Lamm, *Power of Hope*, pp. 65, 141.

> *to bring life out of death. And Jesus brought life out of death, when*
> *he walked over to the crypt, called for his friend to come out of the*
> *tomb, and brother Lazarus rose from the grave and strode towards*
> *his sisters, Martha and Mary.* (Jn. 11:17–44 [author's version])

Two very important principles can be found in this story.

First, Jesus entered into his *friends' hopelessness.* He did not laugh at their tears or analyze their grief. Instead he wept with them, fully embracing their grief. He did not try to promote hope until *after* he had fully partaken of their hopelessness. It is my conviction that prayers for hope are only meaningful to the degree that we have entered into the person's experience empathically. It is only then that we can faithfully give voice to their cry to God and remind them that God will give heed to their cry.

Second, the hope that Jesus promoted through prayer was not a fantasy experience that deluded Mary and Martha into believing that they were better off than they really were. Instead, it was a faith experience in which the painful facts of their situation were miraculously transformed – bringing them face to face again with Lazarus, who they had believed had been lost forever. I am convinced that prayers for hope are only liberating to the extent that they are prayers of faith rather than prayers of fantasy. Fantasy pretends that things are not as bad as they seem. Faith faces reality squarely – with a confidence that either our situation can change or that we can change enough to cope with the situation as it is.

This does not mean that faith is unimaginative. It is quite the contrary. Prayers of *faith* involve encouraging people to imagine their painful reality being totally transformed or themselves being transformed through the pain. *Faith* looks into the face of reality. *Fantasy* ignores it. Jesus would have entered the realm of *fantasy* if he had encouraged Mary and Martha to imagine Lazarus rising and never having to die again. Instead, he imparted *faith* that imagined life coming out of death but still accepted death as an inescapable part of life. Therefore prayers of hope are only liberating to the extent that they face the facts – yet allow for the facts to be transformed by God.

1. What are the implications of the idea that, no matter how hopeless the situation is, there is still hope – because, even in the midst of the hopelessness of death, a source of life still exists that has the power to bring life out of death?

2. What evidence, if any, do you have for this out of your own experience?

3. Why are prayers for hope only meaningful to the degree that we have entered into the person's experience empathically?

4. Why are prayers for hope only liberating to the extent that they are prayers of faith rather than prayers of fantasy?

◊ *Remember to record your reflections in your working notes.*

4. THE PROCESS OF PRAYER

45 minutes

4.1. The Process of Prayer

Prayer is the process of developing an *awareness of*, and *availability to*, God. It involves a conscious *waiting* upon God and a *willingness* to yield to God. It is essentially a *creative response to life in the light of the love of God.*

1. How would you define prayer?

2. How does the definition of prayer given above compare or contrast with your own?

3. If your definition is somewhat different, can you flesh it out with some of the ideas above?

4.2. The Place of Prayer

Prayer is the centre of the community and the catalyst for community development: the *still point* around which the life of the community revolves; the *point of integration* where the conflicts in the community are resolved; the *starting point* at which people begin to live again, and the *point of departure* from which people begin to experiment and explore another way of living.

We emphasize the importance of prayer because we believe that community begins and ends with God, and, in prayer, we could meet God who is the beginning and the end of the community development process.

It is in encounter with God that all that is good can be defined and affirmed, and all that is evil can be exposed and opposed and our task for the future outlined.

It is in encounter with God that a vision of justice can be revealed and an infusion of grace could be realized.

It is in encounter with God that we can develop discernment in the midst of disorientation, energy when we have exhausted our ability, and endurance where we would have otherwise withdrawn.

It is in prayer, therefore, that we can begin to engage with God in the struggle for the salvation of the world.

> Having read and reflected upon the above statements on the place of prayer, write a few sentences in your own words that describe the place prayer has, or should have, in your life.

◊ *Be sure to record your reflections in your working notes.*

4.3. The Inspiration of Prayer

It is in prayer that my vision for justice emerges:

> A vision of equality,
>> in which all the resources of the earth
>> would be shared equally between
>> all the people on earth regardless of
>> nationality, colour, caste, class or creed.
>
> A vision of equity,
>> in which even the most disadvantaged people
>> would be able to meet their basic needs
>> with dignity and joy.
>
> A vision of a great society of small communities
>> interdependently co-operating
>> to practise political, socio-economic
>> and personal righteousness and peace
>> in every locality.

It is in prayer that we begin to feel the inflow of an infusion of grace to enable us to realize our vision for justice.

> An infusion of grace that enables us
>> to begin to deal with the reality
>> of our limitations and contradictions.
>
> An infusion of grace that enables us
>> to move beyond angry reactions to just actions
>> that transcends those limitations
>> and resolves those contradictions.

An infusion of grace that enables us
to respond, if not always with courage at least with
conviction, compassionately, constructively, and
productively.

We know that there are many who pray but do not act and many who act but do not pray. However, it seems that such people have misunderstood the meaning of both prayer and action. Prayer is the inspiration for action.

When we pray,
we come into the presence of a Love so profound
that it challenges all our plans, opinions and prejudices,
and calls us to a cause of pure compassion.

In the presence of that Love we have to act with love;
because to do anything else seems utterly absurd.

In the presence of that Love we are set free
from a preoccupation with meeting our needs
for a vocation of seeking peace
on the basis of justice for all.

What one thought in the meditation above particularly strikes you? Why? And how will it change the way you pray for your community?

◊ *Be sure to record your reflections in your working notes.*

4.4. The Pattern of Prayer

Prayer is not only a *means* of doing justice, but also the *model* for doing justice. To do justice to people, the process of community development needs to not only conform to the pattern of prayer, but also actually *become* a form of prayer itself.

Community development is usually a form of *intervention*. In any intervention we tend to take on the concerns of others as our own. We tend to depend on ourselves and our capacity to help to facilitate the resolution of the problems in the community. When we do this, we will only tend to work with people we think we can help, and we will only work with them as long as we perceive that our help is facilitating the resolution of the problems in the community.

It is only as our notion of community development is transformed, through prayer, into a form of prayer – from an act of *intervention*, which depends on the expertise we have, into an act of *intercession*, which depends on the power God has to do something about the situation that we can not do – that we can begin to engage in the struggle for justice in situations about which we feel hopeless.

For it is only as we approach the process of community development as we would approach prayer – that is, in a spirit of openness and responsiveness, being willing to do our bit without any expectation of ever controlling the outcome – that we can do justice to people.

1. What is your understanding of community development as "intervention"?

2. What is your understanding of community development as "intercession"?

3. What difference does it make to do community development as prayer?

◊ *Be sure to record your reflections in your working notes.*

4.5. The Power of Prayer

Hope of justice, for people without any hope of justice, cannot be developed on the basis of their past experience. Their past experience – characterized by a litany of one injustice after another – may make hope imperative, but it also makes it impossible.

The only hope they have is of an alternative future that would be in total contrast to their present situation and a total contradiction of their past history. Their only hope is to experience the power to act against their conditioning while the personal, social, cultural and political circumstances in which they were conditioned are still the dominant and dominating realities that circumscribe their lives.

That power is beyond most people. Their only hope, therefore, depends on their capacity to access a power beyond themselves through prayer.

Jacques Ellul says that a "self-therapy" takes place in prayer. "There is the giving up of anger and aggressiveness, a validation through responsibility and meditation, a recovery of balance through the rearranging of facts on successive levels as seen from a fresh outlook."[70]

Ellul also says that there is a "power" that can be released through prayer that is beyond the capacity of contemporary psychology and

---

[70] Quoted from Andrews, et al., *Building*, p. 351.

sociology to explain. He calls it "the effectual, immediate presence of the wholly Other, the Transcendent, the Living One."

If people are to access enough power to break the bondage of their conditioning so that they can be free to think and talk and work towards an alternative future, we not only need to help them with as much "self-therapy" as they can get, but we also need to impart something "wholly Other" than anything they have ever tried before.

1. Give an example of "self-therapy" that can occur through prayer.

2. Give an example of something "wholly Other" occurring through prayer.

◊ Record your reflections in your working notes.

Note that we cannot predict what will happen when we pray. All we can say is that something will surely happen.

Sometimes something will happen that is "wholly Other."

There are two kinds of "wholly Other" things that can happen. One "wholly Other" thing that can happen is that our problems will be solved.

Another "wholly Other" thing that can happen is that, though our problems may not be solved, we will be given power to cope with our ongoing problems.

We tend to see only the first thing – and not the second thing – as a miracle. We need to remember that *both are miracles* – and *marvellous* to behold!

4.6. The Practice of Prayer

20 minutes

We need to remember to put prayer at the heart of the process of whatever we're doing in the community.

Prayer in the process of community development

Following are a few ways of praying that people in the community who would not describe themselves as "religious" have still found helpful in the process of community development.

1)   *Be glad to be alive.* We need to make sure we get enough sleep each night so we wake up every morning not groggy, not grumpy, but glad to be alive. As we wake we can be more aware of the love of God in us and around us. We are then able to give ourselves over to the joy of living more fully and more freely.

2)   *Let the grudges go.* In order to prepare ourselves for the day, we can take a bit of time just to sense the tensions in our bodies that signal things we are uptight about. Often these are grievances, real or perceived, about ways that people thwart our plans. We can note the issues they raise that we need to address. Then we can let them go.

3)   *Let the love flow.* Once we have let our grievances go, we can begin to let the love flow. We can try to do this by bringing to mind all the people that we are connected to in our community. Then, one by one, picture their faces, speak their names, and pronounce a blessing upon each and every one them, friend and foe alike.

4)   *Deliberate on the locality.* We can often be in a hurry – on the move from morning to night. At regular intervals throughout the day we can always take the time to stop, to look and to listen to reflect on the activities, conversations and undercurrents in our community.

5)   *Meditate on the community.* Every now and again we can try to get a bit of distance from our community and put it all into perspective. We can meditate on our community – both as it is and as it might be. We can imagine all the things we could do to bring people in the locality together more.

6)   *Contemplate responsibility.* Because there are so many things we could do, it's very difficult to figure out exactly what we should do. We are often confused. We can seek clarity by listening to the still small voice inside us. We can listen until we hear a word that is right for us. Then we can take that word to heart.

7)   *Discern a direction.* We can take this direction to heart but not act on it on our own. We can discuss it with a group of people whose opinions we trust. Then together we can decide what to do about it. We can discern the direction to take on the basis of consensus and consent.

8)   *Reflect on actions.* Going in the right direction doesn't mean we will get the action right. We may actually get it wrong far more often than we'd like to admit. It's really important to be part of a group that can help us monitor our progress by reflecting on our actions.

9)   *Celebrate an achievement.* When we reflect on our actions, we are brought face to face with our failures as well as our successes. If we're not careful, we can let our failures overshadow or discount our

successes. So it's important to be part of a group that can help us not only evaluate our progress, but also validate our progress.

10)   *Focus on Jesus.* Last, but not least, we need to keep coming back to focus on the person of Jesus whom we encounter most enchantingly in the Gospels. We need to prayerfully immerse ourselves in the Scriptures so that the spirit of Jesus engages us, challenges us and changes us.

1. Which of the above suggestions do you already try to incorporate in your daily life?

2. Which of these practices have you found most helpful in your life and why?

3. Which of the above suggestions would you like to incorporate in your daily life?

4. How would you expect the practice to help you?

5. Which of the above suggestions would you like people you work with to incorporate in your daily life?

6. How would you expect the practice to help the people you work with?

7. What will you do in the coming week to incorporate this practice into the way that you work with the people in your community?

◊ *Remember to record your reflections in your working notes.*

◊ Finish this time of reflection with the following prayer by Michael Leunig, Australia's foremost cartoonist, who writes prayers for the *Sunday Age* as his contribution to what he calls "this wonderful, free-form, do-it-yourself ritual of connection and transformation." Here is an excerpt from *A Common Prayer.*

> God help us to change.
> > To change ourselves,
> > and to change our world.
>
> To know the need for it.
>
> To deal with the pain of it.
>
> To feel the joy of it.
>
> To undertake the journey
> > without understanding the destination.
>
> The art of gentle revolution.[71]

[71] M. Leunig, *A Common Prayer* (Melbourne: Collins Dove, 1990).

5.   CONCLUSION

10 minutes

The follow-up reading for this session is:
- *Not Religion, but Love*, pp. 138–43/124–129.

The set community tasks for this session are:

◊ Meet with your learning partner and your community development support group.

◊ Share what you learned in this session about hope and about imparting hope through the practice of prayer in the process of community development.

◊ Encourage your community development support group to answer the following questions:

1. Which of the above suggestions do you already try to incorporate in your daily life?

2. Which of these practices have you found most helpful in your life and why?

3. Which of the above suggestions would you like to incorporate in your daily life?

4. How would you expect the practice to help you?

5. Which of the above suggestions would you like people you work with to incorporate in your daily life?

6. How would you expect the practice to help the people you work with?

7. What will you do in the coming week to incorporate this practice into the way that you work with the people in your community?

◊ *Record your actions, reflections and conclusions in your working notes.*

BRINGING ABOUT SOCIAL EMPOWERMENT

1. PREPARATION

1.1. Objectives

- To review your understanding of the importance of imparting hope – and the role prayer can play in promoting hope
- To consider the importance of promoting empowerment – and how renouncing lies and embracing truth can help to impart power

2. REVIEW

15 minutes

Review your work from the previous session. This will include a review of your appreciation of the issues raised in the course notes and clarified in the follow-up readings and your experience of your set community tasks.

Review the issues raised in the previous session, particularly your understanding of the importance of imparting hope – and the role prayer can play in promoting hope.

Review the reading:

Not Religion, but Love, pp. 138–43/124–129.

Review the tasks:

1. How did your meeting with your learning partner and your community development support group go?

2. What was the most important thing you learned while doing the community tasks for the last session?

Finish the review with a reflection on the plans you have to incorporate this practice into the way that you work with the people in your community.

◊ *Be sure to record your reflections in your working notes.*

3.   EMPOWERMENT

20 minutes

3.1. The Importance of Empowerment

Hope alone cannot bring transformation. Hand in hand with hope must come empowerment. Hope is a fragile quality that is quickly destroyed by any feelings of powerlessness. Unless our feelings of powerlessness are dealt with, the hope infused today will be gone tomorrow. Most of us are, to some extent, paralysed by a sense of powerlessness. Ironically, it is often those of us who have tried hardest to transform the community who feel the most powerless. We know only too well how much the system is stacked against anyone who wants to work for transformation. If we are going to promote personal growth or social change, it is crucial for us to deal with our underlying sense of powerlessness.

3.2. The Example of Jesus

Jesus understood the causes of disempowerment: the self-doubt that debilitates us; the social indifference that breaks us; the traditional obligations that bind us; the political subjection that shackles us body and soul to the *status quo*. However, Jesus did not only discern the causes of disempowerment, but he also indicated the sources of empowerment that could dispel the despair and inspire people with the hope that they could make their dreams come true. Jesus saw power as the ability to control ourselves and empowerment as the process of enabling one another to exercise greater control over our lives – individually and collectively.

Empowerment usually happens gradually, almost imperceptibly, over a long period of time. Sometimes, however, it happens dramatically, in an instant.

Jesus' encounter with a man with a withered hand whom he met one Sabbath at the synagogue was an example of dramatic empowerment.

> To this man, his withered hand represented total powerlessness. Not only was it a frustrating physical handicap, it was a social handicap. According to the religious rituals of his time, his withered arm barred him from participating fully in the temple rites of his own religion. And because it was his right hand that was crippled, he would have to use his left hand for business as well as ablutions. According to the cultural traditions of the time, this meant he could never participate freely in the life of the town in which he lived. For him the withered hand was a handicap that not only debilitated him physically, but also spiritually, culturally, economically, and politically.

> When Jesus saw the man at the back of the synagogue, he called him forward and gently encouraged him to do what he had always wanted to do, but had been powerless to do – stretch out his hand. According to Luke, who wrote the account of the incident, the man obeyed and his hand was restored. In describing the incident, Luke uses an interesting turn of phrase which emphasizes the fact that the restoration of the man's arm did not take place before but after he stretched out his hand. It was in the process of doing what the man knew he couldn't do that he was empowered. (Lk. 6:6–10 [author's paraphrase])

3.3. The Lies that Bind and the Truth that Liberates

Most empowerment does not happen instantaneously. But whether it is immediate or gradual, empowerment entails the renunciation of lies and the practice of truth.

Jesus insisted that *lies bind us* and *truth liberates us*. The lies we believe about ourselves disempower us and stop us from growing and changing.

Conversely, the truth about ourselves explodes our sense of powerlessness and sets us free to grow and change. As Jesus said, "You will know the truth, and the truth will set you free" (Jn. 8:32).

Encouraging people to renounce lies and embrace truth about themselves can be difficult and frustrating. It certainly was for Jesus.

Jesus persisted in the process of empowering disempowered people regardless of how arduous the process was.

To those debilitated by self-doubt, who looked at Jesus as an example of what they would like to be but thought they never could be, he said, "You know, anything I can do, you can do better" (Jn. 14:12 [author's version]).

To those debilitated by social indifference who believed they could never make any difference because nothing ever changes, he said, "Stop cursing the darkness. You are the light of the world. If you do justice, you will shine like the sun" (Matt. 5:14; 13:43 [author's version]).

And to those debilitated by their obligations to tradition or their subjection to the *status quo* who believed Jesus was right, but that it was wrong to buck the system, he said, "Forget about the system. Let the dead bury their dead. You must be prepared to die for your beliefs. If you try to preserve your life, you will waste it. But, if you waste your life for me, and my revolutionary movement of love and justice, you will preserve the spirit that makes life worth living" (Matt. 8:22; 10:34–39 [author's version]).

If we want to help empower disempowered people, we will need to encourage them to renounce the lies that promote counter-productive and self-destructive reactions and to embrace the truth that will enable them to act in a responsible, self-disciplined manner so that they can take control over their own individual and collective lives.

1. What do you think are the lies that bind you?

2. What do you think is the truth that can set you free?

3. What do you think are the lies that bind the people you are working with?

4. What do you think is the truth that can set the people you are working with free?

◊ *Remember to record your reflections in your working notes.*

4.   "THOSE WHO LOSE THEIR DREAMING ARE LOST"

45 minutes

4.1. Mordja Amari Boradja

The indigenous people of Australia have struggled for survival in the harsh conditions of this often quite inhospitable continent for over 40,000 years, battling everything from flood and drought to genocide. They have a saying about survival that we would do well to listen to: "Mordja amari boradja" ("Those who lose their dreaming are lost").

What does this ancient saying mean to you?

◊ *Record your reflections in your working notes.*

Note that unless we seek the dream of who we are *meant to be*, we will never find out what we are really *meant to do*.

Unless we seek the dream of what we are *meant to do*, we will never find out who we are really *meant to be*.

4.2. The Story of the Willywagtail

Maureen Watson, a respected Aboriginal elder, tells a dreamtime story that illustrates this point perfectly.[72] It's the story of the willywagtail, a common and cheeky little Aussie bird.

> The willywagtail and the hawk lived by this big wide river and willywagtail used to look across the river and try to fathom out what was going on on the other side.
>
> But whenever willywagtail talked about crossing, flying across the wide river for a visit, (the) hawk would clip her wings so she couldn't make the journey.
>
> So she'd spend her time planning and waiting for her wing feathers to grow so she could make the journey.
>
> But every time she started to fly she'd get her wings clipped again.
>
> So she laid her eggs and she hatched them out.

---

[72] L. Black "To See the Storyteller," *Network News* (Queensland Community Arts, Brisbane, 1st edn, 1995), pp. 8–9.

Taught the babies how to fly.

Showed them from the tops of the high branches the big wide world around them and the world across the water.

And she waited for them to grow so their wings would be wide and strong and they could all fly across the river.

And time went by and she waited and there were more eggs and more babies and more times when she got her wings clipped.

One day, a pelican who used to live on the river stopped by and said, "I often see you looking over the river."

She said, "I'd love to fly over there."

And the pelican said, "Well, you can."

She said, "No, whenever my wings grow long and strong enough they get clipped and I couldn't make the journey."

Then the pelican said, "You can do anything you want to do. If you want to do it badly enough then you will find a way."

And she said, "Well, that's very nice of you to tell me that – but," she said, "I haven't been able to find a way."

And pelican said, "You will."

Sometime later, pelican stopped by again and asked, "Are you still wanting to cross the river?"

And she said, "Yes."

He opened up his beak and said, "Well, there is enough room for you and your babies to hop in and hide."

The willywagtail gathered up her babies and they settled themselves comfortably in the pelican's roomy beak and they flew away.

And over on the other side, with all the adventuring and the wonderment of new discoveries, her wings grew big and strong – and to this day nobody has ever clipped her wings again.

Most people can relate to the story of the little willywagtail. Like the willywagtail, they want to be themselves, realize their potential, and, in spite of the opposition they may be up against, they want to grow big and strong, stretch their wings and fly as far as they can into the adventure of life together. However, they can't do it without the help of a few pelicans!

How can you be a pelican to the willywagtails in your community?

◊ *Also record your reflections in your working notes.*

4.3. Helping People Reweave the Fabric of Their Dreams

We can reweave the fabric of community networks by articulating, communicating, demonstrating, cultivating and celebrating the dream in our own community.

Step one: articulate your vision yourself
10 minutes

Some time ago, I felt I needed to write out my vision. At the time I felt a bit embarrassed about sharing my vision with others. Nevertheless, I knew I needed to articulate my own vision regardless of how it compared or contrasted with others.

> I dream of a world
>> in which all the resources of the earth
>> will be shared equally
>> between all the people of the earth,
>> so that even the most disadvantaged
>> will be able to meet their basic needs
>> with dignity and joy.
>
> I dream of a great society of small communities
>> co-operating to practise
>> personal, social, economic, cultural and political
>> integrity and harmony.
>
> I dream of vibrant neighbourhoods
>> where people relate to one another
>> genuinely as good neighbours.
>
> I dream of people developing
>> networks of friendship
>> in which the private pain
>> they carry deep down
>> is allowed to surface
>> and is shared

in an atmosphere
of mutual acceptance and respect.

I dream of people
understanding the difficulties they have in common,
discerning the problems, discovering the solutions
and working together for personal growth and social change
according to the visionary agenda of Jesus of Nazareth.

And I dream of every church in every locality
acting as a catalyst to make this dream come true.[73]

My vision statement has since become my mission statement. I share this vision with groups of people who want to build a better world. Every time I share it, it seems to strike a chord that puts people in touch with the beat in their own heart.

1. What is your vision for the world you live in?

2. What is your dream of the kind of community that would embody heaven on earth in your locality?

◊ Take five minutes to write out a rough first draft.

◊ *Remember to record your dream in your working notes.*

Step two: communicate your vision through story
10 minutes

We can often communicate our vision best through stories.

Stories are inclusive and can be apprehended both intellectually and emotionally – at different levels by different people.

Stories are also inspirational. They can put soul into the body and flesh on the bones of our dreams.

Think of a true story of the dream lived out in reality – a story about community that you feel would communicate your vision of community most clearly and most cogently to other people. (It could be anything – from a story you've heard about someone organizing a food co-op to putting on a street party.)

◊ Take ten minutes to write out a rough first draft.

◊ *Record your story in your working notes.*

---

[73] D. Andrews, *Can You Hear the Heartbeat?* (London: Hodder and Stoughton, 1989), p. xiii (edited).

Step three: demonstrate your vision in your own life
5 minutes

Change doesn't begin with *others*, but with *ourselves*. First and foremost, we need to demonstrate changes we advocate in our own lives. For it is only as we demonstrate those changes in our own lives that we can prove it is possible to live them out in our context.

> What is one change you can make in your own life that will demonstrate to others the possibility of community development? (It could be as simple as visiting your neighbours!)

◊ Take five minutes to write out a rough first draft.

◊ *Be sure to record your plan in your working notes.*

Step four: cultivate your vision in the lives of others
5 minutes

When it comes to working for change in our community, it is true that *we alone can do it*. But it's also true that *we cannot do it alone!*

Change may start with us but, if it stops with us, it will stop completely. We need to make changes that encourage others to make changes.

> What is one change you can make that will encourage others to join you in your community development experiments? (It could be something as simple as inviting a friend to join you in visiting a neighbour who is sick.)

◊ Take five minutes to write out a rough first draft.

◊ *Be sure to record your plan in your working notes.*

Step five: evaluate your progress in development
5 minutes

We need to remember that anything that's good enough to do is worth doing badly to begin with – but, if we want to do good, then each time we try something we should try to do it better than we did before.

And if we are going to do something better than we did before, we need to develop the capacity to critically evaluate our progress.

> What is a way that you can help other people evaluate their progress in community development both critically and constructively? (After you've visited your sick neighbour, for example, you can chat with your friend about how it went – talk about what was good about it and what you could do to make it better if you did it again.)

◊ Take five minutes to write out a rough first draft.

◊ *Record your plan in your working notes.*

Step six: celebrate your progress in development
5 minutes

We need to encourage people to continue to work for community development even when they are discouraged. We need to help each person who feels inadequate to realize their capacity to act. Each person who feels afraid needs to find their courage to act. Each person who feels impotent needs to understand the potential of their actions. And each person who feels insignificant needs to recognize the consequences of their actions.

We can encourage people to continue to work for community development even when they are discouraged by commemorating every act of truth as a victory over lies and every act of love as a victory over hatred; by consecrating every act of justice as a victory over brutality and every act of peace as a victory over bloodshed; and by celebrating every risk a person takes to make a stand – no matter how big or small that stand may be – as a victory in the battle for the light of the world against the forces of darkness.

> What is a way that you can help other people celebrate their progress in community development happily – in private, and also in public? (A short spot in a church service, for example, honouring the work people do in the community and commending them for their efforts, can make a huge difference to their morale.)

◊ Take five minutes to write out a rough first draft.

◊ *Be sure to record your plan in your working notes.*

5.   "A Small Group of Citizens Can Change the World"

5 minutes

We must never let the people we work with get discouraged by those who say it's impossible to make our dreams for our community come true. As Lois Brandeus says, "Most of the things worth doing in the world had been declared impossible before they were done!"[74]

---

[74] Shields, *In the Tiger's Mouth*, p. 24.

It doesn't matter how small a group may be, nor how great the odds the group may be up against. Anthropologist Margaret Mead would say to them: "A small group of thoughtful, committed citizens can change the world. Indeed, it's the only thing that ever has!"[75]

And Robert Putnam says there are three specific reasons for people to believe that they can actually reverse the current trends and reweave the fabric of our community:

> People want "real" community networks, not just "virtual" networks. Gen X-ers say flesh and blood friends are 20 times more important than cyber friends.[76]

> People are exploring the development of "real" community networks through participation in small groups. Currently 40% of the population is involved in the "quiet revolution" going on in small groups.[77]

> Contrary to the previous downward trend, "volunteering" is up again. In 1998, 74% of high school students were involved in volunteering in the community, as compared with 62% in 1989. And, in 1998, 42% of first-year university students were involved in volunteering regularly in the community, as compared with 27% in 1987.[78]

---

[75] Shields, *In the Tiger's Mouth*, p. 24.
[76] Putnam, *Bowling Alone*, p. 275.
[77] Putnam, *Bowling Alone*, pp. 148–49.
[78] Putnam, *Bowling Alone*, p. 265.

6. CONCLUSION

10 minutes

The follow-up reading for this session is:
*   *Not Religion, but Love*, pp. 144–51/130–137.

The set community tasks for this session are:

◊ Meet with your learning partner and your community development support group.

◊ Share what you learned in this session about empowerment and promoting empowerment through renouncing lies and embracing the truth.

◊ Encourage your community development support group to answer the following questions:

1. What is your personal dream of community?

2. What are some good stories that illustrate your vision?

3. What can you do to demonstrate your ideal in your reality?

4. What can you do to cultivate those values in the lives of others?

5. What can you do to help others reflect constructively on their actions?

6. What can you do to celebrate any small progress the people you are working with may make towards realizing their dream of community development?

◊ Look for opportunities to put these ideas into action over the next week.

◊ *Ensure you record your actions, reflections and conclusions in your working notes.*

BRINGING ABOUT PROBLEM RESOLUTION

1. PREPARATION

1.1. Objectives

- To review your understanding of the importance of promoting empowerment – and the role renouncing lies and embracing truth can play in imparting power

- To consider the importance of problem solving in community development and ways to promote problem solving by creating a problem-solving culture and using the problem-solving cycle

2. REVIEW

15 minutes

Review your work from the previous session. This will include a review of your appreciation of the issues raised in the course notes and clarified in the follow-up readings and your experience of your set community tasks.

Review the issues raised in the previous session, particularly your understanding of the importance of promoting empowerment – and the role that renouncing lies and embracing truth can play in imparting power.

Review the reading:

Not Religion, but Love, pp. 144–51/130–137.

Review the tasks:

1. How did it go meeting with your community development support group and sharing what you learned in class about empowerment and promoting empowerment through renouncing lies and embracing the truth?

2. What was the most important thing you learned while doing the community tasks for the last session?

Finish the review with a reflection on the ideas you put into action during the week.

◊ *Be sure to record your reflections in your working notes.*

3.   PROBLEMS AND PROBLEM SOLVING

30 minutes

3.1. Problems and Problem Solving

Even after hope has been infused and people feel empowered to take control of their own lives, there is still the nitty-gritty business of getting down to resolving problems. A mechanical problem can be solved once and for all. Problems in human relationships are never solved once and for all – they must be resolved over and over again by the people involved.

A community that is transformed is *not* one that no longer has problems; it is one that has developed a process for resolving problems. In fact, a community is transformed only to the degree that everybody in the community can participate freely and fairly in resolving their problems together. The essence of transformation is in creative problem resolution.

1. How have you seen the truth of the statement that human problems are never solved once and for all but must be resolved again and again by the people involved?

2. Have you seen a transformed community that has developed a process for resolving problems? What does it look like?

◊ *Be sure to record your reflections in your working notes.*

3.2. The Example of Jesus

Jesus never promised us a problem-free life. He said, "In this world the way it is, you are going to have big trouble" (Jn. 16:33 [author's version]). But he did promise us the power to deal with the problems we would confront. "Nothing will be impossible for you," he said (Matt. 17:20). Just be as "shrewd" as you can be (Matt. 10:16).

It is instructive to look at the role Jesus played in settling disputes. Even though Jesus was unafraid to state his opinion publicly, when it came to stating his views on how a particular dispute should he settled, he often refused.

Whenever people wanted Jesus to answer a question that they should have taken the responsibility to answer themselves, Jesus usually refused to answer the question. Jesus wanted people to own their predicaments and accept responsibility for resolving them.

One day two brothers came to Jesus to settle a dispute that they were having over the division of their family property. Jesus, in his typical style, answered the question with a question: "Man, who appointed me a judge between you?" (Lk. 12:14).

Jesus used this technique of questioning the questioner to make people answerable to themselves. It was often in answering a question that the person would be forced to take responsibility for solving his or her own problem.

While Jesus refused to allow people to project the responsibility for solving their problems on to him, he also stated quite clearly that they shouldn't project the responsibility onto anyone else either – particularly the experts. He actually warned people to "beware of experts" (Lk. 20:46). He told people that they were the experts on their own problems. Instinctively they knew the answers. "Why don't you judge for yourselves what is right?" (Lk. 12:57).

Jesus knew that nobody, no matter how expert they might be, could solve someone else's problems for them. Ultimately everyone has to solve his or her own problems. That is why Jesus insisted that, if you have a problem with someone, you must deal with it "just between the two of you" (Matt. 18:15).

Jesus also recognized, however, that many of us need someone to help us solve our problems. This person must act as a helper, though – not an expert to solve it for us. Jesus said about problem solving that if someone wrongs you, "go and show them their fault, just between the two of you . . . But if they will not listen, take one or two others along" (Matt. 18:15–16).

The role of these "one or two others" was not to take sides or give advice. They were there to help clarify the situation by enabling the various parties involved to listen to each other and talk about possible solutions. Jesus called these third-party helpers "witnesses." Their job was to bring the truth to light by faithfully declaring the facts as they saw them emerge from the murky shadows of the dispute. And it was in this role of witness, rather than judge, that Jesus preferred to operate himself.

> One day Jesus was teaching when a whole crowd of noisy people arrived dragging a woman who had been caught red-handed having an affair. They wanted Jesus to pass judgement on her. According to Jewish law, if this woman was an "adulterer," she was meant to be executed and, traditionally, adulterers were executed by stoning.
>
> Jesus had gone on public record as being totally opposed to affairs. As a matter of fact, Jesus had gone much further than the law and claimed that, if anyone even entertained the idea of having an affair with someone that they weren't married to, they were already an adulterer in their hearts. So, when the woman was caught, red-handed, having an affair, it seemed an open and shut case. The woman had been caught in the act. The law required death – by stoning – straightaway. Surely Jesus, by his own standards, would have to judge the woman guilty of adultery and condemn her to death as an adulterer.
>
> Jesus steadfastly refused to assume the role of judge. Instead he assumed the role of witness. When asked for his verdict he simply said to the crowd of men around him, "Let those of you without sin cast the first stone at her."
>
> He witnessed to the truth not only of her sin, but also the sin of her accusers. He then stooped and wrote something in the dust on the ground with his finger, leaving the men, baying for the woman's blood, to make their own judgement. (Jn. 8:2–8 [author's paraphrase])

In encouraging these people to make their own decision Jesus took a huge risk. A woman's life was at stake. Nevertheless, in spite of the grave risk, Jesus did not take the problem from the men and resolve it for them. He simply stayed with them and ensured they arrived at a loving solution – which was just to all the parties involved in the dispute.

The men eventually made their judgement. They departed – one by one – from the oldest to the youngest. And the woman was left alone with Jesus. "Has no-one condemned you?" he asked. "No-one, sir," she said. Then, and only then, did Jesus make his judgement. He said, "Neither do I condemn you. Just don't do it again" (Jn. 8:9–11).

Jesus was prepared to make a judgement – but only in a way that developed people's ability to judge for themselves.

1. How do you feel about the idea that Jesus never promised us a problem-free life?

2. How do you feel about the idea that Jesus promised the power to deal with problems?

3. What do you think was the wisdom in the idea of Jesus wanting people to accept responsibility for resolving their own problems? What do you think are the dangers of people trying to solve other people's problems?

4. Jesus wanted us to act as witnesses rather than judges, mediators rather than arbitrators. Think of a problem you're aware of and how you could assist in solving the problem in a Christ-like way.

◊ Record your reflections in your working notes.

4.   THE POSSIBILITIES FOR PROBLEM SOLVING

20 minutes

4.1. Circumstances in which Problem Solving Is a Possibility

There are some circumstances in which problem solving is possible, and other circumstances in which problem solving is *not* possible. Problem solving is only possible when all parties involved in the dispute are willing to move towards dialogue. When we find ourselves in a dispute with people, we are faced with five possibilities.

1)   The first possibility is that people are *not* interested in interacting with us or the issues we are concerned with – so there is absolutely *nothing* we can do.

- All we can do is give up on our goals and our relationships.
- The only option is *total avoidance.*
- So "shake the dust off your feet" and move on (Lk. 9:5).

2)   The second possibility is that people *are* interested in interacting with us, but are *not* interested in the issues we are concerned with – so we can do *something* to improve our interaction, but we can do *nothing* to work on the issues together.

- All we can do is let go of our goals and some of our relationships.
- The only option is *general accommodation.*
- So "be as innocuous (or inoffensive) as a peace dove" (Matt. 10:16).

3)   The third possibility is that people are *not* interested in interacting with us and but *are* interested in the issues we are concerned with – so we can do *something* to work on the issues, but we can do *nothing* to improve our interaction.

- All we can do is hold onto our goals and let go of our relationships.
- The only option is *unilateral action.*
- So "get on with it while you have the chance" (Jn. 9:4).

4)   The fourth possibility is that people *are* interested in interacting with us and the issues we are concerned with *to a certain extent* – so we can do *something* to improve our interaction and progress our issues *quite substantially.*

- We can hold onto some of our goals and hold onto our relationships.
- And *modest negotiation* becomes an option.
- So "settle matters as quickly as you can" (Matt. 5:25).

5)   The fifth possibility is that people *are* interested in interacting with us and the issues we are concerned with in *an open-ended sense* – so we can do *something* to improve our interaction and progress our issues *very considerably.*

- We can hold onto our goals and hold onto our relationships.
- *Meaningful dialogue* is now an option as well.
- So "find a way that is acceptable to everyone" (Rom. 12:17b).

Note that problem solving is possible where there is modest negotiation, but preferable where there is the chance of meaningful dialogue. One indicator is a willingness to actually get together, another is a willingness to try to resolve the problem.

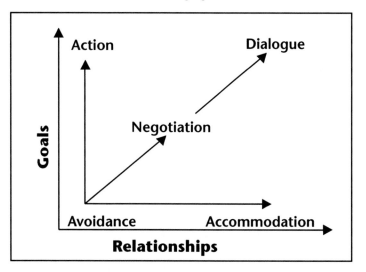

Figure 24. Possibilities for dialogue[79]

Identify a problem you are currently facing. Assess which possibility is realistic for you in this situation and outline a way forward.

◊ *Be sure to record your reflections in your working notes.*

5.   A PROBLEM-SOLVING ATMOSPHERE

20 minutes

5.1. A Problem-Solving Culture

Our role as *witness* is to help develop a healthy problem-solving culture.

A problem-solving culture needs to be *positive* – even about negatives.

A problem-solving culture needs to be *accepting* of problems that exist.

A problem-solving culture needs to be *respectful* of the parties in dispute.

A problem-solving culture needs to be *aware* of the fears and desires that are behind the dispute.

---

[79] S. Fisher, D. Ibrahim Abdi, J. Ludin, R. Smith and S. Williams, *Working with Conflict* (New York: St. Martin's Press, 2000).

A problem-solving culture needs to be *ready* to take some risks in an attempt to resolve the problem.

What are some specific things that you could do to help create a healthy problem-solving culture?

◊ *Be sure to record your reflections in your working notes.*

6.   A PROBLEM-SOLVING APPROACH

25 minutes

6.1. The Problem-Solving Cycle

If we are going to get involved in helping individuals or groups solve their problems, it will be extremely helpful if we understand the five steps in a simple, straightforward problem-solving cycle:
1.   *Defining* the problem
2.   *Identifying* all possible options for solutions
3.   *Selecting* an option as a solution to the problem
4.   *Implementing* the option selected as a solution
5.   *Reflecting* on the results of our effort to solve the problem.

We need to encourage people to ask and formulate answers to strategic questions that follow each step of this cycle.

1)   The first question that people must answer before they can even begin to look for solutions is: *"What is the real problem we are facing?"*

This is often the most difficult stage in problem solving. People confuse the symptoms with the cause. Often the problem is overlaid with unresolved past conflicts.

As witnesses, we must help those with the problem to get beyond a superficial view to a deep understanding of what the problem is.

If people cannot agree what the problem is, then they have no chance of agreeing on a possible solution.

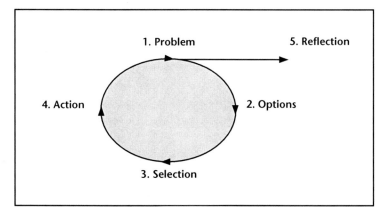

Figure 25. The problem-solving cycle process

2)   The second question people need to ask themselves is: "What are all the possible solutions to this problem we are facing?"

At this stage it is a good idea to brainstorm possible solutions. Each person thinks of as many possible solutions as they can – no matter how wacky or crazy they seem – and a facilitator makes a list of all these possibilities. It is a good idea to ban all criticism of ideas at this stage so that people do not feel inhibited in bringing forward their suggestions.

After the list is completed, it is time to look over each solution more critically. We can do this by playing out each idea in our imagination.

- What would the possible results be if it were implemented? What are its weaknesses? What are its strengths? Is there some way it can be modified?

- There should be lots of discussion about each of the possible solutions. Disagreement will be healthy at this stage.

3)   The third question people need to ask themselves is: *"Which solution will we opt for and implement?"*

Those involved in the problem must now agree on what they consider to be the best solution. The solution must be acceptable to everyone, and everyone must be convinced it has a fair chance of solving the problem.

Once the solution has been chosen, the implementation has to be discussed. The fourth question people need to ask themselves is, *"Who is going to do what by when?"* It is a good idea to write down all the tasks that need to be done and, beside each task, the name of the person responsible and the deadline they have agreed to.

After an agreed-upon period of time, the parties involved need to meet again to ask a fifth question: *"How is our plan to solve our problem working out?"* (This fifth question needs to be asked at regular, agreed-upon intervals during the implementation process.)

Reflection must take place both during and after the implementation of the solution.

During the implementation, people need to get together regularly and report on how they are doing with their allocated tasks. Those involved need to discuss whether the program is actually solving the problem or whether there needs to be some modification to the program. Sometimes the whole program will need to be scrapped and the whole process started again.

Before starting again it will be important to discuss what was learned from the previous effort. Why did it fail? Were we treating the symptoms or the cause? Did it fail because the solution was wrong or because we failed to implement it properly? Experience shows that often people must be willing to "try, try, try again" before they eventually succeed.

Once the solution has been fully implemented, it is important to discuss the results. Each person should have the opportunity to say whether they feel the problem has been adequately solved. Each person should share what they have learned from the experience.

Our role as *witness* in this problem-solving process is to help those involved work through the cycle sensibly. We also need to be sensitive to the needs of everyone involved.

Pick an issue you are concerned about and spend twenty minutes working through the issue using the problem-solving cycle as a guide – with a view to working it through later with your community development support group.

Finish this activity with a reflection on how well it went.

◊ *Be sure to record your reflections in your working notes.*

7.   CONCLUSION

10 minutes

The follow-up reading for this session is:
* *Not Religion, but Love*, pp. 152–61/138–147.

The set community tasks for this session are:

◊ Meet with your learning partner and your community development support group.

◊ Share what you learned in this session about problem solving and about promoting problem solving by creating a problem-solving culture and using the problem-solving cycle.

◊ Then pick a problem in your community concerning which there is a willingness to not only talk about the problem but also to deal with the problem – and, using the problem-solving cycle, do what you can to solve the problem.

◊ *Record appropriate insights, conclusions and actions in your working notes.*

BRINGING ABOUT PROPHETIC TRANSFORMATION

1. PREPARATION

1.1. Objectives

- To review your understanding of the importance of problem solving in community development and of promoting problem solving by creating a problem-solving culture and using the problem-solving cycle

- To consider: the importance of problem solving that is not just spinning our wheels but making some progress; the significance of problem solving in the light of the Gospels; and the place of a Christ-centred problem-solving cycle in the process

2. REVIEW

15 minutes

Review your work from the previous session. This will include a review of your appreciation of the issues raised in the course notes and clarified in the follow-up readings and your experience of your set community tasks.

Review the issues raised in the previous session, particularly your understanding of the importance of problem solving in community development and the way to promote problem solving by creating a problem-solving culture and using the problem-solving cycle.

Review the reading:

Not Religion, but Love, pp. 152–61/138–147.

Review the tasks:

1. How did it go meeting with your community development support group and sharing what you learned in class about problem solving and about promoting problem solving by creating a problem-solving culture and using the problem-solving cycle?

2. What was the most important thing you learned while doing the community tasks for the last session?

Finish the review with a reflection on what you did to help solve a problem.

◊ *Be sure to record your reflections in your working notes.*

3.   PROPHETIC PROBLEM SOLVING

30 minutes

3.1. The Problems with Problem Solving

We have already noted that imparting hope is not enough to bring authentic transformation to a community. People need to be empowered to take control of their own lives. But empowerment alone is not sufficient if people still don't understand how to use that power to resolve their problems. Even helping people solve their own problems, however, is not enough.

People may resolve problems in such a way that does not contribute to the long-term development of themselves or their community. In fact, the problem may be resolved in a way that yields short-term gains but long-term losses. If authentic transformation is to occur, it is absolutely essential that people discover how to resolve their problems together in a way that yields long-term gains for everyone, even if it means short-term losses in the meantime.

1. What is the problem with problem solving that yields short-term gains but long-term losses?

2. Why is it important to promote problem solving that yields long-term gains, even if it means short-term losses in the meantime?

◊ *Remember to record your reflections in your working notes.*

3.2. The Importance of Prophetic Input in Problem Solving

In order for people to settle disputes creatively and constructively, we need to enable people to solve problems together in the light of the prophetic tradition.

Throughout history there have always been prophets who have felt the heartbeat of God. These prophets courageously speak to us, in sympathy with God, about God's passion for love and justice. They call on society to grow, and change, by solving problems in the light of God's agenda. They speak of a world in which all the resources will be shared equally between all people, so that even the most disadvantaged among us will have basic needs met with dignity and joy.

History is the story of the silencing of the voices of the prophets and hence the silencing of the voice of God himself. In rejecting the voice of God, history has become a tale of paradise lost, revolutions betrayed and lives wasted.

If genuine, sustainable transformation is to occur, we must enable people to solve their problems together in a way that takes into account the essential, visionary insights of the prophetic tradition.

It is impossible to create a more loving and just society unless we take into account the agenda of love and justice advocated by sages throughout the ages.

1. What is a prophet?

2. What does a prophet do?

3. What are the consequences of ignoring or rejecting the prophetic voice?

◊ *Be sure to record your reflections in your working notes.*

3.3. The Example of Christ

The prophetic tradition is beautifully personified in the person of Jesus.

Living at the time of Jesus were two men who had a problem they wanted to resolve. Both were rich, while most people around them lived in dire poverty, struggling for survival. One was an aristocrat. The other was an extortionist. Both felt uncomfortable about the disparity between their luxurious lifestyles and the destitution they saw around them. Both decided they didn't like this discomfort and decided to do something about it. Both decided they would get a third party to help them solve their problem. Both sought out Jesus, a recognized prophet.

The rich young aristocrat ignored the advice Jesus gave him. It may have been a good ideal to give everything to the poor, but he didn't think it was a good idea for him to do so. It wasn't that he didn't want to give to the poor – he just wanted to maintain a solid capital base as well. He did not want to waste his capital on unprofitable charities. He probably rationalized his decision by arguing that it was the most sensible course of action. He decided to solve his problem not by giving away his wealth, but by simply refusing to feel guilty about it. If he had any guilt feelings left, I'm sure his priest and psychotherapist helped him cope.

The old extortionist, on the other hand, decided to handle his problem a different way. He followed Jesus' advice. He gave half his wealth to the poor and repaid all those he had ripped off – not just what he had taken, but four times what he had taken, as a form of compensation.

Both had effectively resolved their problems: one by rejecting the imperatives of the prophetic tradition; the other by accepting the imperatives of the prophetic tradition.

Ignoring the advice of Jesus to share his wealth with the poor, the aristocrat opted for a solution that upheld his right to dispose of his private property as he chose *over against* the rights of the poor to access the resources he had at his disposal to meet their basic human needs. The aristocrat thereby chose to solve his problem at the expense of the poor. He enjoyed short-term gains, but the rest of the community suffered long-term losses.

On the other hand, by taking Jesus' advice to share his wealth with the poor, the extortionist opted for a solution that upheld his right to dispose of his private property as he chose, *as well as* recognizing the rights of the poor to access the resources he had at his disposal. In so doing, the extortionist chose to solve the problem at his own expense.

There were short-term losses – giving away half of his wealth to the poor and paying back every dollar he swindled, at the rate of four-to-one, as a form of compensation. But the short-term losses resulted in long-term gains for everybody in the community, including the extortionist himself. The poor would get some unexpected social security payments; the extortionist's victims would get the compensation they'd always hoped for but never expected to get; and the extortionist would get back some self-respect – now that he was no longer an extortionist.

Genuine, sustainable transformation can only be brought about by enabling people to solve their problems together in the light of the prophetic tradition – perfectly personified in the life of Jesus.

1. If you were the aristocrat, how do you imagine you would feel about Jesus' prophetic problem-solving style?

2. If you were the extortionist, how do you imagine you would feel about Jesus' prophetic problem-solving style?

3. In what significant ways does Jesus' prophetic problem-solving style differ from quick-fix methods of problem solving?

◊ *Be sure to record your reflections in your working notes.*

4.   CHRIST-CENTRED PROBLEM SOLVING

20 minutes

4.1. Using a Christ-Centred Problem-Solving Cycle

We need to find a way to facilitate this process of transformation by enabling people to solve their problems together in light of the life of Jesus.

With those who acknowledge Jesus to some degree or other, it is reasonably straightforward.

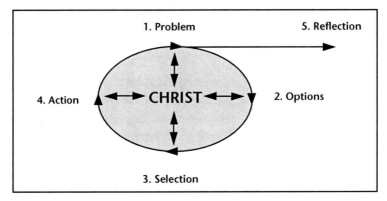

Figure 26. A Christ-centred problem-solving cycle

When we meet together, we encourage each other to share our problems and we help each other resolve these problems in the light of the prophetic tradition. We acknowledge the problems we are trying to solve. Then we discuss the issues with the people who share the problems we are trying to solve. Then we search the Scriptures in general, and the life of Jesus in particular, to discover a story that reveals how God may want us to resolve the problem in the light of his passion for love and justice. This process results in an intimate acquaintance with the heart of God that enables us to resolve our problems in a way that reflects the heart of God.

> Pick an issue you are concerned about and spend twenty minutes working through the issue using the Christ-centred problem-solving cycle as a guide – with a view to working it through later with your community development support group.
>
> Finish this activity with a reflection on how well it went.

◊ *Be sure to record your reflections in your working notes.*

4.2. Using a Christ-Centred Cycle with Non-Christians

20 minutes

The real challenge is being able to facilitate the same kind of process with the majority of people who, for a whole range of reasons, do not acknowledge Jesus as a significant figure in their lives.

Pastor John Perkins says,

> Development cannot happen without evangelism. Evangelism brings us to Jesus who understands the way in which the poor suffer abuse and encourages us through the Holy Spirit. The Holy Spirit heals the gashes of our heart, comforts us in (our) loss, and affirms our dignity in the face of dehumanization. Conversion . . . brings about development.[80]

For me, the love of Jesus is at the heart of every situation that we encounter in a community. And the effective resolution of the problems inherent in each situation depends on people being able to feel something of the love of Jesus for themselves and for others; being able to be free to transcend their anger and guilt and inadequacy; and being able to act in a beautiful, radical, sacrificial, compassionate, Christ-like manner.

Most of the people I work with, however, are not Christians. The challenge for me is to try to introduce them to Jesus in the context of my community work.

I do this by using a simple *centred problem-solving process* (see Figure 26).

I agree to work with people struggling with the issues that are important to them on the basis of *common sense* and *consensus*.

Because I believe Jesus is the source of all truth and the truth is written, as the Scripture says, on the hearts of all people, Jesus' truth is often expressed in the *common sense* that people speak without their even knowing it.

I dialogue with people about their problems and about possible solutions to their problems and try to decide on a particular course of action that we can take together.

Quite often, to the embarrassment of Christians who claim to have exclusive rights to the truth, it is those who do not make any claims to

---

[80] Fisher, et al., *Working with Conflict*, p. 87.

have a corner on the market of truth who seem to be more intuitively in touch with the reality of their problems and the reality of possible solutions to their problems.

I will only decide on taking a particular course of action if I am personally convinced that it will move us in a *direction* that is true to the *compassion* of Jesus and demonstrates his *acceptance* and his *redemption* in relation to the resolution of the problem. However, I can usually – if not invariably – come to *consensus* with the way sensible people want to go about solving their problems. Because – whether they know it or not – there is no fundamental conflict between the way sensible people want to go about solving their problems and the way Jesus wants us to go about solving our problems. Neither wants unethical shortcuts. Both want *genuine, loving, just, long-term, sustainable solutions.*

Sometimes the *implicit* connection – between the way that we have chosen to go and *the way of Jesus* – remains *implicit* (see Figure 27).

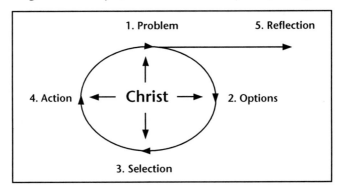

Figure 27. The implicit Christ-centred cycle

Oftentimes the *implicit* connection – between the way that I have chosen to go and *the way of Jesus* – becomes *explicit*. I love to tell people who are celebrating a successful resolution of a problem, that, believe it or not, their success is a result of their having taken the *way of Jesus* without knowing it. Regardless of their attitude to Jesus, they cannot deny the successful resolution of the problem or disregard the value of *the way of Jesus* they have taken thus far (see Figure 28).

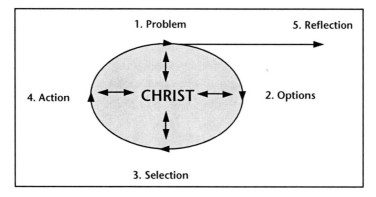

Figure 28. The explicit Christ-centred cycle

As a result, *the way of Jesus* becomes a significant *point of view*. Some see it as one point of view among many. However, some start to see it as the one point of view by which the many may be judged. Thus the *way of Jesus* becomes a significant *point of reference*. If people adopt the *way of Jesus* as the *point of reference* for decision making in their everyday lives, then the process of conversion to Jesus as a person, if not to Christianity as a religion, has begun. Moreover, our dream of personal growth and social change in the light of the love of Jesus has begun to come true (see Figure 29).

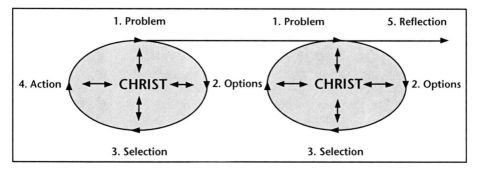

Figure 29. Christ as central reference point in the ongoing problem-solving process

In all of this, we need to use our common sense. Christ's truth is often expressed in the *common sense* that people speak, often without realizing it.

We should only decide on a course of action if we are convinced it will move us in a *direction* that is true to the *compassion* of Christ and if we see that it clearly demonstrates his *acceptance* and his *redemption* in relation to the resolution of the problem.

We should be able to come to *consensus* with the way most sensible people want to go about solving their problems – whether they are Christians or not.

Using an implicit Christ-centred problem-solving cycle *can* be deceptive. We need to be explicit about working on the basis of a *consensus* that will include working on the basis of *our* own views and *our* own values.

Using an explicit Christ-centred problem-solving cycle *can* be oppressive. We need to be clear about being committed to working on the basis of a *consensus* that will take into account the views and values of *others*, not just our own.

1. Why do we need to work with people on the basis of common sense?

2. Why do we need to work with people on the basis of consensus?

3. Think of a problem with which you're familiar and think through how you could move in this situation from an implicit to an explicit Christ-centred problem-solving cycle?

◊ *Record your reflections in your working notes.*

5.   "THE STORY OF THE SQUATTERS"

20 minutes

◊ Read "The Story of the Squatters" and consider it as a case study on Christ-centred problem solving.

The Story of the Squatters

Let me tell you a story of how I put the Christ-centred problem-solving cycle into practice with a group of people who were not only non-Christians, but who were decidedly anti-Christian.

> A group of Christian friends and I decided to get involved with a bunch of squatters. They were totally demoralized. They had no jobs. With no jobs they could not afford to pay rent. Because they had nowhere to live, they squatted on land beside the road. Because this was illegal, they were constantly harassed by the

police – who would either demand a bribe or break down their huts and beat them up. As a result they were constantly on the move, trying desperately to stay one step ahead of the police. But there weren't many places they could go, so they always wound up back where they started, ready to go through the cycle again.

We got to know this group. Bonds of friendship formed between individuals and their families. They were demoralized, but what they lacked in dignity they more than made up for in guts. Their struggle against seemingly overwhelming odds was fought with lots of courage and lots of laughter. We were encouraged and strengthened by their infectious style of heroism and sense of humour. They may have been demoralized, but they taught us valuable lessons about the morality of survival. As our friendships deepened, we not only learned from them the art of survival in an urban slum, we also began to feel the anguish they felt in their struggle to survive. As we discussed with them the issues they had to face every day of their lives, we decided to work together with them and see if together we could find some long-term solutions that would not only minimize the anguish associated with their struggle for survival, but also increase their chances of survival.

One day the group decided that something had to be done about the continuing police harassment. Some wanted to attack the police station immediately with bricks. Bricks were a common means of settling disputes in the slum. As a conflict resolution technique, the people considered it a knockout. We encouraged the people to envisage in their minds what the result of throwing bricks through the window of the police station might be. They concluded that it would probably result in an even more violent visit by the police. The people began to have serious doubts about the effectiveness of bricks as a conflict resolution technique.

So we began to discuss other possibilities for solving the problem. Someone suggested inviting the police over for a cup of tea and discussing the matter. The squatters treated the idea with scorn, but we supported it. The longer we discussed it, the more support it got. Eventually the police were invited. To start with, you could cut the air with a knife, but the tension was soon dispelled with a couple of jokes. The squatters and the police ended up having an amicable chat and, as a result, decided to call a truce. The squatters agreed not to cause the police any trouble and the police agreed not to beat up the squatters.

After the police had gone, we had a talk about how the problem had been resolved. During the discussion, one of us mentioned that the problem had been resolved exactly how Jesus had suggested such problems be resolved. "Bless those who curse you," he said, and "if your enemy is thirsty give him a drink" (which is exactly what the group had done by inviting the police for a cup of tea). Everyone treated it as a joke. They were embarrassed that they had done anything remotely religious, even unintentionally. But the squatters remembered the way they had solved the problem with the police and they also remembered that it was the way Jesus suggested problems be solved.

Time went by. Week after week, month after month, we worked on a whole range of problems together – everything from getting a regular water supply to improving nutrition and sanitation. Each time we resolved a problem together it would be on the basis of *common sense* and *consensus*. After the effective resolution of each of these problems, we would discuss how the decision we had taken fitted with the way Jesus advocated that problems be dealt with. After each successful resolution of a problem there would be a celebration. It was during this euphoria that we would always explain how the success was contingent upon our having worked in harmony with God's agenda, as personified in Jesus; and always there would be the mock groans – that if we carried on the way we were going they would all be Christians before too long!

About a year after inviting the police for a cup of tea, the council decided to clean up the city. Cleaning up the city meant getting rid of the squatters. They were notified that they were to leave immediately. But they had nowhere to go. Then they got news that really freaked them out. The bulldozers were on the way. In a panic they considered their options. But there didn't seem to be any. Any promising options had to be discarded because they felt too powerless to make them happen. "It's typical," they concluded. "Those big people can push us little people around as much as they like and there is not a thing we can do about it." We were tempted to agree. Things looked hopeless. But somehow we knew that we had to believe that the impossible was possible. "Surely there is *something* we can do!" one person said hopefully. "Yeah?" asked one of the squatters. "What? What would Jesus do about it?"

Raising Jesus as a possible *point of reference* for solving the problem had never happened before in our discussions with the squatters. It was a crucial time for this group. A time when Jesus might become more than just *one point of view* among *many points of view;* a time when Jesus might become *the point of reference for all their problem solving.* The time when the group might be converted to a faith in Jesus through which their lives might be transformed. It all hinged upon finding a Jesus story that the group could use to help them to do *something* about their situation.

I racked my brain, wondering where in the Gospels you could find a story that would help a group of squatters deal with the threat of eviction backed by the might of bulldozers. I don't remember who it was, but someone suggested a story they thought might help. It was the story Jesus told of a little old widow who was finding it difficult to get justice from a big crooked judge. She finally got justice by knocking on his door at all hours of the night, week after week.

As we discussed the story with them, hope began to rise out of their hopelessness. As hope was born, so was a new sense of power. They started discussing the possible solutions in a whole new light. They decided to take up a petition to present to the city council and to persist until they got a fair hearing. They gathered hundreds of signatures and organized a march to the city council administration centre to present the petitions. Then they followed up on the people who could change the decision. Finally, through the kind of perseverance they had learned about in the story of the little old widow and the big crooked judge, they were granted an alternative place to stay where the community would have their own houses on their own land. Moreover, the council also agreed to help pay the expenses of their move.

It was more than they had ever dreamed possible. The move also opened up a whole host of new doors. Not only did they now have their own homes on their own land, they could also now develop their own education, health and employment programs. With the decrease in demoralization came an observable increase in morale – and morality – in the community. There was a marked decrease in domestic violence and child abuse. People engaged in more constructive forms of work, and less destructive forms of recreation. It was evident that there were more happier couples and healthier children. Fewer people went to untimely graves. And those who survived not only lived longer, they also lived fuller lives.

And at the centre of all this activity was a group in the community who remembered that the personal growth and social change had come about because they had followed the agenda of God, personified in Jesus. The members of this group weren't content with their growth so far. They looked into the future and saw the changes that were possible if they were to follow in the footsteps of Jesus and, like him, live wholeheartedly for God and his agenda of love and justice.

1. What struck you as really significant about this story?

2. How was the Christ-centred problem-solving cycle used sensitively?

3. What lessons can you learn for your community work from this case study?

◊ Finish with a review of lessons you learned for community work from this case study.

◊ *Be sure to record your reflections in your working notes.*

6.   PLAYING SNAP IN CHRIST-CENTRED PROBLEM SOLVING

10 minutes

Note that to use the Christ-centred problem-solving cycle well, we need to be familiar with the Scriptures in general, and the life of Jesus in the Gospels in particular – in order to be able to think of a saying or a story that reveals how God may want us to resolve a particular problem.

Hence we need to immerse ourselves in the Scriptures in general, and the life of Jesus in the Gospels in particular, as much as we possibly can. We can test the standard of our knowledge by playing a game called "Snap."

To play Snap in a group, someone names an issue and asks the others to try to come up with a saying or a story from Scripture, particularly the Gospels, that addresses the issue. While you will not be able to come up with a Scripture for every issue, you will be able to find Scriptures that provide precedents, principles and convictions that address most fundamental human dilemmas constructively. When someone can match the issue with Scripture they call out "Snap!" – and cite the Scripture.

◊ If you are in a group, take turns naming issues and asking the others to match the issue with Scripture. Go through as many as you can in ten minutes.

◊ If you are not in a group, brainstorm a whole range of issues. Write as many as you can think of on a piece of paper – until you fill up the page. Then, with the paper in front of you, close your eyes and place your finger at random on any point on the paper. Open your eyes, check the issue you have selected, and try to come up with a saying or a story from Scripture that matches the issue, as quickly as you can. When you can match the issue with Scripture call out "Snap!" and cite the Scripture. Then move on. Go through as many as you can in the next ten minutes.

7.   CONCLUSION

10 minutes

The follow-up reading for this session is:

* *Not Religion, but Love,* pp. 162–71/148–158.

The set community tasks for this session are:

◊ Meet with your learning partner and your community development support group.

◊ If the other people in your group would be open to it, share what you learned in this session about Christ-centred problem solving and about how to use implicit Christ-centred problem-solving cycles and explicit Christ-centred problem-solving cycles sensitively with both Christians and non-Christians. Then apply the technique to a problem that you all are trying to resolve.

◊ If the people in your group are not open to a "religious" discussion, just talk about a current problem that you are confronted with. Then try to apply the Christ-centred problem-solving cycle implicitly, rather than explicitly, to the problem that you all are trying to resolve – as sensitively as you can.

◊ *Remember to record your actions, reflections, and conclusions in your working notes.*

◊ *Please note: You need to organize a learning partner to be with you in order to do the next session.*

PART II

COMPASSIONATE COMMUNITY WORK SKILLS

COMMUNITY WORK SKILL 1 – COMMUNICATING

1. PREPARATION

Please note: You need to organize a learning partner to be with you in order to do this session.

1.1. Objectives

- To review your understanding of the importance of transformational problem solving that is not just spinning our wheels but making some progress; the significance of problem solving in the light of the Gospels; and the place of a Christ-centred problem-solving cycle in the process

- To consider a series of basic community work skills – starting with communicating

2. REVIEW

30 minutes

Review the work from the previous session. This will include a review of your appreciation of the issues raised in class and clarified in the follow-up readings and your experience of doing the set community task.

Review the issues raised in the last session, particularly your understanding of transformational problem solving that is not just spinning our wheels but making some progress; the significance of problem solving in the light of the Gospels; and the place of a Christ-centred problem-solving cycle in the process.

Review the reading:

Not Religion, but Love, pp. 162–71/148–158.

Review the tasks:

1. How did your meeting with your community development support group go?

2. What was the most important thing you learned while doing the community tasks for the last session?

Finish the review with a reflection on how you went about trying to apply the Christ-centred problem-solving cycle to a problem *as sensitively as possible.*

◊ *Be sure to record your reflections in your working notes.*

3.   DEVELOPING COMMUNITY THROUGH COMMUNICATION

20 minutes

3.1. The Importance of Communication

Scott Peck says,

> If we are going to use the word "community" meaningfully, we must restrict it to a group of individuals who have learned to communicate honestly with each other, whose relationships go deeper than their masks of composure and who have developed some significant commitment to "rejoice together," "mourn together," "delight in each other" and "make each other's condition their own."[81]

◊ Chat with your learning partner for a few minutes about your experiences of real community. Would you add anything to Peck's definition?

3.2. The Case Study of Martha's Vineyard[82]

Read the following case study aloud, slowly.

> In a small, relatively isolated community on Martha's Vineyard, about every tenth person used to be born without the ability to hear. Everybody in the community – hearing and non-hearing alike – spoke a unique sign language brought from England

[81] Peck, *Different Drum*, p. 59.
[82] J. McKnight, "Why Servanthood Is Bad," *The Other Side* 31.6 (Nov.–Dec. 1995).

when they migrated to Massachusetts in 1690. In the mid-twentieth century, with increased mobility, the people ceased to intermarry and the genetic anomaly disappeared.

But before the memory of it died – and the sign language with it – historian Nora Groce studied the community's history. She compared the experiences of the non-hearing people with those of the hearing people.

She found that 80% of the non-hearing people graduated from high school, as did 80% of the hearing. She found that about 90% of the non-hearing got married, compared with about 92% of the hearing. They had about equal numbers of children. Their income levels were similar, as were the variety and distribution of their occupations.

Then Groce did a parallel study on the mainland of Massachusetts. At the time, Massachusetts was considered to have the best services in the nation for non-hearing people. There she found that 50% of non-hearing people graduated from high school, compared with about 75% of the hearing. About half of the non-hearing people married, while 90% of the hearing were married. About 40% of the non-hearing people had children, while 80% of hearing people did. Non-hearing people had fewer children. They also earned about one-third the income of hearing people and their range of occupations was much more limited.

How was it, Groce wondered, that on an island with no services non-hearing people were as much like hearing people as you could possibly measure – yet, thirty miles away, with the most advanced services available, non-hearing people lived much poorer lives than the hearing.

The one place in the United States where deafness was not a disability was a place with no services for deaf people. In that community, all the people adapted by signing instead of handing the non-hearing people over to professionals and their services. That community wasn't just doing what was necessary to help or to serve one group. It was doing what was necessary to incorporate everyone.

Non-hearing people were *not* healthier in the community where they had access to the most community services. Instead, non-hearing people were healthier in the community where hearing and non-hearing people could actually communicate with one another. Communication, therefore, is more important than service to a healthy community.

1. What strikes you about this case study?

2. What was the difference in the health statistics between the two communities?

3. What reason did the researcher give for the difference?

4. What can you learn from this case study that you can apply in your own community work?

◊ *Be sure to record your reflections in your working notes.*

4.   THE DIFFICULTIES OF COMMUNICATING

30 minutes

4.1. One-way and Two-way Communication

For this exercise you will need two pieces of paper and a pen.

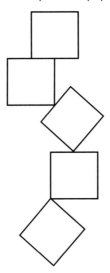

Figure 30. Boxes diagram 1

◊ First make a mental note of the time. Then, making sure that your learning partner cannot see Diagram 1, study it for a minute. And then, *without allowing any questions*, try to describe the boxes in the diagram so that your learning partner can draw them on his or her first piece of paper.

◊ When you are finished this first exercise, record the amount of time that it took.

◊ Without showing your learning partner Diagram 1, ask them to estimate how many squares they have drawn correctly in relation to the others. Write this number next to the recorded time.

◊ Now make a mental note of the time again and study Diagram 2.[83] Then, without showing it to your learning partner, but *inviting and answering any questions for clarification*, try to describe the boxes in the diagram so that your learning partner can draw them on his or her second piece of paper.

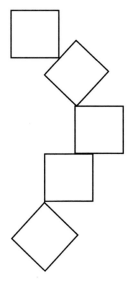

Figure 31. Boxes diagram 2

◊ When you are finished this second exercise, record the amount of time that it took.

◊ Without showing your learning partner Diagram 2, ask them to estimate how many squares they have drawn correctly in relation to the others. Write this number next to the recorded time.

---

[83] McKnight, "Servanthood," p. 38.

◊ Record the actual numbers of correct squares next to the estimates made by your learning partner.

◊ Now show your learning partner the diagrams and discuss the two kinds of communication, one-way and two-way. Assess the relative difficulty – or ease – of the two kinds of communication. Take into account the amount of time taken, the accuracy of the estimations, including any misconceptions, the accuracy achieved and the reasons for these results.

◊ *Record your reflections in your working notes.*

Two-way communication is always better than one-way communication. Extending the right to others to ask questions and seek clarification is critical to two-way communication. Clearly answering the questions asked of us is also critical to two-way communication. Two-way communication may take twice as long, but it can halve the hassles that we often have in trying to understand one another.

5.   ATTENTIVE AND REFLECTIVE LISTENING

45 minutes

A prisoner taps messages on a prison wall.

   "Can anybody hear me?"

There is complete despair when nobody is there to hear.

But, oh the joy, when somebody hears and replies –

   "I can hear you."[84]

5.1. Attentive Listening Skills

◊ Speak for two minutes on a topic of personal interest while your learning partner listens attentively. When you have finished, give some feedback to your learning partner on what you noticed about how attentive they were – or not.

◊ Then change roles and repeat the exercise.[85]

---

[84] Anthony de Mello, *Song of the Bird* (Image Pocket Classics, 1984).
[85] Shields, *In the Tiger's Mouth*, p. 51.

1. What did you feel was inattentive behaviour?

2. What did you feel was attentive behaviour?

3. What do you need to work on to be more attentive?

◊ *Be sure to record your reflections in your working notes.*

Note that we need to be in an environment with minimal distractions to be attentive. We also need to adopt an appropriate posture in order to be attentive:

- Standing or sitting close
- Leaning towards the other
- Looking into the speaker's face
- Maintaining eye contact
- Showing keen interest.

We need to listen silently, and not interrupt, in order to be attentive:

- Nodding understanding
- Encouraging to continue.

We need to set aside significant time for people in order to be attentive.

5.2. Reflective Listening Skills

In order to be effective in our reflective listening:

1. We need to use short phrases to indicate understanding. For instance, "You sound like you're frightened . . ."
2. We need to ask open-ended questions to gain further understanding. For instance, "How does that affect you?"
3. We need to summarize the essence of the speaker's statements in their own language so accurately that they can affirm our version of their words. For instance, "It sounds like you're scared you might make a mistake."
4. We also need to be careful not to add to what the person has actually said, not to put words or ideas in their mouths.

◊ While holding your pen, speak about a personal matter you are really concerned about. For example, "I feel freaked out about my work because I often don't know what to do."

◊ Your learning partner listens attentively and reflects back to you what they heard you say you were feeling – not by parroting it back, but by sensitively paraphrasing what you said. For example, "It sounds like you feel nervous because you're scared you might make a mistake."

◊ If you feel satisfied that you were heard, pass the pen on to your learning partner so that they can take a turn speaking about a personal matter that they are really concerned about.

◊ If, however, you do not feel satisfied that you have been heard, you should hold on to the pen and have your learning partner try again until you feel you have been truly heard.

◊ Once you feel you have been heard, take a turn to listen attentively to your learning partner and reflect back to him or her what you heard them say they were feeling (not by just parroting back, but by sensitively paraphrasing what they said), until they feel satisfied that you have really heard them.

◊ Each of you should then take another turn to try it again.

1. What did you find most challenging about reflective listening?

2. Which aspect of reflective listening do you need to work on more?

◊ *Be sure to record your reflections in your working notes.*

5.3. Some Tips on Listening

Note the following tips on listening:

- Listening takes time.
- Listening requires courtesy.
- Listening attends to the whole person.
- Listening observes the body as much as the voice.
- Listening is about understanding – that is under-standing, for we cannot understand anyone if we look down at them. We can only understand someone if we look up to them.
- Listening occurs at a surface level – what people are saying.
- Listening also occurs at a deeper level – what people are feeling.
- In order to listen respectfully we need to listen deeply to feelings.

1. Which of these tips would you underscore as particularly important for you to work on?

2. What other tip(s) of your own would you add to this list?

◊ *Be sure to record your tips in your working notes.*

6.   SPEAKING

45 minutes

Communication isn't easy. Consider the possible mistakes we can make in a conversation.

> There's what you meant to say.
>
> There's what you actually say.
>
> There's what they heard you say.
>
> There's what they thought they heard you say.
>
> There's what they want to say about
>
> . . . what they thought they heard you say.
>
> There's what they actually say about
>
> . . . what they thought they heard you say.
>
> There's what you heard them say about
>
> . . . what they thought they heard you say.

And so on and so on.

6.1. Effective Speaking Skills

◊ Brainstorm a list of controversial subjects for discussion and write them down – keep writing until you have a long list of interesting topics. A controversial topic is one lots of people you know have disagreements about (e.g., the idea of progress, that things are actually getting better as time goes by). Now pick one of these controversial subjects you would like to talk about. One person argues for it, the other against.

Stage one – articulating your perspective

◊ Take one side of the controversy and speak from your point of view for one minute, advocating your opinion as passionately and as persuasively as you can.

◊ Then ask your learning partner to take the other side of the controversy and speak against your views for one minute – as passionately and as persuasively as they can.

◊ Talk about how you think you both did articulating your own perspectives.

Stage two – advocating other's perspectives

◊ Now reverse roles.

◊ On the same topic, speak for what you spoke against based on what you heard the other person say. Take one minute to advocate your learning partner's views as passionately and as persuasively as you did your own.

◊ Then ask your learning partner to advocate your views for one minute as passionately and as persuasively as they can.

◊ Talk about how you think you both did advocating another's perspective.

Stage three – advancing our own and other's perspectives

◊ Finally, take a few minutes during which both you and your learning partner prepare a one-minute speech that integrates both sides of the argument – your side and their side – in a single presentation. Present a balanced perspective that faithfully represents both sides of the argument.

◊ Then, one after the other, advocate the view that takes both sides into account as passionately and as persuasively as you possibly can.

◊ Talk about how you think you both did trying to present a balanced perspective.

1. What have you learned about articulating your own views passionately but respectfully?

2. What have you learned about advocating another's views both sincerely and persuasively?

3. What have you learned about advancing an integrated perspective genuinely?

◊ *Be sure to record your reflections in your working notes.*

Note that *effective* speaking is

- Personal. It comes from ideas we've made our own.
- Passionate. It comes from the love in our hearts.
- Persuasive. It comes from the logic in our heads.
- Genuine. It is authentic, honest and vulnerable.
- Sincere. It is respectful – especially of opponents.
- Story. It uses examples to make our ideas come alive.

7.   CONCLUSION

10 minutes

The follow-up reading for this session is:
- Bruce Turley's "The Expression of God's Concern," in *Being There for Others* (Melbourne: JCBE, 1982), pp. 46–56 (Reading 6).

The set community tasks for this session are:

◊ Meet with your learning partner and your community development support group.

◊ Share what you learned in this session about communication. Discuss ways that you could all listen more attentively and reflectively and speak more effectively.

◊ Look for opportunities to listen – really listen – to people in your community this week.

◊ Look for opportunities to speak up in your community this week – for yourself, for others and for yourself-and-others.

◊ Ensure that you record your actions, reflections and conclusions in your working notes.

◊ *Please note: You need to organize two learning partners to be with you in order to do the next session.*

COMMUNITY WORK SKILL 2 – NEGOTIATING

1. PREPARATION

Please note: You need to have two learning partners with you in order to do this session.

1.1. Objectives

- To review your communication skills
- To consider negotiating, the next in a series of basic community work skills

2. REVIEW

30 minutes

Review your work from the previous session. This will include a review of your appreciation of the issues raised in the course notes and clarified in the follow-up readings and your experience of your set community tasks.

Review the issues raised in the last session, particularly your understanding of communicating – of attentive listening, reflective listening, and effective speaking.

Review the reading: Bruce Turley's

"The Expression of God's Concern" (Reading 6).

Review the tasks:

1. How did it go meeting with your community development support group and sharing what you learned in class about communication and discussing ways you could all listen more attentively and reflectively and speak more effectively?

2. What was the most important thing you learned while doing the community tasks for the last session?

Finish the review with a reflection on opportunities you had to listen and speak.

◊ *Be sure to record your reflections in your working notes.*

3.   NEGOTIATING DEALS BETWEEN PARTIES

50 minutes

3.1. The Art of Negotiating

Negotiating is the art of

- Turning disagreement into agreement
- Mediating a peace deal between parties in a dispute
- Brokering an arrangement that is acceptable to all parties.

Typical tasks for negotiating in community work include:

- Negotiating entry into (joining) a community organization
- Negotiating access to community resources
- Negotiating support for a community program
- Negotiating settlement of a community dispute.

What are some areas of negotiation that are needed in your community?

◊ *Record your answer in your working notes.*

3.2. The Role of the Negotiator

The negotiator's role in the negotiation process is to:

- Establish contact with the relevant parties
- Approach the enemies as potential allies
- Establish communication between parties
- Help both parties understand one another
- Clear up any misunderstandings

- Encourage both sides to relate as human beings
- Mediate a deal between parties in the dispute
- Broker an arrangement acceptable to all parties.

1. With which of these functions of the negotiator are you most familiar?

2. Think of a dispute you are aware of that you might be able to mediate. In the context of this dispute, which functions of the role of negotiator would you be most comfortable starting with?

◊ *Be sure to record your reflections in your working notes.*

3.3. The Place of the Negotiator

The negotiator works between two parties, at the interface between people; between people and groups; between groups; and between groups and a system of some kind or other.

If we are to work between two different parties, we need to have a thorough knowledge of both.

We need to respect both parties and be acceptable to both parties.

We need to have access to the networks of both as well as be able to work in the gap between them.

We need to be careful that we don't just run messages back and forth between the two parties, but that we effectively set up a process of serious negotiation between the two parties.[86]

1. How can you acquire knowledge of both parties?

2. How can you become acceptable to both parties?

3. How can you avoid running messages back and forth?

4. How can you set up a serious process of negotiation?

◊ *Remember to record your reflections in your working notes.*

3.4. The Pressure on the Negotiator

The negotiator works between two parties, and both of those parties want the negotiator to work for them. So often a negotiator feels as if he or she is working for two masters who are working at cross-purposes. If we are not careful, this can drive us crazy.

Tony Kelly and Sandra Sewell, both experienced community workers, say that "to survive this situation we need a firm self-identity

---

[86] T. Kelly and S. Sewell, *With Head, Heart and Hands* (Brisbane: Boolarong, 1988), p. 91.

and an astute political sense" so we don't get played off against one side or the other.[87]

We need to be clear about who we are, who we are working with, and who we are working for.

Who are we?

We are *mediators*. We are *not* spin doctors or hatchet merchants.

Who are we working with?

We are *working for both parties* not for one *against* the other.

Who are we working for?

We are *working for both parties*. We are *not* working for one against the other.

- As mediators, our *art* is to turn disagreement into agreement.
- As mediators, our *method* is to broker a deal with both parties.
- As mediators, our *aim* is to broker a deal that works for both parties.

In the context of this dispute you are thinking of, answer the following questions:

1. Who are you?
2. Who are you working with?
3. Who are you working for?

◊ *Be sure to record your reflections in your working notes.*

3.5. The Cardinal Rule of the Community Negotiator

The community negotiator's cardinal rule in the negotiation process is to consider the impact of any arrangement on the most vulnerable people in the community.

If it's not "good news to the poor," it's not good.

As community workers Tony Kelly and Sandra Sewell say, "If the starting point for the broker is not the poorest of the poor, he or she runs the risk of being co-opted by the status quo and becoming a public relations machine for the system."[88]

---

[87] Kelly and Sewell, *Head, Heart*, p. 91.
[88] Kelly and Sewell, *Head, Heart*, p. 90.

1. What is the difference between a corporate and a community negotiator?

2. How important is concern for the poor to the welfare of the community as a whole?

◊ *Be sure to record your reflections in your working notes.*

4.   NEGOTIATING DEALS ACCEPTABLE TO ALL PARTIES

90 minutes

The following exercise teaches valuable negotiating skills.[89]

4.1. Stage One: Separate People from Problems

People are humans. Humans can act tough, but all are vulnerable. We need to be hard on issues but soft on people. We need to relate to people and work on the problems, rather than treating people as problems and trying to fix them.

1. What happens when we treat people as problems and try to fix them?

◊ *Be sure to record your reflections in your working notes.*

4.2. Stage Two: Focus on Interests rather than Positions

Positions are predetermined solutions. If people stick to their own predetermined solutions, they are unlikely to think of a solution that's acceptable to other people.

What are some of the positions, for example, on the issue of decision making or the way people think decisions should be made, in your own community?

We need to focus on *interests* rather than *positions*. Interests are people's fears and desires. We can find out people's interests by asking why they take a particular position on an issue.

Why do people take the position that they do on the decision-making issue?

---

[89] Adapted from R. Fisher and W. Ury, *Getting to Yes* (New York: Penguin, 1991).

Usually each side has multiple interests. We need to acknowledge the interests of each side. Some interests may be in conflict, but many interests will in fact be compatible. We need to consider both conflicting and compatible interests.

> 1. What are the various interests in the leadership issue?
>
> 2. Which ones are in conflict with others in the group?
>
> 3. Which ones are compatible with others in the group?

People need to set aside their predetermined positions and find solutions that address as many interests as possible.

> Will people set aside their positions on decision making for the sake of discussion?

◊ *Be sure to record your reflections in your working notes.*

4.3. Stage Three: Invent Multiple Options for Mutual Benefit

We need to invent multiple options for mutual benefit. Don't look for a single solution – look instead for as many solutions as possible. Don't decide what is possible or what will actually work beforehand – do that later. Brainstorm as many wild and wonderful options as possible.

To brainstorm effectively, be relaxed. Don't be critical. Be creative.

> What are all the different ways people could organize your church that could address the concerns people have raised about decision making?

◊ Record all the ideas that you and your learning partners come up with.

> What ideas do you think are most promising?

◊ Can you improve on any of these ideas?

> What other ideas have you seen, heard or read about that might help address your concerns about decision making?

◊ Identify shared interests. Then identify options that address shared interests.

> 1. What would you say are shared interests?
>
> 2. What options address those shared interests?

◊ Underline (in pencil) the option that you think most likely to meet most needs.

What option is most likely to meet most of your needs?

◊ Draft a tentative agreement and keep working on the draft until it is finally acceptable to all parties.

◊ *Be sure to record your answers to these questions and the draft agreement you came up with in your working notes.*

4.4. Stage Four: Set Objective Criteria for Assessment

We need to set up objective *criteria* for assessment.

We need to agree on how to assess whether the agreement is workable in practice or not.

The criteria need to be fair, simple and practical – and acceptable to all the parties in the dispute.

What criteria can you agree on to use to assess whether the agreement is workable in practice or not?

We need to constantly assess whether the way we run our group is safe, accepting, respectful, inclusive and just.

We also need to assess the impact of the way we run our group on the most vulnerable people in the community.

Is the agreement "good news to the poor" or not?

If it is – okay. If it is not – we need to negotiate another agreement.

If we can do that – okay. If we can't do that – we need to have in mind a viable alternative to a negotiated agreement.

◊ *Be sure to record your reflections in your working notes.*

4.5. Viable Alternatives to Negotiated Agreements

If we have trouble negotiating an agreement that is acceptable, we need to have in mind a viable alternative to a negotiated agreement.

We need to help each party think about a bottom-line, fall-back position they can live with if the negotiating process should falter, or fail.

- It will save them from being pressurized.
- It will strengthen their hand in negotiation.

- It will give them a basis for assessing agreements.
- It will give them a way out in case they need to get out.

1. If you couldn't come to an agreement on the leadership style you would like for your group, what would you do? Speak up? Stay silent? Go along with the majority? Or not?

2. Could you cope with the consequences of that choice?

If so – okay. If not – we need to think of another viable alternative.

◊ *Be sure to record your reflections in your working notes.*

5.   CONCLUSION

10 minutes

The follow-up reading for this session is:
- Sue Critall's "A Southport Story – Community Work in Parish Structures," in A. Kelly and S. Sewell, *People Working Together*, II (Brisbane: Boolarong, 1986), pp. 48–61 – a case study on the need to negotiate any community work we do in the church from the start (Reading 7).

The set community tasks for this session are:

◊ Meet with your learning partner and your community development support group.

◊ Share what you learned in this session about negotiating. Discuss the following questions concerning the potential need for negotiating agreements in your community.

1. Are there any issues you need to negotiate or renegotiate?

2. Are there any issues that may need to be negotiated in the near future?

3. What steps would you follow in negotiating agreements on these issues in your community?

◊ Look for opportunities to negotiate informally – if not formally – on small but significant issues that will inevitably come up in your community this week.

◊ *Record your actions, reflections and conclusions in your working notes.*

Please note: You need to organize two learning partners to be with you in order to do the next session. You will also need to supply 300 drinking straws and 100 dressmaker's pins.

COMMUNITY WORK SKILL 3 – FACILITATING

1.   PREPARATION

Please note: You need to have two learning partners with you in order to do this session. You will also need to supply 300 drinking straws and 100 dressmaker's pins.

1.1. Objectives

- To review your understanding of the importance of negotiating
- To consider facilitating, the next skill in a series of basic community work skills

2.   REVIEW

30 minutes

Review the work from the previous session. This will include a review of your appreciation of the issues raised in the course notes and clarified in the follow-up readings and your experience of your set community tasks.

Review the issues raised in the previous session, particularly your understanding of negotiating skills.

Review the reading:

Sue Critall's "A Southport Story – Community Work in Parish Structures" (Reading 7).

Review the tasks:

1. Did any opportunities for you to negotiate informally – if not formally – on small but significant issues come up in your community this week? If so, how did they go and what did you learn?

2. What was the most important thing you learned while doing the community tasks for the last session?

Finish the review with a reflection on how you can make the most of opportunities you have to negotiate.

◊ *Be sure to record your reflections in your working notes.*

3.   FACILITATING GROWTH AND CHANGE

3.1. The Importance of Meetings

15 minutes

Meetings are an important part of any enterprise labouring for personal growth, social change and community development.[90]

They are times when we can share information, give each other some support and accomplish joint tasks together. They are times when we can laugh and cry, share ideas and get down to work.

However, as we all know, there can be good meetings and bad meetings.

◊ Brainstorm a list of the characteristics of a good meeting – the kind of meeting you feel is worth going to yourself. Write down this list of suggestions on the left-hand side of a piece of paper and save it for later on in the session.

Note that a good meeting includes:

- Most of the participants turning up
- The feeling that people can be honest and real with one another
- A high level of energy and enthusiasm
- A sense of involvement in the decisions
- Some commonly-agreed group goals
- Clear processes for reaching those goals
- Clear roles for facilitating those processes
- And so on . . .

---

[90] V. Coover, et al., *Resource Manual for a Living Revolution* (Philadelphia: New Society Publishers, 1978), p. 61.

◊ Keep this list handy – we will come back to it later.

Note too that a good meeting includes a good facilitator.

3.2. The Importance of Facilitating

5 minutes

A "facilitator" plays a role in the group that's similar to that of a "chairperson." The facilitator helps the group members make decisions and carry out tasks. This person takes responsibility to remind the group of its purpose and monitor group maintenance and group function. The facilitator suggests processes and encourages participation. While the word "chairperson" is usually used in corporate groups, in community groups we use the word "facilitator."

As we all know, there can be good "facilitators" and bad "facilitators."

◊ Complete the statement: "A good facilitator always . . ." three times, writing down three qualities of a good facilitator.

◊ Then read out your statements, one by one, to the two others in your group.

3.3. Different Views on Facilitating

60 minutes

Some of the statements from your list may reflect a "full-on" directive view of leadership, while others may reflect a "laissez-faire" non-directive view of leadership or a "fair-go" democratic view of leadership.

Note that there are three very different styles of facilitating:
1. "Full-on" directive view
2. "Laissez-faire" non-directive view
3. "Fair-go" democratic view

◊ Rather than debate the strengths and weaknesses of these different views of facilitating, explain to the group that you are going to put them to the test in an exercise.

◊ You will go through this single group exercise with straws and pins three different times. – Each time you will do it with a different facilitator and a different set of instructions.

◊ Go around and name each person in your group as "A," "B" or "C."

"Full-on" directive leader

◊ Person "A" should take Brief 1 (at the end of this session) and read the instructions silently (no-one else should see them).

◊ After ten minutes, person "A" should call a halt to the construction. Leave the structure and move to another part of the table for the next exercise.

"Laissez-faire" non-directive leader

◊ Person "B" should now take Brief 2 (at the end of this session) and read the instructions silently (no-one should see it).

◊ After ten minutes, person "B" should call a halt to this exercise. Leave the structure and move to another part of the table for the next exercise.

"Fair-go" democratic leader

◊ Person "C" should now take Brief 3 (at the end of this session) and read the instructions silently (no-one should see it).

◊ After ten minutes, person "C" should call a halt to the process and leave the structure.

◊ When the time is up, assess all of the structures in terms of their height, strength and beauty. Remember that in these exercises in facilitation each facilitator was asked to play a particular role. Hence any comments about the roles people played should be about the style of facilitation, not the person.

◊ Bearing that in mind, go through the following set of questions for each group, giving specific examples from each group:

1. Who facilitated group "A" (then "B" and "C")?
2. How did person "A" (then "B" and "C") facilitate the group exercise?
3. What was the climate of the exercise for group "A" (then "B" and "C")?
4. How much did people participate in group "A" (then "B" and "C")?
5. How well did group "A" (then "B" and "C") perform?
6. Was any behaviour of the group "A" (then "B" and "C") related to the way the facilitator acted?

◊ *Be sure to record your observations in your working notes.*

◊ Now the members/workers in each group should discuss together how they felt about the process in each of the group exercises.

To start with . . .

1. How did you feel about the facilitator of the "A" group?

2. How did you feel about the other person in the "A" group?

3. How did you feel about your own work in the "A" group?

4. How did you feel about the structure the "A" group made?

Then . . .

1. How did you feel about the facilitator of the "B" group?

2. How did you feel about the other person in the "B" group?

3. How did you feel about your own work in the "B" group?

4. How did you feel about the structure the "B" group made?

And . . .

1. How did you feel about the facilitator of the "C" group?

2. How did you feel about the other person in the "C" group?

3. How did you feel about your own work in the "C" group?

4. How did you feel about the structure the "C" group made?

◊ Give specific examples as you answer these questions.

◊ *Be sure to record your observations in your working notes.*

◊ Then discuss how you felt facilitating the process in the exercises you led.

Ask the "A," "B" and "C" leaders in turn to answer the questions . . .

1. What was the role that you were asked to play?

2. What did you like about the role?

3. What didn't you like about the role?

4. How do you think it affected the group?

5. How do you feel it affected you?

◊ Give specific examples as you answer these questions.

◊ *Be sure to record your observations in your working notes.*

◊ Finish the exercise with a discussion on the advantages and disadvantages of all three styles of facilitating. Compare and contrast the "full-on" directive leader with the "laissez-faire" non-directive leader and the "fair-go" democratic leader.

Note that a good "fair-go" democratic leader is the best facilitator. He or she:

- Helps the members make decisions and carry out tasks
- Takes responsibility to remind the group of its purpose
- Monitors both group maintenance and group function
- Suggests options but lets the group make its own decisions
- Encourages all members of the group to participate
- Helps the group to realize that it is their group and they are in charge
- Encourages the group as a whole to do the best that it can.

3.4. Selecting a Facilitator

10 minutes

In regular meetings it is helpful to encourage people to either share the role or rotate the role of facilitator. That way as many people as possible can learn how to facilitate meetings in the community.

However, on occasion there will be meetings that we expect to be very difficult – perhaps a large meeting, an emergency meeting or a meeting where some kind of trouble is anticipated. In these circumstances, it is crucial to choose an experienced facilitator.

What would you look for in an experienced facilitator?

◊ *Be sure to record your ideas in your working notes.*

It is important to note that an experienced facilitator

- Has the energy and courage to deal with the meeting
- Is more concerned for the process than for the outcome
- Will encourage participation from all of those present
- Will have the time and interest to prepare well for the meeting.

4.   FACILITATING FUNCTION AND MAINTENANCE

4.1. Facilitating the Group Function of the Meeting

20 minutes

There are two parts to facilitating the group function of the meeting. The first part is *preparing* for meeting. The second part is *running* the meeting.

a) Preparing for meeting[91]

What does a facilitator need to do to prepare for meeting?

◊ *Be sure to record your ideas in your working notes.*

In preparing for a meeting, the facilitator needs to:
1.   Make sure people are informed about the meeting.
2.   Ask for suggestions of items to put on the agenda.
3.   Make sure the setting for the meeting is appropriate.
4.   Put a proposed agenda on the table for discussion.
5.   Gather the necessary writing and recording materials.
6.   Have an alternate facilitator in case of an emergency.

Note that the facilitator is responsible to do these things him or herself *or* to appoint the given tasks to others (e.g., a person in the role of "secretary" could prepare the agenda, etc.).

b) Running the meeting[92]

What does a facilitator need to do to run a meeting?

◊ *Be sure to record your ideas in your working notes.*

In running the meeting, the facilitator needs to:
1.   Make sure that an agenda is agreed upon.
2.   Prioritize agenda items and allocate time for each item.
3.   Take care that a recorder is also nominated.
4.   Start on time – with energy and enthusiasm.
5.   Keep the group focused on one task at a time.
6.   Regulate the discussion so that it is inclusive.
7.   Encourage the louder people to hold back a bit.
8.   Encourage the quieter people to participate.
9.   Make sure the discussion is getting the job done.

---

[91] Coover, et al., *Resource Manual*, p. 63.
[92] Shields, *In the Tiger's Mouth*, p. 96.

10. Slow down the conversation if it is moving too quickly.
11. Speed up the conversation if it is moving too slowly.
12. Sum up the meeting and provide satisfying closure.

4.2. Facilitating the Group Maintenance of the Meeting

40 minutes

◊ Review the characteristics of a good meeting you listed from 3.1, above. Now divide the right-hand side of the paper into two columns, and put "task" on the top of the first and "relationship" on the top of the second column.Place a tick in the appropriate column next to each characteristic, according to whether it is a "task" or a "relationship" issue.

◊ Then ask the following question:

Which is more important – task or relationship?

◊ *Be sure to record your reflections in your working notes.*

There are usually a lot more characteristics listed under "relationships" than "tasks." Thus while both tasks and relationships are important, people often feel that relationships are more important than tasks.

Facilitating maintenance is about facilitating relationships.

Maintaining a meeting[93]

In maintaining the meeting, the facilitator needs to:

- Host – welcome participants, greeting them by name
- Initiate – open up the discussion by making suggestions
- Encourage – invite other people's ideas by being receptive
- Listen – attend to their opinions by being accepting
- Clarify – eliminate any confusion by giving examples
- Diffuse – reduce any tension by laughing or crying
- Affirm – increase the sense of respect by being friendly
- Mediate – reconcile differences and find similarities.

In all of this, it is important to remember that affirming people is essential to maintaining relationships.[94]

---

[93] Coover, et al., *Resource Manual*, pp. 46–47.
[94] Coover, et al., *Resource Manual*, pp. 72–73.

Reflect on the facilitation of a meeting you attended recently (that you did not facilitate yourself). Did the facilitator maintain the meeting according to these criteria? What did he or she miss, and what was the effect?

◊ *Be sure to record your ideas in your working notes.*

◊ At this point each person should take a moment to share what they liked about this session and the role that were able to play in it.

◊ After each person has spoken, someone else in the group should reflect on what they said, noting something that they like and would like to affirm about them.

5.   CONCLUSION

10 minutes

The follow-up reading for this session is:
*   Geoff Huard's "Building an Urban Parish," in *Green Shoots in the Concrete* (Sydney: Scaffolding, 1985), pp. 107–15. This is a case study on facilitating community work in an urban church (Reading 8).

The set community tasks for this session are:

◊ Meet with your learning partner and your community development support group.

◊ Share what you learned in this session about facilitating. Talk about ways in which you could improve your facilitation of meetings in which you take part.

1. How could you prepare better for meetings?

2. How could you run community meetings better?

3. How could you maintain community meetings better?

◊ Look for opportunities to facilitate meetings better in your community this week.

◊ Also look for opportunities to affirm people every time that you meet with them.

◊ *Record your actions, reflections and conclusions in your working notes.*

BRIEF 1

A "full-on" directive facilitator

Your job is to be a dictator. Display this style of leadership without informing your group what you are doing. Just do it.

Tell the group that their task is to build a structure out of the straws and pins. Also tell them that the structure will be judged for its height, strength and beauty.

You could say, for example, "Your job is to build a structure out of these straws and pins. When you are finished, I will judge it according to its height, strength and beauty. Now, start by taking two straws each and forming a square on the table. Now take another set of pins and . . ."

Do not tell them that the structure is to be constructed entirely according to your ideas.

Do not tell the group your ideas about what the finished structure will look like, just give them the work to do. Give them step-by-step instructions as they go.

Don't let them decide what to do.

Don't take any suggestions from anyone. You give the orders.

Don't allow the members to talk with each other. If they have something to say, have them say it to you.

Feel free to criticize or praise their work as you like.

BRIEF 2

A "laissez-faire" non-directive leader

Your job is to be laid back and let it happen. Display this style of leadership without informing your group what you are doing. Just do it.

Tell the group that their task is to build a structure out of the straws and pins. Also tell them that the structure will be judged for its height, strength and beauty.

You could say, for example, "Please build another structure out of these straws and pins. When you are finished, I will be looking at its height, strength and beauty. I look forward to seeing what you come up with . . ."

Do not tell the group that the structure is to be constructed from the member's own ideas.

You should be friendly but not take any initiative at all. Only say something if the members ask you something. Even then you should not direct the group in any way.

You can tell the group what the task is but don't make any suggestions about what is to be done or how it is to be done. Let the members decide for themselves what to do.

Don't criticize or praise anyone's work.

Brief 3

A "fair-go" democratic leader

Your job is to be a democratic facilitator. Display this style of leadership without informing your group what you are doing. Just do it.

Tell the group that their task is to build a structure out of the straws and pins. Also tell them that the structure will be judged for its height, strength and beauty.

You could say, for example, "We are going to build another structure out of these straws and pins. Together we need to work to achieve height, strength and beauty. I wonder if anyone has an idea about how we should begin here . . ."

Do not tell them that the structure is to be the product of the thinking of the whole group.

You should encourage a thorough discussion of what the task is and how to do it by the whole group. As much as possible, allow the people to decide how to divide up the work among themselves.

During the discussion, you should act as a moderator. When a suggestion is made, ask whether the others in the group support it or not. You should encourage the group to come to consensus before decisions are made.

You should encourage members to talk with each other as they go, consulting, clarifying and checking with each other as they need to.

You can criticize or praise people's work if you give a reason for it.

COMMUNITY WORK SKILL 4 – RESEARCHING

1. PREPARATION

1.1. Objectives

- To review your facilitating skills
- To consider the fourth in a series of community work skills – researching

2. REVIEW

15 minutes

Review the work from the previous session. This will include a review of your appreciation of the issues raised in the course notes and clarified in the follow-up readings, and your experience of your set community tasks.

Review the issues raised in the session last week, particularly your understanding of facilitating and affirming.

Review the reading:

Geoff Huard's "Building an Urban Parish" (Reading 8).

Review the tasks:

1. How did it go meeting with your community development support group and sharing what you learned in class about facilitating?

2. What was the most important thing you learned while doing the community tasks for the last session?

Finish this review with a reflection on how you found facilitating meetings and affirming people.

◊ *Be sure to record your reflections in your working notes.*

3.   REFLECTING ON YOUR COMMUNITY

3.1. What Kind of Church are You in?[95]

20 minutes

◊ Consider which of the following statements are true of your church:

- Old church
- New church
- Youthful church
- Ageing church
- Worship orientated
- Fellowship orientated
- Outreach orientated
- Service orientated
- 0–50 members
- 50–150 members
- Over 150 members
- No buildings
- Old buildings
- New buildings
- Debt-free

Are there any other distinctive characteristics of your church?

◊ Fill in the specific stories behind these general descriptors by answering the following questions.

1. What is the history of your church community?
2. What are the significant events that have changed it?
3. What are the various groups in your church community?
4. What are the major issues your church is dealing with?
5. How is your church likely to change in the future?

◊ *Be sure to record your reflections in your working notes.*

---

[95] Adapted from *The View from Outside*, a pamphlet published by The Board of Mission of the Uniting Church of Australia (n.d.).

3.2. What Kind of Locality are You in?[96]

20 minutes

◊ Which of the following statements are true of your locality:

- Rural area
- Urban area
- Inner suburb
- Outer suburb
- Old suburb
- New suburb
- Stable
- Growing
- Declining
- Homogeneous
- Heterogeneous

Are there any other distinctive characteristics of your locality?

◊ Fill in the specific stories behind these general descriptors by answering the following questions.

1. What is the history of your local community?
2. What are the significant events that have changed it?
3. What are the various groups in your local community?
4. What are the major issues your community is dealing with?
5. How is your locality likely to change in the future?

◊ *Be sure to record your reflections in your working notes.*

3.3. Similarities and Differences between Communities

15 minutes

◊ What are the similarities and differences between your church community and your local community.

1. Does your church reflect the range of people in your local community?
2. How similar or different is the age profile of your church and your locality?

---

[96] Adapted from *The View from Outside.*

3. How similar or different is the class profile of your church and your locality?

4. How similar or different is the ethnic profile of your church and your locality?

5. Are there any other similarities or differences between your communities?

6. What do these similarities or differences between your communities signify?

◊ *Be sure to record your reflections in your working notes.*

4.   RESEARCHING YOUR COMMUNITY

4.1. What Do You Need to Know?

10 minutes

Consider what things you need to know about your communities (your local community and your church community).[97]

Make a list of all the different areas you need to look into in order to feel that you know your community and its needs.

You will probably need to know about the people in your communities and the characteristics of these people:

- Faith
- Values
- Lifestyles
- Quality of life
- Areas of need and concern

You will also want to know about the communities themselves:

- Their boundaries
- Their organization
- The various groups within the communities
- Facilities
- Resources
- Relationships between the communities

---

[97] Adapted from T. Kelly, *Community Profiles* (University Lecture Notes, University of Queensland, 1973).

4.2. How Do You Get to Know These Things?[98]

10 minutes

Make a list of all the different ways you can find out what you want to know about your communities.

You will probably need to include all of the following.

Observe your communities

- Walk around.
- Stop, look and listen.
- Consider the significance of what you see and hear.

Interview key people in your communities

- Talk with your leaders.
- Talk with your colleagues.
- Talk with your neighbours, family and friends.
- Talk with people whom no-one else would usually talk to.

Survey the people in your communities:

- Ask general questions.
- Ask specific questions.
- Test opinions by polling people.

Access the data on your communities by consulting resources, for example:

- Read local papers.
- Listen to local radio.
- Watch local television.
- Log onto local websites.
- Study various government reports.

4.3. What Do You Want to Do with the Things You Learn about Your Communities?[99]

10 minutes

Make a list of all the things you might want to do with what you learn about your communities.

[98] Adapted from Kelly, *Community Profiles*.
[99] Adapted from *The View from Outside*.

You may want to consider:

- Developing a profile of your church community
- Developing a profile of your local community
- Comparing your church and local community profiles
- Identifying some ways the church might better reflect the locality
- Identifying some ways the church might better effect the locality
- Talking to the church about its relationship with the locality
- Developing a proposal for further church involvement with the locality.

4.4. Where Do You Want to Go with What You Know?

10 minutes

Write down your ideas for where you want to go from here with your research.

◊ *Be sure to record your reflections in your working notes.*

5.   CONCLUSION

10 minutes

Note: Two learning partners are required for you to do the next session. If you don't organize for two learning partners to be present – you can't do it!

The follow-up reading for this session is:

- Bruce Turley's "The Building of God's Community," in *Being there for Others*, pp. 35–45, a study of church-initiated community research (Reading 9).

The set community tasks for this session are:

◊ Meet with your learning partner and your community development support group.

◊ Share what you learned in this session about researching. Talk about where you want to go from here with your research; what things you want to get to know about your communities; how you can get to know these things about your communities; what you want to do with what you learn about your communities and what you will do about it this week.

◊ Ensure you record your actions, reflections and conclusions in your working notes.

Please note: You need to organize two learning partners to be with you in order to do the next session. You will also need 100 filing cards (or equivalent size pieces of paper).

COMMUNITY WORK SKILL 5 – PLANNING (A)

1. PREPARATION

Please note: You need to organize two learning partners to be with you in order to do this session. You will also need 100 filing cards (or equivalent size pieces of paper).

1.1. Objectives

- To review your researching skills
- To consider the next in a series of community work skills – planning

2. REVIEW

15 minutes

Review the work from the previous session. This will include a review of your appreciation of the issues raised in the course notes, clarified in follow-up readings and your experience of your set community tasks.

Review the issues raised in the last session, particularly your understanding of researching.

Review the reading:

Bruce Turley's "The Building of God's Community" (Reading 9).

Review the tasks:

1. How did it go meeting with your community development support group and sharing what you learned in class about researching?

2. What was the most important thing you learned while doing the community tasks for the last session?

Finish the review with a reflection on what you did in terms of research.

◊ *Be sure to record your reflections in your working notes.*

3.   ANALYSIS

Pick a community or a part of a community with problems that you would like to plan to address. The first phase of planning is *analysis*.[100]

There are four steps to this phase:
1. Participants analysis
2. Problems analysis
3. Objectives analysis
4. Alternatives analysis

3.1. Participants Analysis

20 minutes

The first step is to identify all the people in the community who you think would be interested and whom you would like to invite to the planning table

- List all the possible participants – anyone who might be impacted positively or negatively by the plan.

- Prioritize the most important participants – ones who would be impacted most, for better or worse, by the plan.

- Consider what these people could bring to the planning table – not only their problems, but also their capacity to solve their problems – their interests, connections and resources.

You will need to do the following planning processes with these people in mind – not only because you will need their perspectives to inform the processes, but also because, once you have practised the processes with your learning partners in the next couple of sessions, you will need to get together with the people you have in mind and go through these planning processes with them.

◊ *Be sure to record your reflections in your working notes.*

---

[100] Adapted from *Project Planning for Development* (Durban: Olive, 1994).

3.2. Problems Analysis

30 minutes

The second step is to understand the range of problems that people face in the community.

◊ Based on the knowledge that you already have of them, write down approximately 10 problem statements on 10 separate cards – one on each card.

A problem statement should be framed *negatively* – but as *accurately* and as *specifically* as possible. Don't *exaggerate* or *generalize*. (e.g., "25% of wives in this community report that they are being beaten by their husbands.")

◊ As a starting point, select one focal problem for the analysis. This is not necessarily the core problem, but just a place to start.

◊ Circle the problem statement on this card in red and place it in the centre of a table and organize the other cards around it in terms of cause and effect – the causes below it and the effects above it, so the cards begin to take the shape of a "problems tree."

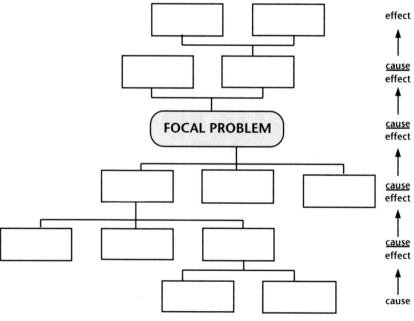

Figure 32. The problems tree with cause-effect analysis[101]

---

[101] *Project Planning for Development* (Durban: Olive, 1994), p. 38.

Developing a problems tree allows you to visualize both the range of problems people face and the interrelationships between these problems.

◊ Add more cards if needed to complete the cause and effect logic. If you have an effect, you need to look for its cause. If you have a cause, you need to look for its effect. Some cards will represent both a cause and effect.

For example, a card stating that 25% of wives in this community report that they are being beaten by their husbands is the effect of multiple causes – inequality of power, misuse of power, lack of respect, poor communication skills, insufficient training in non-violent dispute resolution, and so on. But it is also a cause with multiple effects – physical harm, domestic terror, personal injury, social alienation, family fragmentation, and so on.

◊ Take away cards that are repetitive.

◊ Rewrite cards that are vague.

◊ Review the "problems tree" to make sure everyone present agrees with the problem analysis.

◊ *Don't forget to keep a copy of your problem analysis in your working notes.*

3.3. Solutions Analysis

30 minutes

The third step is to identify desired improvements, and the relationships between these desired improvements, indicating means (causes) and ends (effects)

◊ Restate all the problem statements in the problems tree as *positive, desirable* and *realistic outcomes* – described as if they have already happened (e.g., 100% of wives in this community report they are not being abused by their husbands).

◊ Reword the resolution of the focal problem as an outcome and write it on a card without a red circle just like all the others. To build your "solutions tree," place this card at the top of your workspace.

A solutions tree allows you to visualize the range of potential improvements and the relationships between them. This time you will work not from the centre out, but from *top to bottom*.

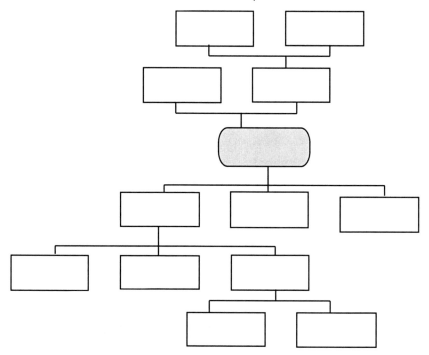

Figure 33. The solutions tree[102]

◊ Review the cards to make sure they are realistic and reword them if necessary.

◊ Add or delete cards to ensure the means-to-end logic is valid. To check the means-to-end logic, read the tree from the *bottom up*.

◊ Place the cards on a paper, and draw connecting lines to show the means-ends relationships between the outcomes.

Note that the solutions tree should look very much like the problems tree, but framed in positive rather than negative terms.

For example: The card stating that 100% of wives in this community report they are not being abused by their husbands is the effect of multiple causes – equality of power, use of power for assertion rather than aggression, mutual respect, rich communication skills, sufficient training in non-violent dispute resolution, and so on. But it is also a

---
[102] *Project Planning for Development* (Durban: Olive, 1994), p. 41.

cause with multiple effects – physical health, domestic peace, personal safety, social integration, family intimacy, and so on.

◊ *Don't forget to keep a copy of your solutions tree in your working notes.*

3.4. Alternatives Analysis

20 minutes

The fourth step is to identify alternative ways of making an impact on the problems identified, assessing the feasibility of the alternatives and selecting a strategy

◊ Study the range of solutions on the solutions tree. Each card should represent a solution objective that could be achieved.

◊ Study the range of objectives on the solutions tree. Each card should represent an objective that could be achieved.

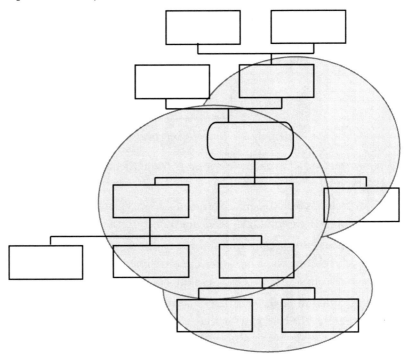

Figure 34. Solutions tree with "means-ends ladders"[103]

---

[103] *Project Planning,* p. 46.

◊ Identify the different "means-ends ladders" that present themselves in the solutions tree and outline these with a pen. These represent different options for different strategies – and some may overlap.

◊ Eliminate the strategies that are:
- Unethical
- Unrealistic
- Beyond your capacity at the moment
- Being conducted by another group in your area.

◊ Select a strategy and discuss the implications for different participants. The matrix below is a simple tool that can help with this selection.[104] For example:

Options/ Alternatives	Positive implications	Negative implications
1. Advocating equality of power	Ethical Realistic Possible	But a direct immediate threat to the traditional societal structures
2. Training in non-violent dispute resolution	Ethical Realistic Possible	None

Figure 35: An alternative options matrix

◊ Don't forget to keep a copy of your matrix in your working notes.

◊ Keep the cards and the pieces of paper for the next session.

4.   CONCLUSION

10 minutes

Note: Two learning partners are required for you to do the next session. If you don't organize for two learning partners to be present – you can't do it!

The follow-up reading for this session is:
- James Bosscher and Carol Doornbos's "Reaching Out – One Church's Story," in *Caring for the Least of These*, pp. 107–13, a case study of church planning for local community work (Reading 10).

---

[104] *Project Planning*, p. 47.

The set community tasks for this session are:

◊ Meet with your learning partner and your community development support group.

◊ Share what you learned in this session about planning. Look for an opportunity for your group to work through the four steps in analysis for planning – participants analysis, problems analysis, solutions analysis and alternatives analysis – with the people from the community you had in mind when you did the planning exercise.

◊ Consider whether there might be a wider group of participants with whom you can work through these steps. If appropriate, plan to do so this week.

◊ *Ensure you record your actions, reflections and conclusions in your working notes.*

◊ *Please note: You need to organize two learning partners to be with you in order to do the next session.*

COMMUNITY WORK SKILL 5 – PLANNING (B)

1. PREPARATION

Please note: You need to organize two learning partners to be with you in order to do this session.

1.1. Objectives

- To review your planning skills
- To extend your understanding of the importance of planning

2. REVIEW

15 minutes

Review the work from the previous session. This will include a review of your appreciation of issues raised in the course notes, clarified in the follow-up readings and your experience of set community tasks.

Review the issues raised in the last session, particularly your understanding of analysis for planning.

Review the reading:

James Bosscher and Carol Doornbos's "Reaching Out – One Church's Story" (Reading 10).

Review the tasks:

1. How did it go meeting with your community development support group and sharing what you learned about planning?

2. What was the most important thing you learned while doing the community tasks for the last session?

Finish the review with a reflection on how it went trying to do some planning with a wider group of participants from the community. If you weren't able to do this, think of a way that you might be able to do so in the near future.

◊ *Be sure to record your reflections in your working notes.*

3.   DESIGN

15 minutes

The second phase of planning is *design*.[105] We will consider using the project approach for this. The project then becomes the "box" in which the planned community development is packaged.[106] There are four steps in the design phase of a project:
1.   Project frame
2.   Project elements
3.   Project assumptions
4.   Project indicators.

The main advantages of the project approach are:
- It provides a new, neat and tidy organized program.
- It requires clear objectives, outputs, inputs and activities.
- It encourages a systematic approach to community development.
- It facilitates the control of funds invested in the project by donors.

The main disadvantages of the project approach are:
- It encourages the idea of adopting a new, neat and tidy program.
- It discourages the idea of muddling through with existing activities.
- If the design is flawed, then the program will be flawed. No matter how well organized the program may be, garbage in = garbage out.
- It focuses on investment concerns and facilitates investor control – which may undermine ownership of the program by local people.

Think of a community development project you know of and identify the strengths and weaknesses of doing community work as a packaged project.

◊ *Be sure to record your reflections in your working notes.*

---

[105] Adapted from Durban, *Project Planning.*
[106] Adapted from B. Broughton, *Project Planning, Monitoring and Evaluation Training Course* (Canberra: Australian Council for Overseas Aid, 1996).

3.1. Project Frame

30 minutes

The first step is to identify a framework for project planning

The logical framework, or log frame, was developed during the late 1960s as a tool for development project planning.

	Project Elements	Indicators	External Factors or Assumptions
Objectives {	Development Objective/ Goal		
	Immediate Objective/ Project Purpose		
Project Area {	Results/ Outputs		
	Activities		
	Inputs		

Figure 36. The log frame for project planning[107]

The logical framework approach is rather jargon bound, and it is important to understand what the commonly used terms really mean. Following is a brief description of how we shall use the terms:

Project elements. This refers to the narrative description of the program at each of the five levels of the hierarchy used in the log frame.

Development goal. This term refers to the program objectives to which the project is designed to contribute (e.g., reduced violence).

Immediate objective. This is what the project is expected to achieve in development terms within the community (e.g., reduced domestic violence in church families). Note that there may be more than one objective.

---

[107] *Project Planning for Development* (Durban: Olive, 1994), p. 75.

Outputs or results. These are the specific results and tangible products produced by undertaking a series of tasks or activities (e.g., reduced incidents of domestic violence in church families). Note that each objective usually has a number of outputs.

Activities or procedures. These are the specific tasks undertaken to achieve the required outputs (e.g., workshops on dealing with domestic violence).

Inputs or resources. These are the resources required to do the work (such as personnel, equipment and materials for workshops).

Risks. These are conditions which could affect the success of the project, but over which the project manager has no direct control (e.g., higher salary costs for personnel).

Pre-requisites. These are conditions for successful program implementation and prior obligations that need to be fulfilled by agencies involved in the project before the project properly begins (e.g., community group formation).

Means-ends relationships. Constructing the project description involves a detailed breakdown of the chain of causality implicit in project design. Each level depends upon the completion of other elements in order to achieve results. In other words:

- *If* inputs are provided, *then* activities can be undertaken.
- *If* activities are undertaken, *then* outputs will be produced.
- *If* outputs are produced, *then* objectives will be achieved.
- *If* objectives are met, *then* the project will have contributed towards achieving the overall development goal.

It is important, therefore, that inputs are sufficient to allow activities to be undertaken, and so on up the hierarchy. It is usual, however, to start constructing the matrix from the goal down, before working back up the hierarchy to ensure that resources are sufficient to undertake the required activities.

It is useful to standardize the way in which the hierarchy of project objectives is described in the matrix. In particular, this helps the reader to recognize more easily what is an objective, an output or an activity.

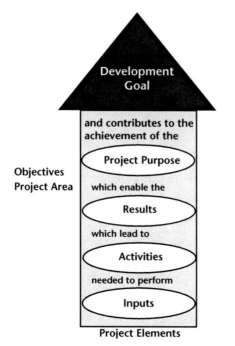

Figure 37. The elements of project planning[108]

The following convention can, therefore, be helpful: describe goals and objectives in the infinitive ("to do something"); describe an output in the future perfect ("something will have been done"); and describe an activity/input in the present ("do something"). For example:

1)   *Goal* – To reduce domestic violence

2)   *Objective* – To reduce domestic violence in the church

3)   *Outputs* –

- Incidents of domestic violence in church families will have been identified.

- Families with a history of domestic violence will have been trained in alternative dispute resolution.

- Families with a history of domestic violence will have begun to practise alternative dispute resolution.

- Incidents of domestic violence in church families will have been reduced.

---

[108] *Project Planning*, p. 76.

4)   Activities –

- Identify families with a history of domestic violence.
- Advise of need for training in alternative dispute resolution.
- Recruit capable trainers in alternative dispute resolution.
- Organize workshops on alternative dispute resolution.
- Run workshops on alternative dispute resolution.

5)   *Inputs* –

- Two church counsellors
- Two alternative dispute resolution trainers
- Church facilities for workshop venue
- Training costs.

Before we move on, check that you all understand the terms in the log frame. Take it in turns to name a term and ask the others in the group to say what it means and give an example of it.

What is a goal?

What is an objective?

What is an output?

What is an activity?

What is an input?

3.2. Project Elements

30 minutes

The second step is to connect the analysis with elements of the project

1)   Start with the development goal. Look at the alternative you selected as your project strategy as a result of your alternatives analysis at the end of the last session. Study those cards you identified as being part of the means-end strategy.

Identify which card expresses the benefit the people will experience.

This becomes the *development goal*.

What is your development goal?

2)   Identify a card at the next level down which expresses how people in your community will need to act differently to bring about your goal.

This becomes your *immediate objective*.

1. What is your immediate objective?

2. What is the relationship between your goal and your objective?

3. What resources does the project need in order for it to run these activities?

3)   Look at your immediate objective and ask: "What must the project deliver for it to achieve this immediate objective?" Brainstorm and write down ideas on cards.

Then come to a consensus on the *outputs or results* of the project.

What results must the project deliver for it to achieve its objective?

4)   Take each result and generate a list of all the activities which are needed to achieve it. Set out these *activities* in a logical sequence and number them.

What activities are needed to deliver these results?

5)   Look at your list of activities and ask: "What does the project need in order for it to run these activities?" Brainstorm and write down ideas on cards.

Then come to consensus on the necessary *inputs or resources* for the project.

What does the project need in order for it to run these activities?

◊ Check that these resources are relevant, necessary and enough, and also that these resources are quantified and costed correctly.

◊ *Be sure to record your reflections in your working notes.*

3.3. Project Assumptions

10 minutes

The third step is to consider the assumptions made in planning the project

◊ Identify factors outside the project's control which could influence the success or failure of the project.

◊ Write these factors on cards – wording them positively, not negatively.

◊ Then assess the importance and probability of these assumptions for achieving the objective of the Project Planning Matrix (PPM).

1. How important – or how crucial – are your assumptions to the success of the plan?

2. How probable – or how likely – is it that the assumptions you are making are valid?

3. How can you design the project so that killer assumptions don't finish it off before it even starts?

The following is a procedure for assessing the importance and probability of assumptions – and for identifying killer assumptions that constitute fatal planning flaws.

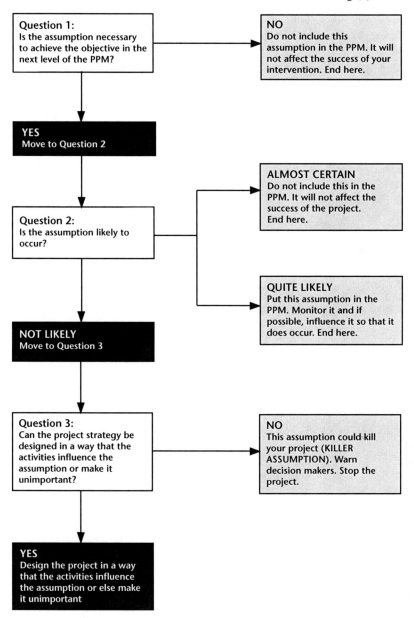

Figure 38. The "Killer Assumptions" test questionnaire[109]

---

[109] *Project Planning,* p. 66.

◊ Run all the assumptions you are making in your plan through the "Killer Assumptions Test Questionnaire."

3.4. Project Indicators

10 minutes

The fourth and final step is to identify indicators for monitoring project planning

It is important to specify each of the *objectives* in detail. These should be:

- Realistic
- Achievable
- Measurable.

What are the specific objectives of the project?

It is important to identify appropriate *indicators* for each specific objective. These should be:

- Independent
- Attainable
- Factual
- Plausible
- Verifiable.

What are the best indicators for each specific objective?

Last but not least, it is important to identify how evidence will be checked. In addition all sources of information for verification need to be cited.

1. What information is needed?

2. By when is it needed?

3. In what form is it needed?

4. Who should provide it?

5. Is all of this possible or not? (If not, try again!)

◊ *Be sure to record your reflections in your working notes.*

◊ Keep the cards and the pieces of paper for the next session.

4.   CONCLUSION

10 minutes

The follow-up reading for this session is:

* Tim Muirhouse's "Participative Action Research," in *Weaving Tapestries* (Mount Hawthorn: LGCSA[WA], 2002), pp. 38–41, on community project planning (Reading 11).

The set community tasks for this session are:

◊ Meet with your learning partner and your community development support group.

◊ Share what you learned in this session about planning. Work through the four steps in analysis for planning: project frame, project elements, project assumptions and project indicators, in your group.

◊ Consider whether there might be a wider group of participants with whom you can work through these steps. If appropriate, plan to do so this week.

◊ Look for an opportunity for your group to work through the four steps in design for planning – project frame, project elements, project assumptions and project indicators – with the people from the community you had in mind when you started this planning exercise.

◊ *Ensure you record actions, reflections and conclusions in your working notes.*

COMMUNITY WORK SKILL 6 – BUDGETING

1. PREPARATION

1.1. Objectives

- To review your planning skills
- To consider the next in a series of community work skills – budgeting

2. REVIEW

15 minutes

Review your work from the previous session. This will include a review of your appreciation of issues raised in class and clarified in the follow-up readings and your experience of set community tasks.

Review the issues raised in the last session, particularly your understanding of design for planning.

Review the reading:

Tim Muirhouse's "Participative Action Research" (Reading 11).

Review the tasks:

1. How did it go meeting with your community development support group and sharing what you learned in class about planning?

2. What was the most important thing you learned while doing the community tasks for the last session?

If you haven't able to do any planning with a wider group of participants from the community, think of whether there may be some underlying issues that you need to deal with before you can proceed.

What do you think that those issues might be?

How do you think you might deal with them?

Finish the review with a reflection on how it went trying to do some planning with a wider group of participants from the community.

◊ *Be sure to record your reflections in your working notes.*

3.   PROJECT BUDGETS

30 minutes

The budget should be a realistic estimate of the costs of the inputs or resources needed for operating the activities of the project. Cost estimates should be broken down into logical categories such as:

- Salaries
- Supplies
- Materials
- Equipment
- Travel
- Telephone
- Postage

◊ Look back over your working notes to see how you answered the question in section 3.2 of Session 23 about inputs or resources.

What resources does this project need in order to run these activities?

◊ Check that:

- These resources are relevant, necessary and enough.
- These resources are quantified and costed correctly.

◊ Write out a simple budget for your project. On the left-hand side of a page list costs; on the right-hand side list income.

◊ *Be sure to record your reflections in your working notes.*

Budgets need to be:

- Realistic
- Achievable
- Measurable
- Not in deficit. If it is, the next big question is:

How are you going to get the income you need to run the project?

4.   PROJECT FUNDS

20 minutes

Most community projects do *not* get external sources of funding. These projects have to rely on internal sources of funding. That is, community development workers have to fund their own projects!

◊ Check the budget to see whether you listed your own voluntary contributions as income or not. If you did list your own contributions, it's great that you recognize the value of your voluntary contributions. If you didn't list your own contributions, it's about time you recognized their value.

◊ Make a list of all voluntary contributions available – time, money, expertise and materials – and assign them a total monetary value in the right-hand column of your budget.

◊ Check whether the budget is still framed in terms of a deficit or not. If the budget isn't in deficit – good! If the budget is still in deficit, you need to ask:

1. Are there any other ways you can reduce the cost of the project?

2. Are there any other ways you can contribute more to the project yourselves?

◊ Revise your budget once again.

◊ *Don't forget to keep a record of your budget in your working notes.*

If the budget isn't in deficit – good! If the budget is still in deficit, you need to ask:

Are there any other ways you can get funds for the project?

The two most usual ways for getting funds from other sources are *fund-raising* and *funds-sourcing*.

4.1. Fund-Raising

15 minutes

Fund-raising involves either raising the funds ourselves or employing a professional fund-raiser. Most groups who need to raise funds, however, don't have the funds to pay a professional to raise funds for them. So they have to do it themselves.

But the decision needs to be made: "How much time and effort do we really want to invest in fund-raising?"

It is often easier to cut costs or increase our own contributions than it is to do fund-raising on top of everything else.

> How much time and effort do you really want to invest in fund-raising?

Once you have decided how much time and effort you want to invest, then you need to consider fund-raising options.

Whether you choose a traditional fund-raiser – like a cake stall – or a modern fund-raiser – like a three-course meal – it will still involve investing voluntary labour in generating activities to raise funds.

The quickest way I know to raise funds is to ask 20 people you know to give a small specified amount.

However, fund-raising is usually very slow. But, if it is done well, it can play a significant role in raising more awareness and encouraging more ownership of a project. Lots of people can contribute towards a project through a fund-raising event and – through the fund-raiser – find out about other ways that they can become more involved in a project.

> What fund-raising activities could you engage in to raise funds for your project?

◊ *Don't forget to keep a record of your ideas in your working notes.*

◊ If you are going to raise your own funds, spend the rest of this session devising a fund-raising strategy.

◊ If you feel the need to source your funds, spend the rest of this session exploring fund-sourcing options, below.

4.2. Funds-Sourcing

40 minutes

If we choose to source funds, we need to remember that all funds from other sources come with strings attached – and there is usually very little room for negotiating or renegotiating the terms.[110]

So we need to choose sources for funds that have terms that we believe we can live with – or not access other sources of funds at all.

1. Brainstorm some possible sources for funds for your group.

2. Think through some of the kinds of stipulations you may be asked to follow when you accept funds from other sources and draft a working policy for your group. What are you willing to give up in terms of control? What are your non-negotiables?

◊ *Don't forget to keep a record of your ideas in your working notes.*

Once you have decided on the terms you can and can't live with, if you still want to access other sources of funds you need to look for a funding source with terms that are consistent with your conditions.

The options include *government grants and contracts, philanthropic foundations, development organizations* and *corporate sponsorships*.

Government grants

Governments recycle resources from the community, and as such they are a major source of funds for the community.

Community needs always exceed the resources available from the government so government agencies allocate resources according to a certain set of criteria.

Most government agencies require a detailed application for funding and rank submissions on the basis of conformity to government guidelines, past performances and policy priorities.

What government funds do you know of that you might be able to tap into for your project?

◊ *Don't forget to keep a record of your ideas in your working notes.*

---

[110] Adapted from S. Kenny, *Developing Communities for the Future* (Melbourne: Nelson, 1994), pp. 189–201.

Philanthropic foundations

Many community groups access charitable trusts. However, in Australia there are relatively few charitable trusts and competition for funds is great.

Charitable trusts vary greatly in their philosophies. Not all are sympathetic to community development, but many do support community development projects.

Most charitable trusts also require a detailed application for funding.

> What philanthropic funds are you aware of that you might be able to tap into for your project?

◊ *Don't forget to keep a record of your ideas in your working notes.*

Development organizations

Many community groups also access development agencies. Most development agencies in Australia focus on addressing issues related to poverty.

Development agencies tend to place a priority on supporting projects in poorer communities overseas. Occasionally in Australia, however, they will support projects in poorer communities – especially projects working with indigenous people.

Most development agencies also require a detailed application for funding.

> What organizational funds do you know of that you could tap into for your project?

◊ *Don't forget to keep a record of your ideas in your working notes.*

Corporate sponsorships

Although many community groups tend to be suspicious of corporations and corporate sponsorships, some groups do receive funds from these sources. Anyone seeking corporate sponsorships would need to be happy to be publicly associated with the company sponsoring them.

> What corporate funds do you know of that you could tap into for your project?

◊ *Don't forget to keep a record of your ideas in your working notes.*

◊ Check the list of funding sources for community projects in the funding options section below, along with the lists that you have made in your working notes in this session, and consider the various funding options these lists present for your project.

1. What are the funding options that might be helpful for your project?

2. Which would you consider to be the top ten funding possibilities?

3. How would you rank the top ten possibilities – from 1 (the most beneficial) to 10 (the least beneficial)?

Don't forget to keep a record of your ideas in your working notes.

◊ Consider the possibilities of securing funding from these sources.

Nominate the most beneficial source of funds for which you are most likely to be eligible.

◊ *Don't forget to keep a record of your ideas in your working notes.*

5.   FUNDING OPTIONS

Micah is a network of agencies and churches with common interests in Christian community development around the world. Appendix D lists some of the over 275 members of Micah with whom you could talk about funding options for compassionate faith-based community work in your region.

6.   CONCLUSION

10 minutes

The follow-up reading for this session is:

• David Bos's "Starting and Developing Community Ministry," in *A Practical Guide to Community Ministry* (Louisville: Westminster, 1993), pp. 45–74 (Reading 12).

The set community tasks for this session are:

◊ Meet with your community development support group and share what you learned in class about budgeting and work through the budgeting process with the group. Consider fund-raising options together. Consider your nomination for most likely external funding option. Try to get as much information about it as you can so you can report back about it next week.

Note: Do *not* talk to the wider community about applying for funds from funding agencies prematurely, lest you raise unrealistic expectations.

◊ *Ensure you record your actions, reflections and conclusions in your working notes.*

COMMUNITY WORK SKILL 7 – REPORTING

1. PREPARATION

1.1. Objectives

- To review your budgeting skills
- To consider the next in a series of community work skills – reporting

2. REVIEW

15 minutes

Review the work from the previous session. This will include a review of your appreciation of issues raised in the course notes, clarified in the follow-up readings and your experience of set community tasks.

Review the issues raised in the course notes in the previous session, particularly your understanding of budgeting.

Review the reading:

David Bos's "Starting and Developing Community Ministry" (Reading 12).

Review the tasks:

1. If you decided to do fund-raising, how did you find devising a funding strategy? If you decided to pursue fund-sourcing, how did it go researching funding agencies?

2. What was the most important thing you learned while doing the community tasks for the last session?

◊ Be sure to record your reflections in your working notes.

3.   APPLICATIONS

45 minutes

3.1. Preparing Applications

The way that we *prepare* our applications for funding is crucial to our funding.[111]

When writing an application for funding for a project it is important to remember that applying is a competitive process. It is crucial that great care is taken in preparing the application.

Applications are all about *packaging* our plans in the most attractive way possible in order to procure the funding we need to make the project a reality.

The integrity and credibility of the plan are important, but so is the delivery, or the "package," of the plan. It needs to attract the attention of those from whom you are seeking funding.

It is therefore necessary to:

- Obtain information about the funding rounds and processes of the agency you are applying to, to be sure of your approach.
- Check if the organization has any guidelines for writing applications.
- Seek information on priorities for funding, such as whether particular issues or types of organization are given preference.
- Make sure that you know your field – what other organizations are doing in this field and whether other organizations are applying as well.
- Seek an opportunity to meet with representatives of the agency, but do not be too pushy. If it is appropriate, meet over lunch – but the conversation should focus on matters that are relevant to the application.

Meeting with representatives of the agency is very important:

- To open up channels of communication with the funder
- To make sure we are approaching our preparation correctly
- To put a personal face to an impersonal application.

---

[111] Adapted from Kenny, *Developing Communities*, p. 199.

1. What were you able to find out about your most likely funding option?

2. How relevant were the criteria they required for funding a project like yours?

If it isn't relevant, forget it. If it is still relevant, then consider other options and try again.

3.2. Writing Applications

The way that we *write* our applications for funding is crucial to our funding.[112]

If the agency has any guidelines for writing applications, always follow these guidelines.

If the agency has no guidelines, we need to research whatever materials we can to give us clues as to the appropriate language and style to use in writing the application.

It is important to state clearly:

- The title of the project
- The rationale for the project
- The objectives of the project
- The strategies of the project
- The management of the project
- The plan for evaluation of the project
- The actual budget for the project.

Further:

- Include a realistic budget, including details such as standard rates of pay.
- Do not inflate costs, but indicate where cut backs might be possible.
- The application should be clear, brief, easy to read and written in the language and style of the funder.

Finally check that you:

- Identify the project objectives in terms of the funder's criteria.
- Describe the project activities in terms of the funder's criteria.
- Package the project so as to meet the funder's expectations.

---

[112] Adapted from Kenny, *Developing Communities*, pp. 202–203.

1. Why is it important to write your application in the language of the funder?

2. What are the dangers of "packaging" your project for the funder?

3. How can you package the project both honestly and attractively?

◊ *Don't forget to keep a record of your reflections in your working notes.*

Note: Funding applications are *very* competitive. It is possible to minimize the competition even in the process of applying. If you are aware that other groups like yours in the area are applying for the same funding, contact them to talk about either writing a joint application – as agencies implementing a single project together – or writing complementary applications – as collaborating agencies implementing complementary projects.

3.3. Submitting Applications

The way that we *submit* our applications for funding is crucial to our funding.[113]

It is quite acceptable to submit an application to more than one funder at the same time, as long as you indicate to each of the funders that this is what you are doing.

It is important to remember, however, that each application needs to be written with the specific expectations of each particular funder in mind.

Wherever possible, deliver the submission by hand and give it to the representative of the agency whom you have met with personally.

If it is not possible to deliver the submission by hand, then phone beforehand to let them know you are sending it in and phone afterwards to make sure that they actually received the application.

After the agency has received the application, ask your contact if he or she would check it over and let you know whether or not they think it is complete. If they don't think it is, ask if they would send it back with any suggestions to improve it.

If this happens, it is important to rewrite and resubmit the application as quickly as possible.

Note: Submit all applications with a covering letter from the person in charge of your project and supporting letters for the project from

---

[113] Adapted from Kenny, *Developing Communities*, p. 204.

other groups and agencies in your area. Both the covering letter and the supporting letters should state:

- Why your project is important to your area at this time
- What you hope to accomplish through the project
- Who will be helped through the project
- Why the project should be funded.

What kind of covering letter would you write for your project?

◊ Draft a covering letter.

◊ *Don't forget to keep a copy of your letter in your working notes.*

4.   EVALUATIONS

60 minutes

◊ Write the answers to the following questions on cards and put them on the table:

1. What is evaluation?
2. Why is it important?
3. Who is it for?

◊ *Don't forget to keep a record of your reflections in your working notes.*

4.1. Appreciating Evaluation

Appreciative inquiry is an evaluation approach that is "valuing" rather than "de-valuing." According to appreciative inquiry:[114]

1)   Evaluation should begin with an *appreciation* of "what is."

The basic principle assumes that every social system 'works' to some degree and that it is a primary task of research to discover, describe and explain those social innovations, however small, which serve to give 'life' to the system and activate members' energies.

---

[114] The following quoted material is from Cooperrider and Srivasta, "Appreciative Inquiry," pp. 129–60.

2)   Evaluation should always be *provocative*, taking the best of "what is" and generating challenging images of "what might be."

> Appreciative knowledge of what is (in terms of peak social innovations in organizing) is suggestive of 'what might be" and can be used to generate images of realistic developmental opportunities that can be experimented with.

3)   Evaluation should always be *collaborative*, including the members and not just the management of the organization in an open, ongoing dialogue.

> There is an inseparable relationship between the process of the inquiry and its content. A collaborative relationship between the researcher and the members of an organization is, therefore, deemed essential.

4)   Appreciative inquiry does not avoid underlying issues – on the contrary, it gladly embraces the "mysteries" of life. It is unashamedly *spiritual*.

> Organization is a miracle of co-operative human interaction of which there can be no final explanation. There simply are no organizational theories that can give account for the life-giving essence of co-operative existence.

5)   This perspective is not seen as disempowering, but rather as *empowering*.

> The re-enchantment of the world gives rise to 'a consciousness' where there is a sense of personal stake and partnership with the universe.

1. How do you respond to these statements?

2. How do they compare with your own views?

◊ *Don't forget to keep a record of your reflections in your working notes.*

4.2. Evaluating Appreciatively

According to appreciative inquiry,[115] research in sociology shows that:

- when people study problems, the number and severity of the problems they identify actually *increase*:
- when they study human ideals, peak experiences and best practices, *these* things – not the problems – tend to flourish.

So it is important to shift the focus of evaluation *from* the gaps *to* the accomplishments.

Instead of asking, "What hasn't worked?" we need to say: "Describe a time when things were going really well around here. What conditions were present at those moments? What changes now would allow more of those conditions to prevail again?"

There are five phases in the *appreciative inquiry* process:

Phase one – definition

This is not a definition of the problem or a definition of a solution, but rather the definition of "what you would like to learn more about."

Phase two – discovery

Through multiple formal interviews and informal conversations, seek peak experiences and best-practice examples on the topic you would like to learn more about.

Phase three – dream

Then generalize from these specific examples, generating images of how the group might be able to function at its best.

Phase four – design

Develop individual and collective options that the group thinks might be worth experimenting with in order to function at its best.

Phase five – delivery

Experiment with options that might deliver more best-practice innovations and celebrate any success at all, no matter how small.

1. How do you personally respond to this approach to evaluation?

2. How do you think this method of evaluation could help your project move forward?

◊ *Don't forget to keep a record of your reflections in your working notes.*

---

[115] Adapted from Cooperrider and Srivasta, "Appreciative Inquiry," pp. 129–60.

Note that anyone can do appreciative inquiry . . .

◊ The next time you have a few moments with your learning partner, say something like: "I'm curious to know what you think of as the really good times we have had together. Would you tell me what stands out in your memory?"

◊ The next time you evaluate a colleague's performance, ask them to tell you about the times when they felt they were most effective in their work – and then ask them what they think they could learn from that in order to increase the frequency of those times of effectiveness in the future.

◊ The next time someone in an organization you are a part of wants to talk with you about the organization, ask them to describe to you what they believe the organization does best. Also ask them to offer any ideas as to how the organization could do more of that in the future.

Note that:[116]

> The learnings that surround the *appreciative inquiry* process begin to shift the collective image that people hold of the organization. In their daily encounters, members start to create together compelling new images of the future. These images initiate small ripples in how employees think about the work they do, their relationships, their roles and so on. Over time these ripples turn into waves. The more positive questions people ask, the more they incorporate the learnings they glean from those questions in daily behaviour, and ultimately in the organization's infrastructure.

And that:

> Unlike many behavioural science approaches, *appreciative inquiry* does not focus on changing people. Instead it *invites* people to engage in building the kinds of communities they want to live in. [It assumes that people are] competent adults – capable of learning from their experiences *and* from the experiences of others.

---

[116] The following quotes are from Bernard Mohr, "Appreciative Inquiry: Igniting Transformative Action," in *The Systems Thinker*, 12.1 (Waltham, MA: Pegasus Communications, Feb. 2001), pp. 1–5.

4.3. Formalizing Evaluations

If we fund our project ourselves, we may be satisfied with *informal* evaluation.

If others fund our project, they will expect regular, *formal* evaluation reports. They are less concerned with the *dynamics* of evaluation. Whether the evaluation process is appreciative or not is not their concern. But they are more concerned with the *indicators* for the evaluation. In other words, they are concerned with whether or not the evaluation report is accurate.

It is a good guideline to ensure that our indicators for the objectives of our project are SMART:

- **S**imple
- **M**easurable
- **A**chievable
- **R**ealistic
- **T**imely

What are the SMART indicators of the objectives of your project?

◊ *Don't forget to keep a record of your indicators in your working notes.*

These indicators of the objectives of our project should be:

- Independent
- Attainable
- Factual
- Plausible
- Verifiable

What are the best indicators you could use for each specific objective?

◊ *Don't forget to keep a record of your best indicators in your working notes.*

Last, but not least, we need to provide evidence to support these indicators. Such evidence may include:

- Observations
- Interviews
- Anecdotes
- Records
- Minutes
- Accounts
- Inventories
- Documents

1. What would be the best kind of evidence for your indicators?

2. How could you gather this evidence? How could you keep it?

3. How could you best present this evidence in a formal report to a funder?

◊ *Don't forget to keep a record of your reflections in your working notes.*

4.4. Framing Evaluations

We can frame our informal evaluation in our own terms, but we need to frame our formal evaluation in the same terms as our application – in the funder's terms.

If the agency has any guidelines for writing an evaluation, it is imperative that we follow their guidelines in our writing.

If the agency has no guidelines, we need to find whatever materials we can to give us a clue as to the appropriate language and style for writing our evaluation.

It is important to state clearly:

- The title of the project
- The rationale for the project
- The objectives of the project
- The strategies of the project
- The management of the project
- The plan for evaluation of the project
- The actual budget for the project.

Further:

- The activities of the project
- The accounts of the project
- The objectives of the project
- The indicators of the objectives
- The evidence for these indicators
- An appreciation of the accomplishments.

Note that:

- If we have not kept to the budget, we should indicate any changes.
- We should also account for, and justify, any changes in the budget.
- It is important to ensure that the evaluation is clear, brief and easy to read, and that it is written in the language and style of the funder.

Finally it is important to:

- Identify the project objectives in terms of the funder's criteria
- Identify the indicators of the objectives in the funder's terms
- Identify the evidence for the indicators in the funder's terms
- Describe the activities and accounts in the funder's terms
- Package the report so as to meet the funder's expectations.

Write a few notes on how you would draft a report on your project to a specific funder.

◊ *Don't forget to keep a record of your reflections in your working notes.*

5.   CONCLUSION

10 minutes

The follow-up reading for this session is:

- Ross Langmead's "Community: The Vision (Revisited)" *A Westgate Paper* (No. 3) (Melbourne: Westgate Baptist, 1984), pp. 1–6, a report on one experiment with church community work (Reading 13).

The set community tasks for this session are:

◊ Meet with your learning partner and your community development support group.

◊ Share what you learned in this session about writing applications and evaluations. Consider whether you need to write a report of your work.

◊ Also look for opportunities to practise "appreciative inquiry" at home and at work, in the church community and in the local community.

◊ Prepare a ten-minute report on the work you've done throughout this course. The report should be framed around: the tasks you attempted; strategies you tried; your successes; your failures; the lessons you have learned.

This report should demonstrate an understanding of community work within the framework of your own spirituality, theoretically and practically. Honesty, authenticity and creativity in these presentations are important.

◊ *Ensure you record actions, reflections and conclusions in your working notes.*

COMMUNITY WORK SKILL 8 – SUPPORTING

1. PREPARATION

1.1. Objectives

- To review your reporting skills
- To consider the last in the series of community work skills – supporting

2. REVIEW

15 minutes

Review your work from the previous session. This will include a review of your appreciation of the issues raised in the course notes and clarified in the follow-up readings and your experience of your set community tasks.

Review the issues raised in the session last week, particularly your understanding of reporting.

Review the reading:

Ross Langmead's "Community: The Vision (Revisited)" (Reading 13).

Review the tasks:

1. How did you find meeting with your community development support group and sharing what you learned in class about writing applications and evaluations?

2. How did you find practising appreciative inquiry at home, at work and at church?

3. What was the most important thing you learned while doing the community tasks for the last session?

◊ *Ensure you keep a record of your report in your working notes.*

3.   Supporting People in Development

3.1. The Importance of Support

10 minutes

It is not easy working for community development. Even when we are working *with* people, we may not feel supported *by* people. At some stage, we may find ourselves being able to support others more than they can support us. At another stage, we may find ourselves in unresolved conflicts with the people with whom we are working.

Jan McNicol, a community worker from Brisbane, says "without a support network for the things I am on about," it is "harder for me to maintain my truth" and keep going.[117]

We all need to make sure that we get the support that we need.

How can you make sure you and your group get the support that you need?

◊ *Be sure to record your reflections in your working notes.*

Note that there are many ways of setting up support for people in development.[118] Some of the ways that we will explore below include:

- Phone check-ins
- Internet connections
- Networking parties
- Clearness meetings
- Senior mentors
- Peer monitors
- Personal coaches

---

[117] Shields, *In the Tiger's Mouth*, p. 104.
[118] Shields, *In the Tiger's Mouth*, p. 115.

4. SUPPORT OPTIONS

10 minutes

4.1. Phone Check-Ins

Many community workers are working in communities in which the people do not have a deep understanding of what they are doing.

So, many community workers look for support from people outside their communities who are doing the same kind of work.

Support from other community workers can be as near as the phone. It's just a matter of phoning up an appropriate person and asking for a few minutes of their time to chat on the phone. It is important, when phoning, to assure the person on the other end of the phone that this matter will only take a few minutes. If it is an unscheduled phone call, it is also important to say that, if it is inconvenient, you would be happy to phone back at a more convenient time.

A phone check-in involves a person simply talking about how the last day, week, fortnight or month has been going and how they feel about it. Generally a phone check-in will only take two or three minutes. It could go as long as five minutes, but it shouldn't go any longer than that. The purpose of the check-in is to have a hearing, not counselling.

1. Do you have someone you can call for a phone check-in?

2. If you do have someone, how do you feel about the kind of support you're receiving from them?

3. If you don't have one, how could you find one?

◊ *Be sure to record your reflections in your working notes.*

4.2. Internet Connections

10 minutes

Many community workers also find support from people outside their communities who are doing the same kind of work.

Sometimes they can find support on the end of a phone, sometimes they cannot. The world wide web helps them to cast their net wider.

The disadvantages of internet connections are that the cyber-poor can't access them – only the cyber-rich can; they create virtual connections rather than real connections; and at worst they can reduce personal communication to impersonal information exchange.

But the great advantage of internet connections is that they can be accessed anytime of the day, anywhere in the world. This gives people access to wider connections, more conversations, more information; and the potential for mobilizing people around a particular cause of concern.

1. Do you have community work internet connections?

2. If you do, what are they and how well do they work?

3. If you don't, where would you go to find some?

◊ *Be sure to record your reflections in your working notes.*

Appendix E lists some helpful support connections that can be accessed on the internet.

4.3. A Networking Party

10 minutes

A networking party is an opportunity to get together with the people we know who have a common interest in community work. All that is involved is inviting a group of people who share an interest in community work to your home for an evening. Provide drinks and munchies and a comfortable, welcoming atmosphere. Then settle in for a night of sharing about what people do, what they need, and what they can do to help meet one another's needs.

This may lead to developing an informal support network, or a formal support network of some kind.

1. Have you ever had a networking party?

2. If so, how did you organize it and how did it go?

3. If not, how would you go about organizing one?

◊ *Be sure to record your reflections in your working notes.*

4.4. A Clearness Meeting

10 Minutes

A clearness meeting is a process through which a community worker asks for feedback from people they trust and respect. It is a process in which clarity is sought – not permission or approval. This process is meant to enable the worker to make a good decision.

A clearness meeting can be called at any time by people who feel the need for input as they consider a decision they want to make.[119]

The worker seeking clearness needs to prepare for the meeting by first considering for themselves the decision they want to make. They need to take time out, pray, contemplate and write down their thoughts and feelings about the decision they are considering.

Then the worker seeking clearness needs to invite a few friends who know him or her well to come to a meeting to reflect on the decision together. Meeting with three to five friends for two to three hours in a relaxed atmosphere after sharing a meal together is the recommended format.

A facilitator needs to be selected to guide the process. This person should outline the purpose of the meeting – to help the worker seek clarity, not permission or approval. The worker then shares his or her thoughts and feelings about the decision being considered. The facilitator then invites other people present to reflect on what they have seen and heard, asking probing questions and making helpful comments. The facilitator invites the worker to respond to these reflections. Finally, people are given an opportunity to affirm the worker and pray for clarity.

If the worker feels the need for any further help, he or she should say so.

1. Have you ever had a clearness meeting?

2. If so, how did you organize it and how did it go?

3. If not, how would you go about organizing one?

◊ *Be sure to record your reflections in your working notes.*

4.5. A Senior Mentor

10 minutes

Senior mentors are people who are older than we are – the kind of people that we would like to be like when we get to their age. We need to encourage people in community work to find older people who are the kind of community workers they would like to be and arrange to meet with them regularly to discuss their work.

---

[119] Coover, et al., *Resource Manual*, pp. 123–24.

Senior mentors in community work may not be called community workers or have any formal qualifications in community work, but they need to be good models of Christ-like community work.

Once you have found a person who could be a senior mentor, you need to talk with them about the possibility of meeting regularly to discuss their community work.

Regular, but not too frequent, meetings seem to work best. Meeting once every month or so is usually helpful for a worker but not too much pressure for the mentor.

The meetings need to be relaxed and flexible enough to allow for discussion about anything and everything to do with people's community work.

Sometimes the mentor will give advice, sometimes he or she may not. The most important thing is that the worker can discuss issues in the context of support from an experienced person.

1. Do you have a senior mentor in community work?

2. If you do have one, how is it going with them?

3. If you don't have one, who could be a senior mentor for you?

◊ *Be sure to record your reflections in your working notes.*

4.6. Peer Monitors

10 minutes

Peer monitors are people who are in the same age bracket as we are, in more or less the same stage of life, who are in the same community and who are interested in the community work we are doing.

We need to encourage people in community work to find peers in the same community who are interested in the work they are doing, to whom they can be accountable in regard to specific issues.

Everyone has issues they need to deal with – from laziness to aggressiveness. How they deal with these issues will affect their work. If they always turn up late, people will get angry with them. If they get angry in return, people will avoid them. All of us need to deal with issues like these and, to deal with these issues well, we need to be accountable to someone else.

When it comes to dealing with personal issues, accountability needs to be mutual, rather than hierarchical, so as not to be depersonalizing.

Hence we need to encourage people to have peer monitors rather than senior mentors to support them in dealing with these issues.

Accountability is simply answer-ability. It means answering the question about "how are we doing" fully, freely and truly. Peer monitors should not be scared to ask the hard questions and should not accept dishonest answers.

Having found a person who could be a peer monitor, a worker needs to talk with this person about the possibility of meeting regularly to discuss the personal issues that they are dealing with.

If the person is in the same community, it will be easy to meet regularly and as frequently as is required. Usually people need to meet more frequently earlier in the relationship and less frequently later on.

The meetings can be very informal – on the run, at the corner, before or after church. The only thing that matters is that the question about "how we are doing" is asked and answered – fully, freely and truly.

Sometimes the monitor may give advice, sometimes he or she may not. The most important thing is that the peer monitor holds the worker accountable for dealing with their issues in the context of support from a counterpart.

1. Do you have a peer monitor in community work?

2. If you do have one, how is it going with that person?

3. If you don't have one, who could be a peer monitor for you?

◊ *Be sure to record your reflections in your working notes.*

4.7. Personal Coaches

30 minutes

A personal coach is not an expert so much as a coach who is able to help people realize their potential and maximize their work performance.

Rather than teaching, personal coaches seek to help people learn, leaving the responsibility for learning with the learner. The personal coach aims to develop internal motivation rather than relying on the external motivations of advising, directing or instructing. The sequence suggested for a session with a personal coach includes four stages to help the learner GROW:[120]

---

[120] J. Whitmore, *Coaching for Performance* (London: Nicholas Brealey Publishing, 1996).

- **G**oals – setting goals for the session
- **R**eality checking – exploring the current situation
- **O**ptions – what options or alternatives for action exist?
- **W**hat is to be done? When, by Whom, and finding the Will to do it.

We will consider each of these four headings separately.

Goals

Goals relate to achievement, so what we are looking at here is what we want to achieve or get out of a particular coaching session. We could ask questions like:

1. What would you like to get out of this session?

2. In the half hour we have, what would you like to achieve?

3. What would be the most useful thing for you to take away from this session?

Ownership of goals is crucial. It is the *learner* who sets the goals.

Reality

Having defined the goals, we now need to clarify the situation. What is the actual situation now? We could use questions like:

1. What is happening now?

2. Who is involved?

3. What have you done about this so far?

4. What results did that produce?

5. What are the major difficulties in finding a way forward?

Options

The aim of this stage is to create as many options or alternatives as possible. It is important to accept all ideas and to build an environment where people will feel safe to make suggestions.

Once a full list has been produced, it will be necessary to analyze all options to select the best solution – that is, to analyze the benefits and costs of each option. Possible questions to use are:

1. What options do you have?

2. What else could you do?

3. What if . . . ?

4. Would you like another suggestion?

5. What are the benefits and costs of each possibility?

What will you do?

The aim of the final phase of the training sequence is to convert a discussion into a decision. It should produce an action plan. The questions to use at this point are:

1. What are you going to do?

2. When are you going to do it?

3. Will this action meet your goal?

4. What obstacles might you meet along the way?

5. Who needs to know?

6. What support do you need?

7. How and when are you going to get that support?

8. What other considerations do you have?

Note that all of the above questions are designed to encourage the person to set their will to actually take action. The "W" is for "Will"!

◊ Rate on a scale of 1–10 the degree of certainty you have that you will carry out this action. If you rate the chances as less than 7 out of 10, you may have to start again.

4.8. The Support of Colleagues

5 minutes

In Session 13, you made a list of some of the local people, groups and organizations that you believed you would be able to co-operate with.

◊ Take a few minutes to look at that map again, to remind yourself of the support that is local, available and accessible – for you, and for the people with whom you are working.

◊ Write a list of the key people you may want to refer to, and/or who you may refer others to.

◊ Keep one copy of this list handy in case of emergency, and *keep another copy of the list in your working notes.*

5.   CONCLUSION

10 minutes

The follow-up reading for this session is:
*   Wayne Gordon's "The Role of the Church in Community Development," in *Caring for the Least* (Scottsdale: Herald, 1992), pp. 81–90, a case study of the church as support system (Reading 14).

The set community tasks for this session are:

◊ Meet with your learning partner and your community development support group.

◊ Share what you learned in this session about the importance of supporting people in community work. Talk about ways in which you can support one another through phone check-ins, internet connections, networking parties, clearness meetings, senior mentors, peer monitors and personal coaches. Share notes so that you can develop a comprehensive and reliable local referral list.

◊ Look for a way to get some support for yourself, as well as to give some support to somebody else.

◊ *Record your actions, reflections and conclusions in your working notes.*

COMMUNITY WORK SKILL 9 – PROMOTING

1. PREPARATION

1.1. Objectives

- To review your supporting skills
- To consider the next in a series of basic community work skills – promoting

2. REVIEW

30 minutes

Review the work from the previous session. This will include a review of your appreciation of the issues raised in the session and clarified in the follow-up readings and your experience of your set community tasks.

Review the issues raised in the course notes in the last session, particularly your understanding of supporting.

Review the reading:

Wayne Gordon's "The Role of the Church in Community Development" (Reading 14).

Review the tasks:

1. How did it go meeting with your community development support group and sharing what you learned in class about finding support for yourself and others?

2. What was the most important thing you learned while doing the community tasks for the last session?

Finish the review with a reflection on how you have begun to
organize support for yourself.

◊ *Don't forget to keep a record of your reflections in your working notes.*

3.   PROMOTING OUR VISION WITH PASSION

45 minutes

Martin Luther King gave one of the great speeches of the twentieth
century, promoting the civil rights struggle, to an enormous crowd in
Washington on 28 August 1963.

Read the extract below or listen to the speech on http://www.hpol.
org/record.asp?id=72 (Dr. Martin Luther King: I have a dream – Real
Audio and transcript). As you read or listen to these words, think about
why this speech was such a powerful inspiration to action.

"I have a dream. . ."

I say to you today, my friends, that in spite of the
difficulties and frustrations I still have a dream.
I have a dream that one day this nation will rise up
and live out the true meaning of its creed:
"We hold these truths to be self-evident –
that all (people) are created equal."
I have a dream that one day on the red hills of Georgia
the sons of former slaves and the sons of former slave-owners
will be able to sit down together at the table of brotherhood.
I have a dream that one day even the state of Mississippi,
a desert state sweltering with the heat of injustice and
oppression,
will be transformed into an oasis of freedom and justice.
I have a dream that my four little children will one day live
in a nation where they will not be judged by the color of their
skin
but by the content of their character.
I have a dream that one day the state of Alabama,
whose governor's lips are presently dripping with the words
of interposition and nullification, will be transformed
into a situation where little black boys and black girls
will be able to join hands with little white boys and white girls
and walk together as sisters and brothers.

I have a dream that one day
every valley shall be exalted,
every hill and mountain shall be made low,
the rough places will be made plains,
and the crooked places will be made straight,
and the glory of the Lord shall be revealed,
and all flesh shall see it together.
This is the faith I shall return to the South with.
With this faith we will be able
to hew out of the mountain of despair a stone of hope.
With this faith we will be able
to transform the jangling discords of our nation
into a beautiful symphony of (fraternity).
With this faith we will be able to work together,
pray together, struggle together, go to jail together,
stand up for freedom together,
knowing that we will be free one day.
This will be the day when all of God's children
will be able to sing with new meaning:
"My country 'tis of thee,
sweet land of liberty,
of thee I sing.
Land where my (ancestors) died,
land of the pilgrim's pride,
from every mountainside
let freedom ring."
When we let freedom ring,
when we let it ring from every village and every hamlet,
from every state and every city,
we will be able to speed up that day
when all of God's children,
. . . will be able to join hands and sing in the words
of the old Negro spiritual,
"Free at last! Free at last!
Thank God almighty, we are free at last!"[121]

Why was this speech such a powerful inspiration to action?

◊ *Don't forget to keep a record of your reflections in your working notes.*

---

[121] S. Oates, *Let the Trumpet Sound* (New York: New American Library, 1982), pp. 260–62.

King eloquently articulated the deep longing in people's hearts. When James Baldwin heard these words he said:

> That day, for a moment, it almost seemed that we stood on a height and could see our inheritance; perhaps we could make (it) real, perhaps the beloved community would not forever remain (a) dream . . .

They killed the dreamer. Just as they killed the dreamers who came before him. But they couldn't kill the dream of "the beloved community." The words that were heard that day are still heard today, echoing encouragement in the conscience of each succeeding generation as we consider the challenge to "make (it) real . . ."

> I have the audacity to believe that peoples everywhere
> can have three meals a day for their bodies,
> education . . . for their minds, and . . . freedom for their spirits.
> I believe that what self-centred (people) have torn down
> other-centred people can build up.
> I still believe that one day humanity
> will bow before the altars of God
> and be crowned triumphant over war
> and non-violent redemptive goodwill
> will proclaim the rule of the land.
> And every one shall sit
> under their own vine and fig tree
> and none shall be afraid.
> I still believe that we shall overcome.[122]

What can you learn from King about how you can promote your vision?

◊ Write down as many ideas as you can come up with on separate cards.

◊ Spread the cards on the table and select one that you want to work on. Explain why you chose that one to work on and how you intend to work on it.

◊ *Be sure to record your reflections in your working notes.*

---

[122] A. Hope and S. Timmel, *Training for Transformation* (Gweru, Zimbabwe: Mambo Press, 1984), p. 130.

4.   PROMOTING OUR MISSION WITH COMPASSION

In this session I'd like to introduce you to two brilliant Australian examples of people promoting mission with compassion.

There are a whole range of case studies on promoting mission with compassion through the centuries from every continent available from the "stories" section of the *Compassionate Community Work* site at www.daveandrews.com.au. You can see the full list of these stories in Appendix B.

But first, let me introduce you to Caroline Chisholm and Mary MacKillop.

4.1. Caroline Chisholm

45 minutes

I'm not one of those who ask "What will the Government do for us?" The question of the day is – "What shall we do for ourselves?"

Caroline Jones was born into a wealthy family in rural England in 1808. The Joneses were evangelical Christians. Her father brought his daughter up to stand by what she believed in, and her mother brought her daughter up to serve the poor. So the fun-loving young Caroline grew up with a serious faith, a strong mind and a social conscience.

But when Caroline's father died, the erstwhile wealthy family was suddenly plunged into desperate poverty. It was one thing for her to care for the poor; it was another thing for her to *be* poor herself. It was an experience Caroline never forgot.

When she reached a marriageable age, Caroline met Archibald Chisholm. He was an English officer in the Indian Army and cut a dashing figure in his uniform. When she got the chance to talk with him, Caroline found Archy had substance as well as style. They decided to get married, but in an "equal partnership" rather than in the traditional "superior-subordinate relationship" which was more common at the time between husband and wife. Although Caroline, who was Protestant, agreed to become Catholic like Archy, she only agreed on the proviso that she would be free to pursue any nondenominational philanthropic work that she felt called to "without impediment."

After their wedding Archy was recalled to India and Caroline followed him later to Madras. Upon her arrival, the officers' wives drew her into their party circuit. But Caroline loathed the petty gossip that filled the empty lives of the *burri memsahibs*. The poverty Caroline saw around her attracted her attention more than the opulence. She immediately began to pray that God would show her a way to respond to the plight of the hapless child prostitutes that swarmed around the outskirts of the garrison town. Caroline eventually decided that the only way she could save these poor children from prostitution, or marriages so degrading they were almost as bad, was to start a school which could teach them marketable skills.

The officers and their wives were scandalized by Caroline's "unbecoming" behaviour and told Archy to pull his wife into line or risk becoming a "social outcaste." But Archy refused to be bullied. He threw his lot in with the social outcastes by personally underwriting the expenses of the school himself. So, with Archy's support, Caroline set up a modern school in Madras. The school taught street children not only reading and writing, but also cooking and cleaning, budgeting and bookkeeping, and even nursing.

Some years later, due to ill health, Archy and Caroline applied to take a long leave in Australia. They arrived in Sydney with their two children in 1938 and settled into a comfortable house in Windsor. After a couple of years in Australia, Archy had to go back to his regiment, but they decided it was best for Caroline and the children to stay on at their new home in New South Wales. Caroline thought she might open a school in Sydney like she had in Madras. As she prayed about it, she became convinced that she needed to set the idea of a school aside for a while and first get involved with the poor immigrant women, penniless widows and orphaned girls who slept in tents in the Domain, or in the streets around The Rocks.

Many of the women that Caroline met told tragic tales of fleeing destitution in England by emigrating to Australia, only to fall into the hands of abusive crews on board the ships and unscrupulous brothel owners once the ships docked in Sydney harbour. Upon hearing these stories, Caroline made it her business to meet every ship as it came in. At first Caroline took these women into her own home in Windsor. Then, when there were too many, she persuaded the wife of Governor Gipps to have her husband give her the old barracks on Bent Street to use. She turned the rat-infested shed into an emergency shelter accommodating more than a hundred women at any one time.

Caroline also accompanied the shelter residents around town in their search for work. When she couldn't find enough jobs around Sydney she set up voluntary committees all around New South Wales to act as employment agencies for her. She would personally take her charges from Moreton Bay to Port Macquarie to secure proper employment for them. In the process, Caroline secured employment for over fourteen thousand women. To protect the rights of these women, Caroline introduced employment contracts in triplicate to ensure the provision of good basic conditions in their places of employment.

When Archy returned in 1845, Caroline talked to him about the need to take her campaign to Britain in order to lobby the British government directly. Archy agreed to return with Caroline to England to take the fight for the rights of migrants to their point of origin. Back in England, Caroline met with the Secretary of State, the Home Secretary, and the Land and Emigration Commissioners. She provided them with detailed reports on human rights abuses and presented them with specific policy options which they could adopt to address these issues. While waiting for these reforms to be adopted, Caroline went ahead and organized a society to aid migrants independent of, but in co-operation with, the British government. The central committee of the society she organized, under the high-profile presidency of Lord Ashley MP (Earl of Shaftesbury) and with the public support of Charles Dickens, set up a scheme to help poor migrants with everything from safe travel to personal loans. Caroline also did all she could to expedite family reunions for ex-convicts who were separated from their wives and children for years. She lobbied for free passage for these reunions and for land reform to enable these families to get small farms of their own.

In 1854 Caroline joined Archy in Melbourne where, since 1851, he had been running the Australian end of their operation. Back in Australia Caroline continued her relentless campaign through the press and the parliament for women's entitlements. By 1866 the Chisholms had exhausted their considerable intellectual, emotional and physical resources. They had worked passionately, without pay, in the service of humanity for more than a quarter of a century. When they retired to England they were worn out. Caroline died in 1877, and her beloved Archy died a few months later.[123]

---

[123] Adapted from S. De Vries, *The Immigrants' Friend: Strength of Spirit* (Alexandria: Millennium Books, 1995), pp. 91–110.

What can you learn from Caroline about how you can promote your mission?

◊ Write down as many ideas as you can come up with on separate cards.

◊ Spread the cards on the table and select the one that you want to work on. Explain why you chose that one to work on and how you intend to work on it.

◊ *And be sure to record your reflections in your working notes.*

4.2. Mary MacKillop

45 minutes

Never see a need without trying to do something about it!

Mary MacKillop was born in Fitzroy in 1842, into a Scottish migrant family. Mary was the eldest of eight children and their father, who had attended Scots College in Rome, educated the children at home.

Having squandered most of the family fortune, the MacKillops were very poor. At the age of fourteen Mary was sent out to work. By the age of sixteen, Mary had become the primary family breadwinner. Even in her youth Mary showed herself to be a very capable person. At Sands & Kenny, the stationers where she worked, Mary was given a position of responsibility usually reserved for older employees.

At the age of eighteen Mary assumed the role of governess to her cousins in Penola, South Australia. There she met Father Julian Tenison Woods. Mary had already decided that she wanted to be a nun, so she asked Father Woods to be her spiritual mentor. Julian Woods and Mary MacKillop became close friends. They shared a vision for developing an Australian religious order that would serve the needs of the poor.

In 1866 they founded the Sisters of St. Joseph. This was an indigenous mission made up of small, mobile communities of two or three sisters caring for children in frontier towns, rural farms and roadside and railway camps. The itinerant lifestyle of the sisters was very simple. They took a vow of poverty to identify with the poor. Because they had no money, they were only able to get by through begging. The hierarchy of the church did not approve of the practice. However, mindful of her mission, Mary encouraged the sisters to carry on regardless.

Mary started Australia's first free Catholic school. At the time only the rich could afford to pay the fees to send their children to school. The sisters provided education for the children of the poor whether they could afford to pay the fees or not. In 1867 Mary moved to Adelaide, and it wasn't long before she and her sisters had seventeen schools up and running. Instead of supporting their efforts, the Bishop of Adelaide, who was a paranoid alcoholic, tried to clamp down on the congregation. When Mary resisted, he excommunicated her and discharged her sisters.

For Mary, being thrown out of the church was a terrible blow. She was totally devastated. But, in spite of the desolation, she was determined to maintain her faith. She refused to become bitter and twisted about the way she was treated. The Holy See sent a delegation to investigate the disturbance in the Antipodes, and as a result of their inquiries they decided to back Mary against the Bishop. In 1872, when the Bishop lay dying, he apologized to Mary, absolved her from excommunication and reinstated her and her sisters.

In 1873, Mary travelled to Rome. There she sought permission from the Pope for her congregation to run its own affairs in future, free from the interference of the Bishops. Because of the quality of her work, her request was well received and the Josephites were given the independence for which Mary had fought. In 1875 Mary was elected superior-general of her order. Under Mary's guidance the Josephites became the primary provider of Catholic education to Australian girls regardless of race, class or creed. Because they had a policy of being non-proselytizing, the sisters enjoyed a lot of support from Protestants as well as Catholics in the communities where they worked around Australia.

In 1885 the Josephites found themselves in conflict with the Bishops again. The Holy See supported the Josephites, but they asked Mary if she would stand aside and let someone else (less controversial) lead the congregation for a while. So, in 1888, Mary stood aside and Mother Bernard was elected to lead the order in her stead. In 1898 Mother Bernard died and Mary was elected again by the congregation to lead the order into the twentieth century.

The Josephites not only taught students, but also the teachers who taught the students. They opened orphanages for those with no homes and refuges for those fleeing violent homes. They provided family support and residential care services for those with intellectual, physical, psychological and developmental disabilities.

In 1909 Mary died. And in 1995, this "little battler," this "feminist trailblazer" and "ecclesiastical troublemaker," this "extraordinary never-say-die pioneer of education for all" was appropriately recognized as our first "fair dinkum" Aussie Saint.[124]

What can you learn from Mary about how you could promote your mission?

◊ Write down as many ideas as you can come up with on separate cards.

◊ Spread the cards on the table and select the one that you want to work on. Explain why you chose that one to work on and how you intend to work on it.

◊ *And be sure to record your reflections in your working notes.*

5.   CONCLUSION

10 minutes

The follow-up reading for this session is:
*   Susan Kaldor's "Reaching Out – Some Principles," in *Green Shoots in the Concrete* (Sydney: Scaffolding, 1985), pp. 133–43, a case study of church-initiated local community work. (Reading 15).

The set community tasks for this session are:

◊ Meet with your learning partner and your community development support group.

◊ Share what you learned in this session about promoting. Consider what action you might take together to promote your vision and your mission.

◊ Look for opportunities to present your ten-minute report on the work you've done during this course. The report should be framed around the tasks you attempted, strategies you tried, your successes, your failures and the lessons that you have learned along the way.

◊ This report should demonstrate a theoretical and practical understanding of community work within the framework of your own spirituality. Honesty, authenticity and creativity in these presentations are always appreciated.

◊ *Ensure you record your actions, reflections and conclusions in your working notes.*

---

[124] Mary MacKillop, www.sosj.org.au; www.trinity.wa.edu.au/plduffyrc/subjects/re/action/saints/mackillop.htm.

COMMUNITY WORK SKILL 10 – PERSEVERING

1. PREPARATION

1.1. Objectives

- To review your promoting skills
- To consider the last in a series of basic community work skills – persevering

2. REVIEW

15 minutes

Review the work from the previous session. This will include a review of your appreciation of issues raised in course notes, clarified in follow-up readings and your experience of set community tasks.

Review the issues raised in the last session, particularly your understanding of promoting vision and mission.

Review the reading:

Susan Kaldor's "Reaching Out – Some Principles" (Reading 15).

Review the tasks:

1. How did it go meeting with your community development support group and sharing what you learned in class about promoting?

2. What was the most important thing you learned while doing the community tasks for the last session?

◊ Be sure to record your reflections in your working notes.

3.   COURSE EVALUATION

30 minutes

◊ Begin your evaluation by looking at the course from a new angle with a slightly different question, such as:

If this course were a piece of fruit that you tasted, what kind of fruit would you say it was?

◊ Then move towards classic inquiry questions, such as:

1. What was the best thing about this course?
2. What is the one thing you will not forget?
3. What would you do differently if you were to do it again?

◊ *Be sure to record your reflections in your working notes.*

4.   MEDITATION

60 minutes

◊ Use the extracts provided below to meditate on self-care, self-control and self-sacrifice.

Carl Jung says that "Any genuine personality (will) sacrifice self for (their) vocation."[125] But, for that process to be life affirming, rather than life negating, as paradoxical as it may seem, self-sacrifice always needs to take place in the context of self-care and self-control.

4.1. Self-Care

At the centre of the creative use of self is self-care.

> I am struck repeatedly by the degree to which people who are committed to "good work," to making this world "better" to live in, do not include themselves as valid environmental concerns . . .

> If you are saving the world and killing yourself (even if only by self-neglect) you will not be effective in your work. The people whom you are trying to convince will not believe you.

> You can't abuse yourself and advocate that society should not abuse the environment.[126]

---

[125] C. Jung, *Collected Works*, 17.vii (Princeton: Princeton University Press, 1967), pp. 167–87.
[126] W. Bryan, *Preventing Burnout in the Public Interest Community* (Helena: Northern Rockies Action Group Paper NRAG III.3, 1980).

Katrina Shields explains the process of exercising self-care:

> (It) means, in the most simple sense, to attend to basic requirements – nourishing food, quality sleep, pleasant exercise and fresh air.
>
> However, taking care of ourselves extends well beyond this. Dealing with projects, people, and challenges on a daily basis (especially if it is done under pressure, with uncertainty and few external rewards) slowly drains our inner reserves.
>
> One way to "top up" again is to nurture ourselves, perhaps by little treats and pleasures, deep relaxation exercises or meditation.[127]

What are simple, practical, inexpensive ways you can care for your self?

◊ *Be sure to record your reflections in your working notes.*

- Read the "Ten Commandments for Community Workers" at the end of this chapter.

4.2. Self-Control

At the circumference of the creative use of self is self-control.

> The essential problem in any situation of injustice is that one human being is exercising control over another human being and exploiting the relationship of dominance.
>
> The solution to the problem is not simply to reverse roles in the hope that once the roles have been reversed the manipulation will discontinue. The solution is for people to stop trying to control one another.
>
> All of us to one degree or another exploit the opportunity if we have control over another person's life. Common sense therefore dictates that the solution to the problem of exploitation cannot be through . . . controlling others, but controlling ourselves individually and collectively.[128]

---

[127] Shields, *In the Tiger's Mouth*, p. 124.
[128] Andrews, *Not Religion*, 32.

Stephen Covey explores the process of increasing self-control:

> We each have a wide range of concerns (from the welfare of our
> family through to the fate of the world). As we look at those
> things . . . it becomes apparent that there are some things over
> which we have no control, (and do nothing about) and other
> (things over which we have some control and) can do something
> about.
>
> We could identify the former as a *circle of concern* and the latter
> as a *circle of influence*. (Increasing self-control) depends on
> focusing our efforts on our circle of influence and gradually
> expanding those efforts to affect more and more of our circle of
> concern.[129]

We share in the spirit embodied in the prayer used in Alcoholics
Anonymous:

> Lord, grant me
>
> > the serenity to accept
> >
> > the things I cannot change,
> >
> > the courage to change
> >
> > the things I can,
> >
> > and the wisdom to know
> >
> > the difference'.[130]

How can we take greater control of ourselves, without controlling
others?

◊ *Be sure to record your reflections in your working notes.*

• Read the "Guidelines for the Long Haul" at the end of this chapter.

4.3. Self-Sacrifice

At the interface, in the community, between ourselves and other
selves, the creative use of self involves self-sacrifice.

After years of often quite difficult experiences with an intentional
Christian community, Art Gish wrote:

> It is important that we come to terms with our own selfishness.
> Unless we do that, our communities will be little more than
> reflections of the . . . society we hoped to overcome. It is not

---

[129] Covey, *Seven Habits*, pp. 81–85.
[130] Covey, *Seven Habits*, pp. 81–85.

enough to reject the selfishness of the larger society. The condition of our inner selves needs to be transformed.

Community is not based on the extent to which we see the community fulfilling our own needs or the extent to which the interest of the total community matches our self-interest, but rather the extent to which we give up self in order to live (a) new life.

Without this surrender, community is impossible. Each of us brings with us our own agenda from the past, our different patterns of living. To the extent that each of us insists on our own way community is impossible.

Community is more than an association of independent individuals, for membership involves the very heart of a person's being in all its dimensions. One is not truly in community unless (one) is committed.

Community always includes a price. It means giving up something else, being here rather than there, giving up other options. But the sacrifices are nothing in light of what is received. In fact, the . . . higher the cost for us, the more valuable . . . community will be for us.

Those who give little also receive little. The degree of success of communities is directly related to the strength of commitment in those communities.

What we are talking about is . . . a whole new world in which each individual lays down his/her life in love for each other. Renunciation of individual ego is no guarantee that a collective egoism will not take its place. The selfishness of "mine" and "thine" can be exchanged for the selfishness of "ours" and "yours."

So surrender, not only of each individual, but also of the total community, (is) demanded. Unless we are prepared to die for each other we are not (able) to live for each other.[131]

What would sacrificing yourself for the sake of community mean to you?

◊ *Be sure to record your reflections in your working notes.*

---

[131] A. Gish, *Living in Christian Community* (Sutherland: Albatross, 1979), pp. 47–54 (quotation has been edited).

- Read Ange Andrews's poem, "Who of you will join me?", at the end of this chapter.

◊ Make a time this week to copy the three 'posters' found on the following pages and display them where you can meditate on them regularly – on the wall of your kitchen, the board in your office or the back of your bathroom door.

- Also make time to read "How Far Are We from the Edge?" and reflect on the issues that it raises for you (from *Third Way* [Sept. 2001], p. 35; Reading 16).

POSTER 1

Ten Commandments for Community Workers
adapted and developed by Dave Andrews
1. Thou shalt learn to say NO as well as to say YES.
2. Thou shalt NOT let people's deadlines kill thee.
3. Thou shalt leave some things undone sometimes.
4. Thou shalt NOT be responsible for everything.
5. Thou shalt be as friendly as much as thou canst be.
6. But thou shalt NOT try to be everybody's best friend.
7. Thou shalt be good to one and all – even unto thyself.
8. Thou shalt NOT neglect thine own family or friends.
9. Thou shalt schedule time for thyself and thy supportive network.
10. Thou shalt relax regularly – and thou shalt NOT even feel guilty!

Poster 2

Guidelines for the Long Haul
Be continually converted to Jesus.
Constantly relate to reality through Jesus.
Be accountable to one another.
Answer the hard questions as honestly as you possibly can.
Don't be responsible for everything, but be responsive to everyone.
Never react; always respond; as constructively as you can.
Don't try to do big things; try to do little things with a lot of love.
Extend love unconditionally, but trust only conditionally.
Don't have high expectations; have high hopes with low expectations.
Cultivate seeds of hope in the grounds for despair.
Never forget – there's no salvation without grace, and no grace without suffering.
Always remember – that strength is made perfect in weakness.
by Dave Andrews

POSTER 3

"Who of you will join me?"

by Angie Andrews

There is precious little acceptance in our society
    of the changes in our bodies, brought about by sacrifice,
    by the giving of life to others.
People want us to look unscathed, unscarred.
Without the sagging in our breasts,
    the stretchmarks on our stomach,
    the lines of strain and struggle.
People want us to look ageless, timeless.
With the model body of a young girl.
With long flowing hair, fair skin, firm upright breasts,
    tight muscled tummy, slim thighs and long legs.
The image of the lithe and slender is what men lust for.
The image of what men lust for is what women strive for.
Where is the place for the beauty derived from love
    and developed through sacrifice?
Where are the people who will celebrate
    the signs of someone who has given themselves to others
    through touch, in tears, with love, unnumbered times?
Who of you will join me in forsaking the images
    we idolize in our society?
Who of you will join me in turning away
    from the mirror towards the door
    that leads to the needs of others?
Who of you will join me in the risk of being worn out,
    of being wrinkled, of being thrown away?
We are not fools,
    who give what we cannot keep
    to gain what we cannot lose!

APPENDIX A

COMPASSIONATE COMMUNITY WORK ARTICLES

Reading 1: "Our Ideal in the Real World" in Dave Andrews, *Building a Better World* (Sutherland: Albatross, 1996), pp. 52–68

Reading 2: "The Crucial Process of Community Development" in Dave Andrews, *Building a Better World* (Sutherland: Albatross, 1996), pp. 163–65

Reading 3: "The Ottawa Charter For Health Promotion" (First International Conference on Health Promotion, WHO, Ottawa 21 Nov. 1986), pp. 1–5

Reading 4: "On the Potential and Problems of Community" (An Interview with Robert Putnam on Radio National, ABC, 26 Sept. 2001), pp. 1–12

Reading 5: "Our Life Together" and "Community Connections" in Peter Kaldor, et al., *Connections for Life* (Adelaide: NCLS, Open Book, 2002), pp. 37–44 and 51–61

Reading 6: "The Expression of God's Concern" in Bruce Turley, *Being there for Others* (Melbourne: JBCE, 1982), pp. 46–58

Reading 7: "A Southport Story – Community Work in Parish Structures" by Sue Critall in A. Kelly and S. Sewell, *People Working Together*, II (Brisbane: Boolarong, 1986), pp. 48–61

Reading 8: "Building an Urban Parish" by Geoff Huard in P. Kaldor (ed.), *Green Shoots in the Concrete* (Sydney: Scaffolding, 1985), pp. 107–15

Reading 9: "The Building of God's Community" in Bruce Turley, *Being there for Others* (Melbourne: JBCE, 1982), pp. 35–45

Reading 10: "Reaching Out – One Church's Story" by James Bosscher and Carol Doornbos in D. Caes, *Caring for the Least of These* (Scottsdale: Herald, 1992), pp. 107–13

Reading 11: "Participative Action Research" in Tim Muirhead, *Weaving Tapestries* (Mount Hawthorn: LGCSA(WA), 2002), pp. 38–41

Reading 12: "Starting and Developing Community Ministry" in David Bos, *A Practical Guide to Community Ministry* (Louisville: Westminster, 1993), pp. 45–74

Reading 13: "Community: The Vision (Revisited)" in Ross Langmead, *A Westgate Paper* (No. 3) (Melbourne: Westgate Baptist, 1984), pp. 1–6

Reading 14: "The Role of the Church in Community Development" by Wayne Gordon in D. Caes, *Caring for the Least of These* (Scottsdale: Herald, 1992), pp. 81–90

Reading 15: "Reaching Out: Some Principles" by Sue Kaldor in P. Kaldor (ed.), *Green Shoots in the Concrete* (Sydney: Scaffolding, 1985), pp. 133–43

Reading 16: "How Far Are We From the Edge?" by Dave Andrews in *Third Way* (Sept. 2001), p. 35

Extra Readings

Reading 17: "Universal Declaration of Human Rights" (Resolution 217 A [III], UN General Assembly, 10 Dec. 1948)

Reading 18: "The Micah Declaration" at The Micah Network, www.micahnetwork.org (2001)

Reading 19: "Statement of Ethics" (Christian Counsellors Association of Australia, July 2000)

Reading 20: "Living Together" by David Washington in *On Being* (May 1995), pp. 20–24

APPENDIX B

COMPASSIONATE COMMUNITY WORK STORIES

Jesus Christ of Nazareth represents the very best that we can be. It might be too much for any of us to expect to be Christlike in terms of our *ability*. Very few, if any, could ever calm a storm, or raise the dead, like Christ did. But it's not too much for any of us to expect to be more Christlike in terms of our *sensibility*. Now, more than ever, we need to learn to care for people like Christ did.

Fortunately, the path of Christlike compassion is one that others have trodden before us, and there are people from the past whose lives can serve as examples of the way we need to take in the future. We need to remember and reconsider these people as they really were – *imperfect people in pursuit of the practice of perfect compassion.*

Following is a list of short stories of some of these imperfect people in pursuit of the practice of perfect compassion. In writing these stories I have tried to be accurate. But because they are sketches – outlines, not portraits – a lot of details are missing. To get the fuller picture you will need to read their biographies and autobiographies yourself. But these sketches of people from all over the world are excellent for meditation and discussion about the dynamics of compassionate community work. All of these are available from the "stories" section of the *Compassionate Community Work* site at www.daveandrews.com.au

Telemachus – "The Mad Monk" (4th c.)

John Chrysostom – "The Man with the Golden Mouth" (347–407)

Wenceslaus – "The Good King" (903–35)

Hugh of Lincoln – "The Hammer of Kings" (1140–1200)

Francis of Assisi – "God's Juggler" (1182–1226)

Elisabeth von Thuringia – "The Queen who Served Beggars" (1207–31)

Menno Simons – "The Radical Reformer" (1496–1561)

Nikolaus Ludwig – "The Count who Cared" (1700–60)

John Wesley – "The Whole World Is my Parish" (1703–91)

Charles Finney – "Christ's Lawyer" (1792–1875)

Sojourner Truth – "Ain't I a Woman!" (1797–1853)

Caroline Chisholm – "The Tireless Campaigner" (1808–77)

Florence Nightingale – "The Lady with the Lamp"(1820–1910)

Joseph De Vuester – "Damien the Leper" (1840–99)

Henri Dunant – "Founder of the Red Cross" (1828–1910)

Mary MacKillop – "The Little Battler" (1842–1909)

Pandita Ramabai – "The Learned One" (1858–1922)

Charles Freer Andrews – "Christ's Faithful Apostle" (1871–1940)

Helen Keller – "The Light in the Darkness" (1880–1968)

Toyohiko Kagawa – "The Faithful Traitor" (1888–1960)

Albert Luthuli – "The Apartheid Opponent" (1898–1967)

Dorothy Day – "The Woman who Wanted to Change the World" (1897–1980)

Dietrich Bonhoeffer – "The Man who Stood by God" (1906–45)

Simone Weil – "The Red Virgin" (1909–43)

Helder Camara – "The Red Bishop" (1909–99)

Clarence Jordan – "The Race-Mixing Communist" (1912–69)

Jose Maria Anznediarretia – "The Co-op Priest" (1915–76)

Desmond Tutu – "The Voice of the Voiceless" (b. 1931)

APPENDIX C

BIBLIOGRAPHY OF SOURCES

Andrews, D. *Not Religion but Love* (Oxford: Lion, 2001/Cleveland: Pilgrim Press, 2003/Armidale: Tafina Press, 2005)

—. *Christi-Anarchy* (Oxford: Lion, 1999)

—. *Building a Better World* (Sutherland: Albatross, 1996)

—. *Building Better Communities* (Brisbane: Praxis, 2000)

Banks, R. *Paul's Idea of Community: The Early House Churches in their Cultural Setting* (Peabody, MA: Hendrickson Publishers, rev. edn, 1994)

Bos, D. *A Practical Guide to a Community Ministry* (Louisville: Westminster, 1993)

Bradshaw, B. *Bridging the Gap: Evangelism, Development and Shalom* (Monrovia, CA: Marc Publications, 1993)

Broughton, B. "Evaluating Development Projects," in *Project Planning, Monitoring and Evaluation* (Canberra: ACFOA, 1997)

Chambers, R. *Rural Development: Putting the Last First* (Essex: Longman, Harlow, 1983)

—. *Whose Reality Counts: Putting the First Last* (London: Intermediate Technology, 1997)

Chester, T. *Justice, Mercy and Humility: Integral Mission and the Poor* (Carlisle: Paternoster, 2002)

Clarke, J. *Democratising Development* (London: Earthscan, 1991)

Caes, D. *Caring for the Least* (Scottsdale: Herald, 1992)

Covey, S. *7 Habits of Highly Effective People* (Melbourne: Business Library, 1989)

Craig, J. *Servants among the Poor* (Littleton, CO: OMF, 1998).

Duncan, M. *Costly Mission* (Monrovia, CA: Marc Publications, 1996)

Etzioni, A. *The Spirit of Community* (New York: Simon & Schuster, 1993)

Gill, A. *Life on the Road* (Homebush: Lancer, 1989)

—. *The Fringes of Freedom* (Homebush: Lancer, 1990)

Gish, A. *Living in Christian Community* (Sutherland: Albatross, 1979)

Grigg, V. *Companion to the Poor* (Sutherland: Albatross, 1984)

Henderson, P., and D. Thomas. *Skills in Neighbourhood Work* (Melbourne: Allen & Unwin, 1980)

Kaldor, P., et al. *Connections for Life* (Adelaide: NCLS, Open Book, 2002)

Lapierre, D. *The City of Joy* (London: Arrow, 1985)

Lovell, G. *The Church and Community Development* (Pinner: Grail, 1972)

—. *Human and Religious Factors in Church and Community Work* (Pinner: Grail, 1982)

Kaldor, P. (ed.). *Green Shoots in the Concrete* (Sydney: Scaffolding, 1985)

Kelly, A., and S. Sewell. *With Head, Heart and Hand* (Brisbane: Boolarong, 1988)

—. *People Working Together*, II (Brisbane: Boolarong, 1986)

Kraus, N. *The Community of the Spirit* (Grand Rapids: Eerdmans, 1974)

Myers, B. *Walking with the Poor* (Maryknoll: Orbis, 1999)

Muirhead, T. *Weaving Tapestries* (Mount Hawthorn: LGCSA(WA), 2002)

Nouwen, H. *Compassion* (London: Dartman, Longman & Todd, 1962)

Peck, S. *A Different Drum* (London: Rider & Co., 1988)

Putnam, R. *Bowling Alone* (Sydney: Simon & Schuster, 2000)

Ringma, C. *Catch the Wind* (Sutherland: Albatross, 1994)

Samuel, V., and C. Sugden. *The Church in Response to Human Need* (Grand Rapids: Eerdmans, 1987)

Sen, A. *Development as Freedom* (New York: Knopf, 1999)

Shields, K. *In the Tiger's Mouth* (Newtown: Millenium, 1991)

Sider, R. *Evangelism and Social Action* (London: Hodder, 1993)

Turley, B. *Being there for Others* (Melbourne: JBCE, 1982)

—. *Expanding Horizons of Care* (Melbourne: JBCE, 1979)

Twelvetrees, A. *Community Work* (Basingstoke: MacMillan, 1991)

Vanier, J. *Community and Growth* (Sydney: St. Paul, 1979)

APPENDIX D

FUNDING OPTIONS FOR COMPASSIONATE COMMUNITY WORK

Micah is a network of agencies and churches with common interests in Christian community development around the world. Listed below are some of the over 275 members of Micah with whom you could talk about funding options for compassionate faith-based community work in your region. Please use the blank space at the end to add your own contacts.

Advocacy and Relief for Children Association Inc., Australia, www.arc-global.org

All Nations Christian College, UK, www.allnations.ac.uk

Armonia, Mexico, www.homestead.com/armonia/files/homepage.htm

Asociacion Paz y Esperanza, Perú, www.pazyesperanza.org/index1.htm

Association for Community Care, Education and Social Services (ACCESS), India

Association of Evangelicals in Africa, Zimbabwe

Baptist World Aid Australia, Australia, www.shareanopportunity.org

CCT – Center for Community Transformation, Philippines, www.cct.org.ph

CEDAR Fund, China, www.cedarfund.org

Christian Reformed World Relief Committee, USA, www.crwrc.org

EFICOR, India, www.eficor.org

El Shaddai Resource Centre, India

ESCAPE – Children at Risk Ministry, LEADS, Sri Lanka

International Nepal Fellowship, Nepal, www.inf.org.np

Kale Hywet Church, Ethiopia

Koinonia, Bangladesh, www.koinoniabangladesh.org

Kumi Pentecostal AOG Planning & Dev Comm., Uganda

Lakarmissionen, Sweden, www.lakarmissionen.se

Malaysian CARE, Malaysia, www.mcare.org.my

Mercy Ministries (Le Rucher), Switzerland, www.lerucher.org

NEICORD, India

ORA International, Germany

Relief & Social Development Ministry, Evangelical Alliance, Sri Lanka

RURCON, Nigeria

SEL France, France, www.selfrance.org

Servants to Asia's Urban Poor, Australia, www.servantsasia.org

Servants to Asia's Urban Poor, Cambodia, www.servantsasia.org

Share and Care, Nepal, www.share-care.org

TEAR Australia, Australia, www.tear.org.au

TEAR Fund Belgium, Belgium, www.tearfund.be

TEAR Fund Holland, Netherlands, www.tearfund.nl

TEAR Fund NZ, New Zealand, www.tearfund.org.nz

Tear Fund Schweiz, Switzerland, www.tearfund.ch

Tearfund UK, UK, www.tearfund.org

The Amani Centre, Tanzania

The Leprosy Mission International, UK, www.leprosymission.org

United Mission to Nepal (UMN), Nepal, www.umn.org.np

VIVA network, UK, www.viva.org

World Relief Canada, Canada, www.worldreliefcanada.org

YWAM – Mercy Ministries International, Thailand, www.ywam-mercy.org

APPENDIX E

ON-LINE RESOURCES AND SUPPORT FOR COMMUNITY WORKERS

The following is a list of some helpful Internet support connections. Feel free to add your own links.

Community Work Resources

http://www.barefootguide.org/
  Provides a free guide to working with organizations for social change

http://www.eauk.org
  The Evangelical Alliance creates resources responding to current trends in the UK to support Evangelical Christians in social leadership

http://www.lastfirst.net
  On-line shop with 10,000 books on aid, development and community work

http://www.scn.org
  Seattle(US)-based organization that resources and links interfaith community workers and projects

Community Work Consultants and Trainers

http://www.ccda.org/ and http://www.urbanministry.org/ccda
  Inspires, trains, and connects Christians working in marginalized communities through resources and a yearly conference in the US

http://www.ccwa.org.uk
  UK-based churches' community work alliance

http://cied.schoolpro.com.au/
  Australian Christian organization for community-integrated educational development in vulnerable communities

http://www.communitypraxis.org
  An Australian not-for-profit workers cooperative for community development workers

http://www.faithandcommunityatwork.com/

An academy for training faith-based community practitioners from various religious backgrounds

http://www.gdrc.org/spheres/community.html
> The Community Sphere of the Global Development Research Centre looks at NGOs and the civil society, gender and development issues, and micro-financing

http://www.livability.org.uk
> UK-based charity creating opportunities for disabled people and bringing life to communities

http://www.ncls.org.au
> Provides resources and training to help local churches connect with their communities

Opportunities to Explore Christ-Like Community Work

http://www.daveandrews.com.au
> Website of the author

http://www.waitersunion.org/
> An organization, of which Dave Andrews is a member, that provides supervised training/learning opportunities for people who want to explore Christ-like Community Work

http://www.wecan.be
> A global campaign started by Dave Andrews to encourage people to 'be the change you want to see in the world' by practicing the 'Be-Attitudes', from the Gospel Beatitudes of Jesus

Christian Community Development Papers

See Appendixes A and B

"Faith-Based Community Development in America", by Robert V. Kemper and Julie Adkins

http://faculty.smu.edu/rkemper/Faith-based_community_development.htm
> The authors argue that "little has been written by anthropologists about a long-standing feature of American religious practices: the role of faith-based organizations in transforming communities."

"Faith-Based Community Economic Development: Principles and Practices", by T. David Reese and Christina A. Clamp

http://www.bos.frb.org/commdev/faith/

"How Faith-Based and Secular Organizations Tackle Housing for the Homeless", by Malcolm L. Goggin and Deborah A. Orth

http://www.religionandsocialpolicy.org/docs/research/10-23-2002_grand_rapids_study.pdf
> Investigates how the way faith-based organizations deliver services differ from the way government agencies do it

"The Theory and Practice of Community Participation: Engagement the First Step", by Sally Jope

http://www.bsl.org.au/pdfs/Jope_ASPC2005_theory&prac_community_participn.pdf

The Micah Network

The Micah Network is a comparatively new and rapidly growing network of nearly 300 practitioner agencies and churches that have significant involvement in Christian relief, development and/or justice ministries. The aims of the Micah Network are to facilitate collaborative reflection and action in "integral mission" by:

- Strengthening the capacity of participating agencies to make a biblically-shaped response to the needs of the poor and oppressed through sharing our learning with one another,

- Speaking strongly and effectively regarding the nature of the mission of the Church to proclaim and demonstrate the love of Christ to a world in need, and

- Prophetically calling upon and influencing the leaders and decision-makers of societies to "maintain the rights of the poor and oppressed and rescue the weak and needy".

The phrase "integral mission" aims to capture for this generation the nature of Christian mission. Its description comes from the declaration produced at the 2001 Micah Network consultation in Oxford, UK:

> Integral mission or holistic transformation is the proclamation and demonstration of the gospel. It is not simply that evangelism and social involvement are to be done alongside each other. Rather, in integral mission our proclamation has social consequences as we call people to love and repentance in all areas of life. And our social involvement has evangelistic consequences as we bear witness to the transforming grace of Jesus Christ. If we ignore the world we betray the word of God which sends us out to serve the world. If we ignore the word of God we have nothing to bring to the world. Justice and justification by faith, worship and political action, the spiritual and the material, personal change and structural change belong together. As in the life of Jesus, being, doing and saying are at the heart of our integral task.

Detailed information about the Micah Network, including its history, governance, up-coming events, papers and resources, strategic directions, membership and associate membership can readily be seen at www.micahnetwork.org.

Dave Andrews and his wife, Ange, have lived and worked in communities with marginalised groups of people in Australia, Afghanistan, Pakistan, India and Nepal for more than thirty years. They are currently part of the Waiters Union in Australia, an inner-city Christian community network supporting Aborigines, refugees and people with disabilities.

Additional articles and stories on community work can be found on Dave's website: www.daveandrews.com.au

Copies of *Not Religion But Love*, the set text for this course, can be purchased on the LastFirst website at: www.lastfirst.net

Dave is also available, by arrangement, to run workshops, seminars and residential intensives. Contact him by snailmail at PO Box 5519, West End, Brisbane, QLD, Australia 4101 or by email at dave@tear.org.au

Copies of *Compassionate Community Work* can be purchased on the Piquant Editions website at:

www.piquanteditions.com

COMPASSIONATE COMMUNITY WORK

DAVE ANDREWS   AN INTRODUCTORY COURSE FOR CHRISTIANS

ISBN: 978-1-903689-36-3